Remapping Modern Germany after National Socialism, 1945–1961

Syracuse Studies in Geography

Don Mitchell, Tom Perreault, and Robert Wilson, *Series Advisers*

The series Syracuse Studies in Geography is distinguished by works in historical geography, political economy, and environmental geography but also publishes theoretically informed books across the breadth of the discipline.

Also in Syracuse Studies in Geography:

Market Orientalism: Cultural Economy and the Arab Gulf States
    Benjamin Smith

Remapping Modern Germany

after National Socialism, 1945–1961

Matthew D. Mingus

Syracuse University Press

Copyright © 2017 by Syracuse University Press
Syracuse, New York 13244-5290

All Rights Reserved

First Edition 2017

17 18 19 20 21 22   6 5 4 3 2 1

∞ The paper used in this publication meets the minimum requirements
of the American National Standard for Information Sciences—Permanence
of Paper for Printed Library Materials, ANSI Z39.48-1992.

For a listing of books published and distributed by Syracuse University Press,
visit www.SyracuseUniversityPress.syr.edu.

ISBN: 978-0-8156-3550-5 (hardcover)
      978-0-8156-3538-3 (paperback)
      978-0-8156-5416-2 (e-book)

Library of Congress Cataloging-in-Publication Data

Available from publisher upon request.

Manufactured in the United States of America

To Lindsey, to Isaac, to the adventures ahead . . .

Contents

Illustrations

Acknowledgments

This book would have been an impossible project without the very generous support of several institutions and individuals. My editors at Syracuse University Press, Alison Shay and Kelly Balenske, helped push the manuscript forward, answered all of my (many) questions, and made the revisions process a generally pleasant experience. Don Mitchell and the other series advisers for the press as well as two anonymous peer reviewers offered invaluable criticism that made this work stronger and, I think, more convincing. Annie Barva did an incredibly thorough job of copyediting this book. I am grateful for her extraordinary patience. The University of Florida, the University of New Mexico at Gallup, the Georg Eckert Institute, the Leibniz-Institut für Länderkunde, and the American Geographical Society Library provided financial support. The staff and faculty of these institutions—and of every library, archive, and society cited throughout this manuscript—work tirelessly to make their material accessible to the public (and, by extension, to me). In our contemporary political climate, mired in a myopic and fanatical obsession with the "excesses" of "big government," I hope that this book speaks to the value of the librarians, faculty, bureaucrats, historians, and archivists charged with maintaining and preserving our historical commons.

Intellectually, I owe this project to my mentors, teachers, and colleagues. Peter Bergmann, Alice Freifeld, and Sheryl Kroen guided and influenced every page. My friend and adviser Geoffrey Giles carefully and brilliantly helped me craft a jumbled mess of ideas into what I hope is now a fair reflection of his effectiveness as both a scholar and a teacher. Geoffrey Martin continually encouraged my research and provided me with advice and lively conversation. My fellow faculty at the University of

New Mexico at Gallup have been instrumental in keeping me sane while I tackled this book alongside a seemingly inhuman fifteen-credit-hour teaching load each semester: Stephen Buggie, Bruce Gjeltema, Ken Roberts, Jim Sayers, Kristian Simcox, Kristi Wilson, and John Zimmerman supported me in my teaching, in my research, and in friendship. Carolyn Kuchera, in particular, donated her time and energy to reading and commenting on various parts of this manuscript. Raymond Calderon, Kyle Chancellor, Whitney Conroy, my brother, Aaron Mingus, Richard Reyes (who I hope enjoys all the serial commas!), and Lane and Toni Towery provided many necessary, off-campus distractions. They all have helped make Gallup, New Mexico, my home.

Of course, my source of greatest support has been my family. My in-laws, Tom and Kelly Smith, and my parents, Marty and Becky Mingus, never seemed to doubt that this book would become a reality. I am most indebted, though, to my best friend and partner, Lindsey Smith-Mingus. She supported me through graduate school, moved multiple times for my career, tolerated my extensive research travel, and continues to listen patiently to my occasional wild ranting. She is a phenomenal teacher and the world's best mother, and she has a fantastic laugh. I have never loved anyone more. It is to her and to our new son, Isaac, that I dedicate this book.

Remapping Modern Germany after National Socialism, 1945–1961

1 | Orientation

> Soon enough we have forgotten [the map] is a picture someone has
> arranged for us (chopped and manipulated, selected and coded).
> Soon enough . . . it is the world, it is real, it is . . . *reality.*
> —Denis Wood, *The Power of Maps*

Few German geographers lived through as much territorial upheaval and uncertainty as Emil Meynen, and none was so successful at transforming himself. By the time Meynen died, on August 23, 1994, at the age of ninety-one, he had worked for the Nazis, their Allied conquerors, the American military occupation, and the government of West Germany. Despite this varied sequence of employers, his opportunism and determination helped him maintain a relatively autonomous office and staff that produced cartographic material and geographical studies during what was, in the mid–twentieth century, the greatest period of map creation and dissemination in the history of the world. Indeed, by the time of his death, his efforts had been significantly rewarded and internationally recognized. In 1969, Meynen was awarded both the University of Bonn's Alexander von Humboldt Medal and the Federal Republic of Germany's Grand Cross of Merit.[1] In 1967, he received the Robert Gradmann Medal for his contribution to German cultural studies. In 1977, he was the recipient of the Berlin Geographical Society's Carl Ritter Medal. As the geographer Ute Wardenga notes, Meynen was presented with honorary memberships in several international geographical and cartographical organizations, including the International Cartographical Association (1984). Moreover, he was granted honorary chairmanships of the Central Committee of German Area Studies (1987) and Germany's Standing Committee on Geographic Names (1987). On four separate occasions—his fiftieth,

seventieth, seventy-fifth, and ninetieth birthdays—colloquia were organized to appreciate, comment on, and contribute to his academic work.[2]
He was, quite frankly, a very celebrated geographer.

Yet when one examines Emil Meynen's early life and career, these
resulting accolades seem obscene. Although he was born in 1902 and
came of age under the Weimar Republic's democratic government, he—
like many other Weimar-era geographers—was heavily influenced by pan-
Germanism as well as by the study and glorification of the German *Volk*.
As explained in subsequent chapters, after completing his habilitation at
the University of Cologne, he went on to serve as a prominent geographer
in the Third Reich. He established himself as both the director of the
Office of German Folk Research Organizations and as an advocate of the
aggressive and expansionist Lebensraum policy, even serving for a short
time along the eastern front in Poland during the Second World War.

After the defeat of National Socialism in 1945, the American military
plucked Meynen and several of his staffers from German territory that was
to become part of the Soviet Union's zone of occupation. After an initial
period of working for the Allied military occupation, Meynen was arrested
and interrogated. Once he was convincingly denazified, he was even more
deeply integrated into the production and study of maps in postwar Germany. As determined by his British and American interrogators, Meynen's
potential usefulness outweighed his earlier cooperation with the Nazis.

The transformation of Emil Meynen's life and career mirrors the
transformation of cartography in Germany. As this book argues, both
transformations were important for re-creating Germany after the Second World War. Every government and military institution that employed
Meynen recognized that geography was to play a vital role in the reconstruction of Germany's political identity. Mapping Germany had been a
problem since the March Revolution of 1848–49, but the Allied powers
were confident that—with the help of Meynen and other German geographers—they could create a convincingly static, peaceful, and final draft of
what had been a territorially erratic German state.

Understanding the gravity with which the Allies approached Germany's remapping after the Second World War requires a brief primer on the
disputed legitimacy of German state territory in the nineteenth century.

Located in the often contentious center of the European continent, German territory has regularly served as a primary tool through which to study Germany's economic, cultural, and political development. Even prior to Germany's unification in 1871, many Germans sought to establish a spatial framework within which their culture could play a vibrant role. Nineteenth-century German politicians and journalists invented the idea of Mitteleuropa in an effort to conceptualize and later to assert their authority over Middle Europe. Although initially utilized during the March Revolution,[3] Mitteleuropa eventually became the rallying cry for Germans interested in the consolidation of Europe's center and wary of the perceived cultural cohesion of Britain, Russia, and the United States during the First World War.[4] After the defeat of the Central powers in 1918, the fantasy of a German *Mitte* became more powerful than ever before. As the historian Henry Cord Meyer convincingly argues, after 1918 Mitteleuropa "was reborn ideologically on the German ethnic frontier. While a majority of Reich-Germans were temporarily preoccupied with Western associations, or concentrated on the social and political issues of the Weimar Republic, the Germans in the borderlands fashioned the new *gesamtdeutsch*, mid-European outlook."[5] But Mitteleuropa was only one manifestation of a much larger trend in the vernacular of Germany's geographical imagination. As discussed at length in the next chapter, many German geographers throughout the nineteenth and early twentieth centuries became deeply invested in several forms of geopolitical determinism, the idea that a nation's territorial holdings (or losses) dictated every other aspect of its existence.[6] In part, this book agrees with that worldview: cartographic expressions of national territory, real or imagined, heavily influence cultural and national identity.

Appealing to the importance of a nation's place on the map, though, need not suggest that all claims of geographic influence and determinism are equal. During the *Historikerstreit*, "historians' quarrel," of the 1980s, right-wing revisionist historians in Germany attempted to soften the image of the Third Reich by approaching totalitarian regimes comparatively. Michael Stürmer, one of the controversy's central participants, wrote in his book *Das ruhelose Reich: Deutschland, 1866–1918* (The Restless Empire: Germany, 1866–1918) that geography played a prominent role in developing Germany's aggressive foreign policy.[7] According to Stürmer, Germany's central position in Europe exposed it to an environment entirely unlike that of other western European states. His argument is explicitly one of German geographic uniqueness—a geographic *Sonderweg*, "special path," which explains, if not excuses, the atrocities of the Third Reich. Democracy in Germany, stuck in the *Mitte* between France and Russia, he argued, was doomed to be inevitably problematic. Surrounded by hostile "others," the German state required the installation of an authoritarian government for its existence.

Stürmer's argument denies many historical realities, is too obviously informed by his nationalist brand of politics, and has been rightly criticized by leading scholars both inside[8] and outside Germany.[9] Stürmer's critics, however, have been too quick to dismiss all potential forms of a "new geopolitical *Sonderweg* thesis."[10] It is easy to claim, as the British historian Richard Evans does, that "history is made not by geopolitics but by people."[11] People, though, are integral to the construction and production of the mapped spaces upon which geopolitical narratives depend. Maps are the primary way through which national territory is codified and disseminated. Although every nation-state has its own unique spatial development—the story of how it fought (or is fighting) for its place in our collective cartographic dogma—Germany's geographic *Sonderweg* after the Second World War is particularly alluring. Initially burdened with spatial terminology associated with Nazi expansionism—*Lebensraum, Heimat,* and *Geopolitik*—German geographers were denazified and then forced to remap an already established cartography of their nation-state under the supervision of the Allied occupation. This remapping was an explicit attempt to reproduce a new national identity through the disciplines of geography and cartography—an identity that would still be shaped by an image of Germany but that would also be so forcefully emblazoned into the minds of the German public that potential territorial expansion would be undesirable.

In an effort to study this redrafting of space, this book offers a history about maps of Germany, the interests behind their (re)production, and their political and cultural consequences. As previously mentioned, this story is couched within one of history's largest mapmaking and map-dissemination projects—a moment that literally redefined Germany and emphasized the value of cartography to the governments, corporations, and people operating within its borders (and sometimes, problematically, on them). It should come as no surprise that this moment occurred during and immediately after the Second World War, one of the geographically largest military conflicts in history. As John K. Wright, the International Geographical Union president who served on its Committee of Cartography, so astutely observed in 1949, "Modern war is the most powerful of all stimulants to human mobility."[12] Wright might have also mentioned that those forces most heavily invested in modern war were usually those most interested in the subsequent stimulation of that mobility. The nation-state with the greatest interest in all postwar German cartographic projects, besides Germany itself, was the United States, the most powerful military and economic force involved in the German occupation. Yet the beginning of the Second World War found the US military scrambling to pull together a coherent cartography of Europe and the rest of the world. With practically no maps to guide the massive conflict it had committed to, the United States became obsessed with standardizing and centralizing its mapmaking efforts. The consequence of this prioritization was the recruitment of cartographers into well-funded and highly respected military agencies, such as the Office of Strategic Services (OSS), the War Department, the State Department, and the Army Map Service. Together, these cartographers, along with the foreign geographers they recruited and on a scale never before realized, collected, analyzed, and produced maps of the various world regions in which the United States was militarily involved. Whereas the United States had produced roughly 9 million maps during the First World War (few, if any, of which were ever cataloged or stored by the government after the end of the conflict), it produced more than 500 million maps between 1941 and 1945.[13]

But it was not simply the Second World War itself that spurred the production of maps. Throughout the postwar period, the US military, alongside the French, British, and Soviet forces, demanded the delineation of a defeated Germany's new borders and prompted the difficult process of drafting, interpreting, and publicly explaining a very consciously constructed cartographic narrative. The most obvious and useful mapmakers of these new cartographic propositions were German geographers

themselves. As I hope to make clear in the following chapters, Emil
Meynen as well as the institutions under his direction played a particularly vital role in legitimizing the postwar cartographic identity of Germany. Government agents and institutions, however, were not the only
vehicles of map creation after the war. The rise of international public-
relations firms in the early twentieth century provided a unique outlet
through which to effectively convince the world and its nation-states of
Germany's new boundaries. Coupled together, the efforts of the American military, the German geographers it employed, the postwar German
government(s), and the public-relations firms hired all attempted to create
and impose a purposeful and carefully prepared map of Germany tailored
to perpetuate a cultural occupation of spatial perception.

Although the story of the remapping of Germany after the Second
World War includes pieces of US history, it is primarily a story of an active
and continuously self-mapping Germany—a nation-state and culture with
a long and influential cartographic history. Germany had been one of the
most technologically advanced states to consistently contribute to the creation of the cartographic and geographic disciplines. Its mapmakers, government land surveyors, and academic cartographers and geographers are
vitally important to this study if we are to understand how a nation-state is
authoritatively and for the most part unquestionably *redrawn*. Moreover, it
is only through a study of postwar Germany that we can begin to see the
cultural effects that radical cartographic change at a level never before
attempted can have on individuals who suddenly do not know (in the
abstract sense) where they are but have long been taught to defer to the
authority of the map. Space, then, is not simply a concept that deserves to
be parsed and fretted over by academic theoreticians. The transformation
of space has real, tangible, empirical consequences that require inclusion
into the historical record.

Critical Cartographies, Critical Histories:
Destroying the Map's Objectivity

Created by geographers and cartographers with various interests, the
maps shown and discussed throughout the following chapters were clearly

developed within a larger context of post–Second World War reconstruction and denazification. As a discipline dependent on both the deconstruc-
tion of seemingly objective structures (i.e., maps) and the perpetuation
of empirical archival authority (i.e., historical scholarship), the history of
cartography can serve as a medium through which to study the important
convergences of time and space.

The discipline of history is spatializing itself, and as contemporary
culture grows increasingly dependent on location-based media and
an ever-"globalizing" economy, historians have begun to recognize the
importance of spatial constructions when building their respective histories. Of particular interest are the early-modern and modern periods—
eras in which a cartographic explosion of navigational charts, colonialism,
and nation-state building demanded the abstraction, production, and dissemination of real space through the instrumental medium of the map.
Although ancient Greek and Roman societies used maps to orient themselves and exploit natural resources, and although various religions took
turns depicting the medieval world according to their respective imagined
communities, it was only during the European Enlightenment that cartography gained the scientific confidence it defends to this day. Moreover,
the necessity of disseminating cartographic material and, consequently,
popularizing particular orientations became imperative only in the modern world—where to be left off of the map might mean the loss of one's
place in real space.[14]

Many historians have understood the importance of studying these
spatial developments and have investigated them through several different
thematic lenses.[15] The history of cartography as an academic discipline, as
an art, as a technological development, and as an instrument of exploration and subsequently exploitation has become the subject of hundreds,
if not thousands, of published works. Space itself has also recently been
a well-worn subject of interest, invoking the concepts of borders, bodies,
geopolitics, environmental history, and (perhaps most relevant to this
project) imperialism. Journals such as *Imago Mundi*, *Cartographica*, and
The Portolan, among others, have provided academic forums in which
to investigate these particular issues. Maps, however, have also appealed
to a more broadly theoretical body of scholarship. Henri Lefebvre's book

The Production of Space,[16] the Annales school's *géohistorie*, Michel Foucault's call for a "history of spaces," and David Harvey's critique of the relationship between capital and space are a few of the more famous and interdisciplinary examples of useful academic exercises undertaken so as to deconstruct our respective perceptions of our environments. More recently, the geographers Geoffrey Martin, Neil Smith, Dalia Varanka, and Jeremy Crampton have offered important histories of how society has mapped itself. Critical cartographers such as J. B. Harley, Denis Wood, John Krygier, John Pickles, and Mark Monmonier have chosen to focus on the institutionalization, professionalization, and political and economic interests involved in mapmaking and the academic disciplines of geography and cartography. By undertaking deconstructive projects, historians, theorists, geographers, and cartographers alike call the map's assumed objectivity and scientism into question. As I point out throughout this book, many scholars have examined the cartographic history of Germany in both German and English. Few, however, have examined its developments after the Second World War, and very few have discussed these developments within the context of the Allied occupation.[17]

This lack of attention to postwar Germany is surprising. The history of cartographic development throughout Europe and its role in determining sovereignty, defining the concept of the nation-state, and coping with contentious territories has been fruitful. The previous work of historians, geographers, and theorists has in many cases successfully exhumed the subjective contexts from which all narratives—including maps—emerge. This book applies their deconstructive insight to an exceptional period of cartographic fluidity, a period in which a country full of skilled modern mapmakers was remapped under a foreign occupation force. In doing so, this project hopes to serve as a foundation for further research. Much more needs to be done on this particular time and place so that we might better understand the relationship between governance and maps, especially during episodes of postwar occupation.

Such critical approaches to cartographic history are hardly universal. Many historians, in particular those interested in the modern era, might understand their chosen temporal category, "modernity," as being full of consciously self-creating subjects,[18] but they too often overlook cartographies in favor of more traditional literary forms. Furthermore, the contemporary student of history is hard pressed to find any scholarly work in which early-modern or modern maps are used as explanatory narratives alongside text and simultaneously cited *as narratives*. The geospatial information utilized to create such narratives, the mathematical projections assumed, and the professionals or amateur cartographers who drew the narratives are rarely ever exposed. Rather, the map is too often used as an aesthetic representation of the past, ready to perpetuate the student's undying loyalty to the combination of spatial abstraction, cartographic objectivity, and capital-T Truth. This is particularly troubling when one considers how much emphasis contemporary historians have placed on the discourses surrounding "the nation." *Nations and Nationalism* by Ernest Gellner and *Imagined Communities* by Benedict Anderson provoked an explosion of interest in this topic,[19] but that interest has largely ignored cartographic propositions of nations despite the "primary function of cartography" being its ability "to help citizens imagine the state as a unified territory."[20]

The relationship between a mapped territory and a nation's identity is tricky, especially when it is being mediated by an occupying force. The means by which such a relationship is forged, its continuous renegotiation, and the perpetuation of this relationship into our contemporary era shed light on how the narratives within which we find our respective places are built and maintained. Maps, the United States, and Germany blended into a triune that would recast and redefine one another in a complex combination of manipulation, politics, war, and capital. But as cartographer John Pickles notes, "[Cartography] has always been a multitude of practices . . . coded and recoded by forms of institutionalized power, but always with leakage."[21] This book focuses on one such "leaky" construction of space, during one historical period, that saturated the world with maps and through constant self-affirmation erected a new Europe. By employing the deconstructive instincts of critical history and critical cartography, it exposes some of the individuals, institutions, and interests seeping through the plans, maps, and efforts used to reestablish Germany after National Socialism.

Outline of the Book

The following chapters are organized chronologically. Chapter 2 examines the history of German cartography before 1945 and the end of the Second World War. This era is important for three primary reasons. First, the chapter explores the historical development of German cartographic history. German territorial instability had been an issue in Europe ever since the creation of the Holy Roman Empire. From the conquests of Napoleon through the Frankfurt Assembly of 1848–49 and the First World War, the flexibility of central European borders produced military conflict and inculcated potential spatial solutions to the German "national question." Chapter 2 also investigates the creation and popularization of geography and cartography as academic disciplines. It argues that German intellectuals committed themselves to these disciplines and were among Europe's foremost experts regarding the study of territory and space. The uniqueness of German cartographic history is wrapped up in its nineteenth- and early-twentieth-century geographical expertise. After the Second World War, Germany was remapped through participatory occupation—that is, through the use of academic disciplines that German professors had helped to establish and popularize. This chapter's exploration of Germany's pre-1945 geography also aims to introduce the reader to two significant groups of geographers: American geographers working for US intelligence agencies and German geographers working for the Third Reich. During the Second World War, the US government began drafting plans for how to remap Germany once the National Socialists were defeated. The eventual decision of how and where to divide Germany was deeply problematic and helped to set the stage for future intra-German territorial disputes throughout the Cold War. Many of the German geographers introduced in this chapter ended up working for the Allied occupation after 1945, despite their initial loyalty to Nazi expansionism. Of particular interest is the aforementioned Emil Meynen—director of the Abteilung für Landeskunde (Department of Regional Studies), one of the only German geographical institutions to survive Germany's defeat and to be utilized by the Allied powers. Chapter 2, then, provides historical context and sets a trajectory for this book's larger interest in the institutions and personalities involved in the remapping of Germany after 1945.

Chapter 3 focuses on the immediate postwar state of Germany's geography throughout the initial postwar years, 1945 to 1949. From the earliest days of Germany's defeat until the eventual division of Germany into two separate states, the United States and other Allied powers were interested in collecting as much information about the Germans (and, in some cases, about each other) as possible. Geographers maintained a prominent position in these undertakings, and the US military extracted many of the Third Reich's most successful mapmaking academics in Operation Dustbin to be utilized throughout the postwar era. German geographers were seen as an important asset: they could contribute legitimacy to a new map of Germany, and they could potentially provide materials and skills that might give the Americans an intelligence advantage over the Soviet Union. Denazification played an obvious role in this transition. This chapter deals specifically with the denazification of German geographers and, more broadly, the denazification of schoolroom geography. Again, as an important and accessible case study, this chapter invokes Emil Meynen's attempts to maintain a group of geographic intellectuals (not to mention the academic discipline of geography) in a nation-state defeated primarily because of its obsession with territorial expansion through expulsion or liquidation. By 1949, Meynen controlled one of the only independent mapmaking and map-analyzing agencies in Germany, worked for the US military occupation government, and simultaneously helped to reestablish Germany's network of geographers. The many ways these functions overlapped are an important part of German history, not only in regard to Germany's spatial reconstruction but also with respect to the complexity and murkiness of postwar individual opportunism and generosity.

Chapter 4 grapples with the polarization of geography between geographers in the East and geographers in the West after 1949 but before the fortification of an inner German border in 1952. As both the Federal Republic of Germany and the German Democratic Republic struggled to gain some semblance of sovereignty after the Allied occupation, the participation of their geographers in this struggle was vital but often difficult to politicize (especially after the days of Lebensraum and *Geopolitik*). This chapter tracks the German geographers' shifting attitudes away from inter-German collaboration and comradery and instead toward hostility and suspicion. Although this chapter focuses primarily on the Federal Republic, it also explores the formal split between East and West, their different approaches to geographic education, and the increasing ideological tension along the "Iron Curtain" as important historical developments in which mapmakers were deeply involved and interested. Understanding literally how those lines were drawn and who was drawing them is an aspect of Cold War history that has largely been overlooked. This chapter seeks to rectify that. Moreover, the culture of distrust between East German geographers and West German geographers—a culture that was encouraged by their respective governments—serves as an instructive example of how important the presentation of German cartography remained, even after 1949.

Chapter 5 outlines the territorial history of the Federal Republic from the construction of Germany's internal "control strip" border in 1952 to the erection of the Berlin Wall in August 1961. As the Cold War became more combative, the relationship between West German geographers and the Allied occupation powers grew increasingly tense. Disagreements regarding mapmaking and, in particular, aerial photography became more frequent and brought to the fore serious questions about West German sovereignty. As this chapter argues, each Germany worked to legitimize its own claims of sovereignty by actively undermining the territorial legitimacy of its counterpart. Obviously, this legitimation regularly relied on the work and participation of geographers. Emil Meynen continued to play a prominent role in helping to draft and disseminate maps of West Germany. By the late 1950s, Meynen wore several professional hats and was simultaneously employed in the American military and the Federal Republic's Bundesrat (Federal Council). The fifth chapter continues with an examination of how the growing popularity of "public relations" came to help dictate the spatial patterns of German territory and how that space was projected to both German and non-German audiences. The disciplines of public relations and cartography were merged into a style of persuasive maps far more effective than those drawn by geographers such as Emil Meynen. This chapter argues that although academic mapmakers in

Germany were concerned with cartographic accuracy, the public-relations firms hired by the West German government created and disseminated maps meant only to project narratives favorable to their employer. This chapter ends with the construction of the Berlin Wall—where the abstract spatial posturing of Cold War rhetoric merged with the radical fortification of an intranational border, causing continual eruptions of violence.

The spatial history of Germany from 1945 to 1961 is a long slope downward from the abstract to the concrete, from the mind to the map, from ideology to border brutality. The maps produced, the governments involved in their production, and the geographers literally drawing the lines were crucial to the creation of convincing new national identities in Germany after the Second World War.

2

Germany's Cartographic Collapse

Before we present you the matters of fact, it is fit to offer to your
view the Stage whereon they were acted, for as Geography without
History seemeth a carkasse without motion, so History without
Geography, wandereth as a Vagrant without a certaine habitation.
—John Smith, *The Generall Historie of Virginia,*
New-England, and the Summer Isles (1624)

The spatial condition of Germany after the Second World War can only
be understood as one key moment in a long and continual process. The
development of German identity and nationalism, particularly regarding
the inclusion or exclusion of territory deemed "German," has a turbulent
history. This is not a remarkably unique or unusual history. Nearly every
contemporary nation-state has worked hard at forcing itself onto the world
map, typically either by pulling itself out from under the shattered framework of an imperial hegemon or by stamping out the territorial claims
of an "Other" usually proclaimed as perennially inferior. In this sense,
then, Germany mirrors other modern nation-states in its awkward march
toward the combination of space and sovereignty as well as the subsequent
territorial solidification necessary for such an abstract amalgamation. Only
after the Second World War, when Germany was quartered under Allied
occupation and its cartography was used as a tool for spatial diminution,
did it experience a kind of geographic *Sonderweg*. Getting to this turning
point, however, required a significant shift in cartographic practices and
understandings—a participatory undertaking that, when studied, nicely
sets the stage for what came after Germany's collapse in 1945.

Medieval and early-modern maps of German states recall an almost
entirely foreign procedure for mapmaking. Not only were the boundary

lines often drawn as nothing more than "porous" dashes or dots, but hundreds of Germania's maps also were variants of a mere seven sixteenth-century base maps.[1] Only by the mid–seventeenth century did cartography begin to enjoy its own renaissance throughout various German territories as map production shifted from the somewhat useful—yet almost always artful—depictions of private space to public undertakings commissioned more and more often by burgeoning nation-states. Emboldened by the Peace of Westphalia (1648) and spurred on by a new and uneasy balance of powers, European nations and empires began experimenting with large-scale cartographic representations of sovereign territory. The post-Westphalian Holy Roman Empire was no exception, even if its spatial expression differed slightly from that of its neighbors.

Created in 800 CE by Charlemagne and Pope Leo III, the Holy Roman Empire was, in the words of David Blackbourn, "a product of historical accretion, loosely draped over an array of independent, highly diverse territories"—not so much a "territorial unit" as "an archipelago of jurisdictions." Blackbourn categorizes these "jurisdictions" into three groups: major powers (Prussia, Austria, Saxony, Bavaria, Hanover, and Württemberg), small "statelets" (Lippe and Lichtenberg), and ecclesiastical units (Mainz and Cologne).[2] Despite minor territorial quibbles and borderline ambiguity, the Holy Roman Empire's major states remained largely unchanged until Napoleon established the Confederation of the Rhine in 1806. Prior to German defeat, however, and very much in accordance with the problems of other nation-states, the Germans were forced to grapple with the definition of state citizenship in the late eighteenth century. In 1794, the administration of Prussia's Frederick the Great proposed new Allgemeines Landrecht (General State Laws), which, among other precepts aimed at centralizing the government, defined state membership.[3] The Allgemeines Landrecht managed in great detail to codify Prussia's feudalist economy and absolute monarchy. Yet although this 17,000-paragraph document succeeded in making citizenship an important status for both the state and the individual, it simultaneously failed to describe exactly how citizenship was determined and simply made broad and ambiguous gestures as to what citizenship was. Nevertheless, the Prussians living under Frederick the Great now had an irretrievable new relationship to the state and to the territorial negotiations that took place between Prussia and the neighbors along its borders.

By 1806, France had dismantled the Holy Roman Empire. In 1792, after declaring war against Austria and Prussia in a bout of revolutionary fervor, the French military began seeping into Germania's northwestern borders. After the rise of Napoleon and the intensification of the French invasion, the German territories along the left bank of the Rhine River fell under the occupation of the French.[4] By 1802, the entire Rhineland had been ceded to the French through a series of treaties made between Napoleon, Prussia, and Austria—settlements that typically ceded parts of the Holy Roman Empire to the French in order to maintain the autonomy of the empire's major powers (i.e., Prussia and Austria).[5] As the historian Thomas Nipperdey notes, during 1803 the "map of Germany was redrawn . . . [and] effectively simplified."[6] The *Mittelstaaten*, or middle states, which had been territorially chipped away at over the previous decade, were consolidated into one territorial bloc and finally allowed a brief taste of the sovereignty and power that had until this point been enjoyed almost exclusively by the political and military polar juggernauts Prussia and Austria. After a series of battles in which the Austro-Russian coalition against Napoleon was repeatedly overwhelmed—most importantly at the Battle of Austerlitz in December 1805—Austrian ruler Franz I abdicated his throne as Holy Roman emperor in August 1806. As a consequence, large swaths of Austrian territory were ceded to the *Mittelstaaten* and to Italy.[7]

Franz I's abdication had a great deal to do with the shifting territorial development of greater Germany. On July 16, 1806, Napoleon established the Confederation of the Rhine, a new territorial bloc created by a geographic mass exodus of *Mittelstaaten* from the Holy Roman Empire. Under the protection of the Napoleonic Empire, this new confederation was meant to serve as a "third Germany" that could counterbalance Prussia and Austria—a territorial and military buffer zone for France. Although the confederation maintained the sovereignty of several of its German member states, the larger kingdoms and principalities such as Baden, Württemberg, Bavaria, and Hesse-Darmstadt effectively sucked up many of the small ecclesiastical territories.[8] As with many of the territorial changes Napoleon imposed onto the European map, the cartographic consolidations and borderlines created at this time lasted well beyond the political unit established to maintain them. By 1813, after incrementally pushing French forces out of the region, the Sixth Coalition of anti-Napoleonic allies, including Austria, Prussia, Russia, and the United Kingdom, dissolved the Confederation of the Rhine. Almost immediately, Prussia annexed the state of Saxony and was soon granted Westphalia and the Rhineland for its participation in liberating the Confederation of the Rhine. These adjustments were solidified at the Congress of Vienna (September 1814–June 1815) and after the defeat of Napoleon at the Battle of Waterloo on June 15, 1815, effectively doubling the population of Prussia and providing it with a rich endowment of resources vital to the growth of its economic and political influence.

The year 1815 also saw the creation of the German Confederation, a loose conglomerate of German states that almost entirely mirrored the territorial demarcations of Napoleon's Confederation of the Rhine, with the important exception of including Prussia and Austria as member states. From 1815 to 1866, the German Confederation succeeded at maintaining relative peace between its German participants and thus was also able to maintain the cartographic status quo. The one exception to Germany's territorial stability during this period was the national revolution of 1848. In 1848–49, an elected German national assembly met in Frankfurt and attempted to establish a unified nation-state. Although parliamentary discussion concerning national borders "took up only a small amount of time,"[9] and although the Frankfurt Assembly was eventually dissolved in 1849, problematic German-speaking states such as Schleswig to the north, Posen to the east, and Tyrol to the south made clear the difficulties of establishing the borders of a greater Germany. The Frankfurt Assembly, for the first time in German history, pushed the issue of territorial unity to the forefront of the *national* consciousness and forced members of the German public to begin searching for spatial solutions to their national "question."[10] Mobility increased tremendously during this period as the relatively long-lasting transnational German Confederation allowed easier interstate movement for German residents.[11] By the mid-1800s, many German states had also built a substantial network of railways—a development that Wolfgang Schivelbusch convincingly argues helped to "annihilate" previous cultural understandings of space and time in Europe.[12] The combination of (relatively) high-speed transportation and diluted intra-German borderlines had steep political consequences as migrant workers became more and more prominent throughout greater Germany. When foreign labor became more influential in state economies and the foreign poor became more taxing on public budgets, German states began passing legislation to expel migrants. Prussia, for example, created a law in 1842 establishing its right to unilaterally oust the foreign poor. In doing so, the state also had to establish what it meant to be "foreign," laying the legal groundwork for modern German citizenship.[13] It should come as no surprise that as mobility increased, and as German states began to define who did and did not belong to their respective territorial holdings, the 1840s also brought with them the first maps of a greater German nation.[14] Although war and conflict may have carved the boundaries of the German nation, the production of spatial representations of that nation were spurred by both a changing infrastructure and by the urgent need to categorize those who were "German" and those who were not.

But if war did not necessarily prompt the initial gestures toward modern citizenship and nation drawing, it most certainly solidified those concepts as fundamental complements to nineteenth-century German nationalist movements. Moreover, war in the latter half of the nineteenth century drove the development of cartographic techniques and map dissemination in German states (particularly in Prussia) to unprecedented levels of spatial acumen. The first maps produced for the General Staff of the Prussian military, for example, were finished in 1841.[15] That is an embarrassingly late date when we compare it to map development in France, a state that had been drafting maps for its military commanders (and *by* its military commanders) since the sixteenth century. Maps were, in fact, particularly useful and heavily relied upon during France's War of Devolution (1667) and War of the Reunions (1683–84) against Spain.[16] Yet by the Franco-Prussian War (1870–71), not thirty years after Prussia began integrating maps into its military, the Prussians had developed far more maps, more accurate maps, and more comprehensive maps than their French counterparts. As the historian Michael Howard notes, the French had been caught cartographically unprepared for war against the

Prussians, having almost no up-to-date maps of even their own nation-state's terrain. French military officers were often forced to "requisition maps from [France's] local schools and estate offices."[17] The Prussian map-makers, in contrast, had been preparing for this conflict for some time, sending many of their most talented artists into the French borderlands to plot the terrain there clandestinely.[18] Although historians usually (and rightly) recognize the Prussians' victory over the French in 1871 as a result of Prussia's dense network of railways, its allies in the German Confedera-tion, and the productivity of the Prussian steel industry, it certainly did not hurt to have accurate spatial data to rely on. In fact, the detail-oriented focus of German military geography left a deep impression not simply on the French military but also on France's civilian population.[19]

What accounts for this shift in cartographic expertise—this inversion of French and German productivity regarding land surveys? How in the span of roughly thirty years did the Germans so quickly find themselves on the cutting edge of mapmaking? One small piece of this puzzle can be found in the development of Germany's academic geography depart-ments and associations, a story dealt with at length in this chapter. Several other historians and sociologists have also fleshed out important factors related to this problem. Rogers Brubaker has argued that Germans had always seen themselves as being on some sort of cultural frontier. Whereas France found spatial stability not only in its geographic position but also in the relatively early solidification of its national boundaries, German space often overlapped with a perennial Slavic "Other."[20] Brubaker goes on to claim that this geographic situation caused German nationalism to identify as primarily ethnocultural rather than (as in France) political, and because this nationalism came to full fruition prior to the establish-ment of a modern German nation-state in 1871, the creation of that state was bound to be imperfect: some Germans (especially Austro-Germans) somewhere were going to be left out, just as some French, Danes, Poles, and Slavs somewhere were going to be brought in. As has already been mentioned, this problem became particularly clear during the Frankfurt Assembly's discussions on national territory during the revolution in Ger-many in 1848. So when modern Germany was established in 1871, mil-lions of Austro-Germans were kept out of the new state because Austria was excluded from German integration and centralization. But with the inclusion of Alsace-Lorraine, North Schleswig, and East Prussia in the new Germany, tens of thousands of French, Danish, and Polish people were suddenly living under centralized German rule.[21] By constantly reassessing and working to analyze their (literal) position on the European map in relation to the Slavic "Other," nineteenth-century Germans may have emphasized the importance of maps and orientation more than their French counterparts simply because of the perceived vulnerability of their national character and the instability of their spatial structure.

The creation and consolidation of a modern Germany in 1871 were, then, a triumphant ending to a national narrative couched in largely spatial terms. Prussian chancellor Otto von Bismarck's vision of a modern (Prussianized) German state was accomplished through an orchestrated series of battles concerned with reshaping the map of central Europe. The Prussians successfully goaded the Austrians into a territorial dispute with Denmark over Schleswig-Holstein in 1863 (and subsequently into a war in 1864). After jointly defeating the Danish, the victors agreed at the Gastein Convention of 1865 that Prussia would control Schleswig and Austria would control Holstein. Shortly thereafter, Bismarck called for an end to the German Confederation and a renewal of commitment by smaller German states to the Zollverein, the German Customs Union, which excluded Austria from the economic benefits of interstate commerce among greater-German continental territories. The changes proposed by Bismarck so blatantly favored Prussian hegemony at the expense of Austrian influence that the Austrians declared war against Prussia in 1866. Within a few short months, Prussia had handily defeated the Austrians and by the following year had established the new North German Confederation.[22] Postwar annexations, consolidations, and occupations led to a Germany dominated by Prussia and a clear-cut territorial demarcation between this new Germany and its Austrian counterpart. Yet only after the defeat of the French in 1871 did Prussia finally unify Germany under its influence, declaring at Versailles the creation of the Second German Reich.

As previously mentioned, the inclusion of territories into this new Reich that had traditionally vacillated between two different cultural polar points (the northern Prussians and the southern Austrians) was problematic. As the "long nineteenth century" wore on, German nationalists and their various counterparts along an ever-solidifying "linguistic frontier" worked to destroy whatever national ambiguity was left among border dwellers. By 1880, Germany had begun releasing an imperial census, making it easy for fervent nationalists to pinpoint the whereabouts of linguistic infiltration—the small leaks in the cultural dam of Germanism.[23] Historians have done an excellent job of studying these situations and pointing out the superficial construction of these "frontiers." Nancy Wingfield has analyzed the competing cultural icons throughout these contested territories, identifying the term *frontier* as nothing more than the categorization of a place (real or imagined) where Germans spoke another language.[24] Pieter Judson has written about the Moravian Compromise of 1905, which split large swaths of land into Czech or German provinces. According to Judson, these types of agreements were not unusual and concerned themselves with contentious spaces such as Bukovina, Galicia, and Budweis throughout the early twentieth century.[25] Tara Zahra, too, notes the rising nationalist rhetoric along the German–Czech borderlands during the fin de siècle. Although Zahra mentions the importance of "maps and census statistics," which, according to her, "have notoriously served to obscure bilingualism and national ambiguity in East Central Europe," her primary focus is the targeting of children for the purposes of border solidification. Children, she argues, were problematic for nationalists because of their ability to learn languages quickly and live happily as bilingual (or even trilingual) residents of a space that was difficult to culturally categorize. In an effort to curb this development, Czech and German nationalists promoted a political culture in which children were identified as belonging more to their respective "nation" than to their parents—a dichotomy so popular that it lasted deep into the twentieth century (and, arguably, still lingers to this day).[26]

For all of these cultural attempts at identifying various ethnic and linguistic distinctions and cordoning off their respective places to the most appropriate state power, it was another military conflict that most effectively wreaked havoc across the continental map (yet again) and determined the new borders of German space. As other historians have noted, maps prior to the First World War (1914–18) tended to be isolated representations, spatial narratives drawn as individual responses to Europe's territorial questions.[27] After the First World War, however, mapping became a much more deliberate and systematic undertaking, with an entire enterprise constructed for the dissemination of this new (and increasingly abundant) cartographic information. Part of this shift had to do with the increasing prominence of geography as an academic discipline—a development discussed at further length in the following pages. Another and perhaps more urgent contributing factor to the systematization of mapmaking was the collapse of Europe's imperial powers after the defeat of Germany in 1918. The division of the Austro-Hungarian and Ottoman Empires, the territorial uncertainty surrounding a defeated Germany, and Russia's self-imposed territorial reductions led to the emergence of what geographers would later call Europe's "shatter zone."[28] In response to this cartographic "shattering," the Entente powers (in particular the United States) took an active role in reshaping Europe according to the ethnographic and linguistic "frontiers" that had been so contentiously constructed by various nationalist functionaries and organizations. Both geographers and historians have carefully studied this redrafting of the European map (although the geographers tend to pay a bit more attention than the historians to the maps themselves). Neil Smith has argued that this Anglo-American remapping, done under the careful watch and supervision of President Woodrow Wilson's (and later President Franklin D. Roosevelt's) geographer Isaiah Bowman, helped to usher in the age of globalization.[29] Wesley Reisser, in his analysis of the famous *Black Book* that bound together all of the Entente map proposals, argues that this project was far less devious than Smith would have us believe. According to Reisser, what geographers and historians refer to as "the Inquiry" was an attempt by the US State Department to fairly and objectively redraw Europe after the Great War, an effort that, according to Reisser, was largely successful. Today's European maps maintain many of the same lines drawn by "the Inquiry."[30] To read Reisser's account of Europe's postwar mapping, though, is to read a history of doe-eyed idealists doing their utmost to save Europe from its territorial ambiguity—a kind of "salvation by place-name."

The historians' analyses are more cynical. Rather than a shift to globalization, as Neil Smith would have us believe, the cartographic "shattering" and rebuilding of central and eastern Europe were a point of continuity, one episode in a long series of territorial reconfigurations. And rather than adopt Reisser's glossy apologia for the US State Department, historians are right to point out just how messy things got after the First World War. Rather than tempering growing nationalist sentiment, the lines drawn by "the Inquiry" did not end territorial categorization and in fact forced even more people into classifying themselves with a particular national affiliation.[31] Armed with the righteous proclamations of Wilson's Fourteen Points, many new European nation-states began to mold public space into an affirmation of self-created and self-determined historical narratives. The Germans, for example, worked hard to "de-Austrianize" Czechoslovakia, while the Czechs tore down the German, Habsburg, and Roman Catholic monuments and symbols that littered their newfound political boundary line.[32] The most (in)famous of these cases, of course, was the Sudetenland—that stubborn German nation within a Czechoslovakian state. Under the guise of pan-German protectionism, the Third Reich would use the nation-states drawn by "the Inquiry" to make its own case for ignoring the boundaries of those states in service to the nations living within them. The lines on the map, rather than annotating internationally recognized points of demarcation, would come to symbolize "the incompleteness of the national project."[33]

Germany lost roughly 13 percent of its territorial holdings after adopting the Treaty of Versailles (1919), including Alsace-Lorraine, the Polish Corridor, and northern Schleswig-Holstein.[34] It should come as no surprise, then, that after both the defeat and remapping of Germany by the Allied powers, "the discourses of German self-determination became thoroughly cartographic." Moreover, the initial geographic framework for justifying the Third Reich's expansionist foreign policy came not from proto-Nazis but from angry Weimar-era mapmakers.[35] Few Germans were pleased with the new postwar boundaries imposed on them by the Triple Entente. And although Germany's spatial development had always been fluid, the Treaty of Versailles marked the end of an era that had experienced particular border mutability. The historian Annemarie Sammartino writes that any German fifty years old and living in Germany in 1920 would have "lived through at least four German states with five different borders." And, she adds, "not one of these states perfectly expressed the unity of ethnic, linguistic, and cultural homogeneity that lay at the basis of the nationalist imaginary."[36]

As border changes intensified and became more politically important and contentious after the First World War, geographers and cartographers became more and more committed to the dissemination of a particular national picture. The study of "geopolitics" had existed prior to the First World War, but many of its adherents began arguing for a geopolitical *Sonderweg* in Germany after the war. Germany was geographically situated to orient itself on a special middle path and to refuse to completely adopt either Western liberalism or Eastern socialism.[37] Political statements reflecting this middle path often became favored over cartographic "accuracy" as territorial tensions increased.[38] The Germans, of course, were not the only nation using maps to bolster their territorial objectives. Along their eastern boundary, for example, the Czechs became more and more vigilant in blocking mobility along the border. Those happy (but unlucky and increasingly hard-to-find) residents of nationally ambiguous towns and villages were forced into choosing between Czech nationalists and "their own cross-border social networks."[39] As the twentieth century drove on, the maintenance of transborder social relationships became more difficult when spatial fluidity was increasingly seen as a threat to state sovereignty and cultural insulation. Yet as international borders solidified, nations expanded within cultural imaginations. If geographers learned anything after the First World War and "the Inquiry's" attempts to map an ethnographically accurate Europe, it was that finding "true" borders was an impossible task. The mental maps established by cultural histories and engraved into the nationalists' psyches were rarely reflected in full by the internationally sanctioned maps of Europe. Solutions to this contradiction varied, but the German response—eventually just to ignore other territorial claims—rightfully became the most notorious. As Nazi Schutzstaffel (SS) commander Heinrich Himmler was so fond of saying, "Blood is our border."[40]

The historian Theodore Hamerow has written—in a melodramatic display of *Sonderweg* history—that "to study German history is to witness the unfolding of a national tragedy."[41] Many historians still give too much purchase to the idea that the German past is a "site of pathology, where social and political development had from the beginning gone 'wrong.'"[42] As David Blackbourn and Geoff Eley make so clear, historians had assigned a "special path" to Germany long before the First World War.[43] Since that war, Germany's "path" has not been portrayed as a positive one, but rather as a mark of backwardness and aggressiveness, of dark turns and "national tragedy."

Although I reject the carving of a uniquely evil German notch into the bedpost of modern historiography, I refuse to dismiss outright the concept of exceptionalism in historical development. Germany *is* exceptional. As Max Otte points out, Germany was at the epicenter of Europe's most radical twentieth-century remappings in 1919, 1945, and 1990.[44] Whether one is working to discover the origins of cartography and geography as academic disciplines, the most systematic ethnic cleansing in the history of the world, the front lines of the Cold War, or the viability of today's European Union, one cannot help but find Germany as a source (usually the primary source) driving these histories. Germany—this engine of countless historical narratives and analyses—is a spatial creature, and its geography deserves continuous investigation.

Geography: A German Profession

As professional and academic disciplines, geography and cartography were born in Germany. In fact, the historian of geography Geoffrey Martin argues that classical geography—a geography that could be mastered by scholars of all stripes—died in 1859 alongside its final (and perhaps most notable) adherents, Carl Ritter (1779–1859) and Alexander von Humboldt (1769–1859).[45] It was these two German scholars who helped usher geography from the periphery of academic study into the Age of Specialization. As Martin so aptly notes, by the late nineteenth century any hope of one individual embracing "universal knowledge" was dead.[46] But Humboldt and Ritter, two of the last great preeminent scholars, were considered by most of the educated world to have gotten pretty close and were hugely influential in establishing the study of space among specialized academic disciplines. Humboldt's work on *Erdbeschreibung*, "earth description," and Ritter's book *Die Erdkunde*, "Earth Studies" (1817–18), helped lay the groundwork for more detailed investigations of geography within an ever-growing network of German higher education.[47]

In 1874, Prussia became the first state to create a chair for the study of geography in each of its universities. Having just consolidated the German territories into a modern nation-state three years earlier, and having seen the advantages brought on by having proper maps during the Franco-Prussian War, the Prussian government saw these chairs as an important academic investment. By 1880, Prussia had ten chairs of geography, with another three yet to be filled.[48] This commitment to studying space helped spur on development throughout Prussia and in other parts of Germany. In 1882, the Zentralkommission für wissenschaftliche Landeskunde (Central Commission for Scientific Regional Geography) was founded, and geography continued to expand throughout German universities, prompting one British observer to note in 1886 that "now [as opposed to a dozen years ago] geography is on an equal footing with other [academic] branches in more than half of the German universities."[49]

Germany also became an increasingly important participant in international geographical undertakings. Indeed, it was a German geographer—Albrecht Penck (1858–1945)—who recognized that in order to truly draw an accurate world picture, international cooperation and uniform mapping processes and procedures were necessary. In 1891, Penck proposed the drafting of an "International Map of the World," a project that was doomed to eventual failure but that nonetheless made clear Germany's role as a world leader in the community of mapmaking and map-studying states.[50] It was in this period of avant-garde geographic internationalism that academics in German geography departments would begin to develop concepts such as Lebensraum and *Geopolitik*.

Friedrich Ratzel (1844–1904) was the first to popularize the concept of Lebensraum with the publication of *Politische Geographie* in 1897, which became the literary bedrock of modern political geography.[51] Within thirty years of its publication, *Politische Geographie* had been reissued three times and had become enormously popular in German universities.[52] The book also received a great deal of praise from English-speaking geographers for its ability to turn political geography into a respectable discipline that had "hitherto [been] treated in [English] textbooks . . . [as] the driest and most unprofitable of all tasks."[53]

Indeed, Ratzel's theory of political geography did just that. A trained zoologist turned journalist-geographer, Ratzel focused largely on implementing a Darwinian view of struggle into an organic, almost Hegelian understanding of the state. He saw the state as a natural result of geography. As one historian notes, "It was, in fact, the land itself, according to Ratzel, that called forth the state."[54] In this sense, geography played an important role in the lives of the people who inhabited it. Each nation (or, as Ratzel called it, *Volk*) and land (*Boden*) went through a semiotic exchange on which both eventually came to rely. Ratzel understood this exchange to be very explicit; his use of the term *Boden* not only invokes the abstract idea of territory but also translates literally to "soil." Thus, for a nation to lose its geographic space or for the same geographic space to be ripped away from its *Volk* was, in essence, to kill both.[55] By characterizing the state in such a way, *Politische Geographie* glorified the agrarian life—that is, the closest relationship possible between *Volk* and *Boden*.[56] Moreover, in true Hegelian form, Ratzel emphasized the importance of movement, growth, and struggle for both human life and the life of the organic state. To draw "inorganic" borders, to artificially limit the state from its natural desire to undertake the dialectical expansion necessary for the existence of any organic life-form, Ratzel argued, upset the natural balance of both the nation and the land (an idea that the German nationalists later utilized in full force after the Treaty of Versailles).[57] Ratzel later introduced the concept of Lebensraum as a prerequisite for a state's existence. It was, in fact, necessary for *Volk* and *Boden* to exist in a dynamic geographic space where both could naturally grow free from seemingly arbitrary, unnatural restriction.

However, an overtly political and racial theme would not be added to Ratzel's geodeterminist concepts until the academic ascension of his student, the Swedish Germanophile Rudolf Kjellén (1864–1922). Kjellén had been trained in the German discipline of *Staatswissenschaft*, which combined law, politics, economics, and history. He was strongly influenced by Ratzel's geographical theories and in 1917 (notably in the throes of the First World War) published *Der Staat als Lebensform*, which was an explicit attempt to politicize Ratzel's work.[58] Kjellén argued that Ratzel was far too simplistic in analyzing the nature of the organic state. The expression of the state as a territory—which Kjellén termed *Geopolitik*, the coining of this term—was only one of five ways the life of the state made itself manifest. The other four included *Demopolitik* (the politics of population, in which there consisted a racial hierarchy), *Wirtschaftspolitik* (the politics of the economy), *Soziopolitik* (the politics of society), and *Herrschaftspolitik* (the politics of power). Through the use of these five ways, the state preserved its own existence.[59] According to Andreas Dorpalen, Kjellén considered the state an instinctual, organic being whose existence was contingent upon obeying "the categorical political imperative of expanding [its] space by colonization, amalgamation, or conquest."[60] Only by solidifying its power internally and externally through the use of its five media could a state truly thrive.

Although these ideas had been circulating throughout Germany for years and had grown in popularity within the confines of academia, it took the outbreak of the First World War and Germany's subsequent humiliating defeat to unify the majority of the German populace behind them. The new and unnatural territorial lines drawn by the Entente powers' meeting at Versailles contradicted the fundamental principles of German geographic study as outlined by Ratzel and Kjellén. It would be through the use of these two thinkers' theories that German geographers would attempt to reconstruct post–First World War Germany. Nearly all academicians and politicians would clamor for a renewed national character, but the different politicizations and interpretations of Lebensraum and *Geopolitik* would make the decision on how to go about doing this incredibly difficult and hotly contested.

Ironically but unsurprisingly, the first calls for an overtly political cartography were made by a geographer who had studied the persuasiveness of British and American maps. In 1921, Joseph März, an employee of the new Weimar Republic's Reichswehrministerium (Ministry of Defense), published an article in which, according to Guntram Henrik Herb, he contrasted British maps with "the bland, ineffectual, and overly scientific style of German maps."[61] He claimed that although the British had falsified geographic locations on their maps, the more interesting and necessary aspect of their cartography was a "clever presentation" of geographic information that bolstered the national identity of the British populace. März's critique of German cartography fell short of establishing a concrete method of implementing his suggestion, but he did offer one important practice he hoped would be implemented: a call for German geographers to publish only maps that showed "the pre–First World War boundaries . . . to ensure that the lost German territories would never fade from the memory of the German people."[62] This call prompted many German geographers to begin creating inventories of territorial descriptions for potential use in making territorial claims throughout eastern Europe.[63] Moreover, many postwar German maps began to emphasize German settlements beyond its eastern borders and as far as Polotsk, Minsk, Kamenets-Podolsky, and Siebenbürgen/Transylvania. The borderlines of these maps were often heavily exaggerated to favor German expansion and were "intensively propagated" until 1945.[64] (For example, see figure 1.[65])

A mere month after the publication of März's cartographic critique, the Weimar Republic's national geography convention met and passed a resolution proclaiming "that it is a national necessity and duty that the link to Germandom of the areas which were torn from the German Empire in the Treaty of Versailles, including the colonies, remains clearly visible in atlases and maps" and "advocat[ing] that only those works for which this is the case, be used for instruction in all school grades."[66] By 1922, General Karl Haushofer (1869–1946)—a geographer at the University of Munich and a hero of the First World War—began to offer through a series of articles published in the academic journal *Grenzboten* (Messages from the Border) a more comprehensive way to implement a kind of suggestive cartography. Haushofer demanded that cartographers and geographers alike utilize maps and atlases as overt political media for inculcating a desired national German character (as he, like März, claimed the British had been doing for decades by this time).[67] Rather than merely rely on older maps dated before the Treaty of Versailles, German cartographers should focus on presenting a contemporary world drawn contrary to the maps created by the Entente powers. As Haushofer would write several years later, "Nothing is more dangerous than to resign oneself to a loss which is not the result of natural necessity, but of an artificial and arbitrary act."[68]

1. Ministry of Public Enlightenment and Propaganda, Third Reich, *Deutsches Grenzland in Not*, scale not given, in "A Geography Lesson for Young Germany," *New York Times*, Mar. 17, 1935. This map is a great example of post–First World War mapmaking, with its emphasis on territorial diminution and the greater German Reich.

In order to gain academic acceptance for his ideas as well as to include different perspectives on geopolitics from other disciplines, Haushofer gathered together a group of like-minded political geographers and founded the *Zeitschrift für Geopolitik* (Journal of Geopolitics) in 1924. Far too many historians have overblown the importance of this academic monthly journal, however, along with that of Haushofer's own political influence. Haushofer did not mold Hitler's understanding of geography, dictate Nazi wartime strategy, or, as several postwar historians have parroted, direct the operations of the fictional Institut für Geopolitik.[69] His ability to shift academic discussions about Germany's spatial developments was much more important (and more real) than any ability he had to shift German foreign policy. His work did eventually come to dictate the intellectual discussion on geography in the Weimar Republic as well as influence several prominent politicians and institutions over the next decade. Within a few years of initial publication, the *Zeitschrift* would enjoy an annual circulation that fluctuated between 3,000 and 5,000 until its suspension in 1944.[70]

The members of the *Zeitschrift*'s editorial board had very different ideas about how the concepts of Lebensraum and *Geopolitik* should be applied to their journal or to the German national identity they hoped to revive. The four primary geographers who made up the journal's editorial core for the duration of its publication were Haushofer, Kurt Vowinckel, Erich Obst, and Otto Maull. Both Haushofer and Vowinckel were committed relatively early on to the political goals of the Nationalsozialistische Deutsche Arbeiterpartei (German National Socialist [Nazi] Party) and wanted to use their journal as a catalyst through which to combine Kjellén's theoretical thought with the National Socialist movement. Maull was particularly upset by this approach and felt that the racial and political implications of such a merger were a distraction from the real theoretical underpinnings of political geography.[71] In an editorial published in 1928, Maull explicitly declared Ratzel and his theory of natural territory as the only manifestation of the state to be the true foundation of geopolitics. He implicitly suggested that Vowinckel and Haushofer's glorification of Kjellén, their political activism (including their inclination to produce publications focusing on political science rather than on geography), and their racial understandings of the state had forced the *Zeitschrift* into a "regrettable digression" of nongeographical orientation.[72] According to Maull, geopolitics and political geography were one and the same and were distinct from political science and contemporary political institutions.

Haushofer and Vowinckel immediately responded, producing essays that attempted to undermine Maull's assertion and declared geopolitics and political geography to be two separate disciplines. They believed that whereas political geography mapped out a political distribution of the world through the use of cartography, geopolitics was the use of political institutions and ideologies to educate and shape a national collective consciousness in respect to that distribution.[73] This rift between Maull and his editorial peers is important when one considers the connection Haushofer and Vowinckel were attempting to build between politics and geography as well as their early political endorsement of the Nazi Party. Ratzel's theory of Lebensraum did not argue for a unified nationalism defined by biological or ethnic differences, which was a key tenet of the National Socialist movement. Rather, during his lifetime Ratzel openly criticized scholars who attempted to racialize his Lebensraum concept.[74]

Yet as the political climate of the Weimar Republic began to favor the conservative nationalist movements, Haushofer and Vowinckel's intellectual persuasion won out in the *Zeitschrift*, and the journal increasingly became more a political instrument than a vehicle of scholarly debate. After Adolf Hitler was appointed chancellor of Germany in January 1933, Vowinckel became especially interested in establishing *Geopolitik* as a central tenet of Nazi ideology. However, the Nazi leadership found the *Zeitschrift*'s efforts to legitimize geopolitical study unreliable. Hitler himself found Haushofer personally intolerable (although this may have had to do with Haushofer suggesting in 1938 that Germany should be satisfied with its foreign-policy achievements).[75] Although Haushofer and Vowinckel's (and Kjellén's) ideas seemed to serve as a convenient intellectual buttress for German geographical expansion and cartographic propaganda, their direct influence over the Third Reich's policies was severely limited.[76]

The National Socialist movement may not have been interested in these ideas, but the government of the Weimar Republic had been convinced. Thus, by the time the Nazis rose to power, there was already a scattered government infrastructure dedicated to mapping and planning the ecological resources and provincial boundaries of nearly all of Germany's regions. The various leadership organizations that founded these area planning centers were often explicitly influenced by the *Zeitschrift* and its editorial board.[77]

Hitler's rise to power and the subsequent Nazification of German universities was a welcome change for the vast majority of geographers, who embraced this new regime in the hope of finally putting into place their academic vision of a reinvigorated national identity.[78] In 1942—a year in which the German Reich seemed committed to eastward territorial expansion and colonization—there was a growing interest among geographers regarding the concept of Lebensraum. In an attempt to save this idea from serving as nothing more than a practical military concept, Ernst Friedrich Flohr published an article attempting to "clarify" it. He claimed that only a "true *Volk*" could really benefit from the existence of Lebensraum.[79] During the Weimar Republic, health professionals and educators had done an excellent job of linking "race hygiene" to geography in an effort to influence public policy.[80] This had also been a fairly common argument in intellectual circles and had already been used extensively throughout all levels of the German geographical education system as a means for promoting the idea of a "wandering" Jewish people. The Jews were not entitled to any place of their own because, in fact, they were not a *Volk* at all.[81] Flohr, however, added to this notion the need for a definite distinction between a "true" and "false" orbit of Lebensraum. The "false" was simply a pragmatic zone, occupied for economic use (his example for this definition was an African colonial territory) in order to secure the "true" Lebensraum. Several other geographers contributed to this discussion, all of them consistently agreeing that there was a great deal more to the concept of Lebensraum than some sort of simple, "applied geography" that had "a much more practical commitment to fight for German space."[82] The Nazis discarded all of these geographers, including the *Zeitschrift* group, in favor of those who promoted a more militarized version of Lebensraum—a version that was both seemingly beneficial to the national character of Germany and to Hitler's own personal vision, a vision he seemed to have developed long before these academic disagreements.[83] Regardless, the development of geography and cartography, of Lebensraum and *Geopolitik*, characterized a German discipline that was internationally admired and that the universities and faculty of other nation-states (such as Great Britain and the United States) attempted to emulate.[84]

German Geography under the Third Reich

After coming to power in 1933, the National Socialists inherited a vibrant class of intellectuals studying geography and cartography.[85] Determined to revise German education to meet its political goals, the Nazi Party made a habit of exploiting ideological tension between university faculty to its benefit. Opportunistic faculty members often had no qualms about exposing the racial or political identity of their colleagues in an effort to advance their own careers more quickly and easily.[86] Although several geographers happily worked to propagate the Nazis' racialized geographies through textbooks and maps,[87] many more simply remained silent on political issues under the Third Reich. This was relatively easy to do as so few geographers were fired after the passage of the Gesetz zur Wiederherstellung des Berufsbeamtentums (Law for the Restoration of the Professional Civil Service) in April 1933. Whereas 25 percent (that is, 188) of German university mathematicians went into hiding or exile during the Third Reich because of their Jewish heritage, only six geographers left or were removed from their respective posts.[88]

There was also, however, some resistance to the changes imposed on German universities by the National Socialists—for example, from Carl Troll, a geography professor at the University of Munich and an individual who became increasingly prominent after the Second World War. One of Troll's colleagues, Alfred Philippson, was a geographer who studied the Mediterranean region and happened to be Jewish. Philippson was first fired, then imprisoned at Theresienstadt, and finally slated for deportation to Poland. Troll interceded on Philippson's behalf by contacting his friend the Swedish geographer Sven Hedin. Hedin was a sympathetic Nazi collaborator who shared political values and a mutual admiration with Hitler. Pressured by Troll into vouching for Philippson, Hedin made sure that the Nazi higher-ups kept Philippson out of the Polish death camps. Philippson managed to survive the Holocaust and died in 1953 after resuming his work.[89] Troll was never reprimanded or punished for advocating on his behalf.

Another important Jewish geographer whose career was negatively affected by National Socialism was Alfred Hettner. A student of Fried-rich Ratzel and a staunch political conservative, Hettner had held the first chair in geography at the University of Heidelberg and had retired to emeritus status in 1928.[90] Even in his retirement, he continued to encourage the development of geographical ideas through a newsletter he had founded in 1895, the *Geographische Zeitschrift*. The Nazi regime forced him to give up his editorial position in 1935 because he was "Nichtvolla-rier," or "not full Aryan."[91] Hettner died in 1941 before the full implementation of the Holocaust but lived out his final years labeled a *Mischling*, "mixed blood," under the Third Reich.[92] His work on regional geography had an immediate impact in his field (particularly on Carl Sauer at the University of California, Berkeley) and influenced countless students of geography. His dismissal, however, was not met with opposition. In fact, by 1936 geography professors at the University of Heidelberg had begun organizing special seminars that focused on the borders of the new Nazi Germany and worked to establish institutional links between their department, their community, and the *Volksgemeinschaft*, "people's community" (a term used to invoke a sense of national, collective identity). Examples like this of institutional cooperation with the National Socialists' racist agenda have led some historians to argue that the majority of academic resistance to Nazi-imposed personnel changes was prompted not by sympathy for the Jews but by the threat of losing departmental autonomy.[93]

This brings up some interesting questions: Just how involved were German geographers in the spatial politics of Nazi Germany? Although some of them (notably Carl Troll) advocated on behalf of particularly close colleagues, did any of them help plan the invasion and occupation of surrounding European nation-states? How, exactly, was a new Nazi geography imposed onto German mapmaking? These are important questions to address before moving on to the reconstruction of Germany after the

Second World War. Many of these pro-Nazi (or at the very least complicit) geographers would help to reshape their nation-state under the supervision of a victorious Allied coalition after Germany's defeat in 1945. The radical changes to German maps and the maps' authors from 1933 to 1945, then, deserve some investigation.

As has already been mentioned, after the appointment of Hitler as chancellor in 1933 and the institutionalization of National Socialism, the discipline of geography saw more funding opportunities and increased political relevance. Suddenly, at least for many geographers, the global depression of the 1930s came to an end, and funding for conferences, research studies, and publications became available once again.[94] But there were deep and significant changes to the structure of academic geography. German cartophiles, for example, had an extensive network of geography societies and associations by the early twentieth century. Like so many other nations, German mapmakers and map admirers had begun establishing these organizations by the mid–nineteenth century. Germany's first professional society for geographers and cartographers was the Gesellschaft für Erdkunde zu Berlin (Berlin Geographical Society), founded in 1828.[95] That is only seven years after the Parisian Société de Géographie (Paris Geographical Society) was established, and more than twenty years before the creation of the American Geographical Society in New York City. And although the first "prototype" association for geographical societies was founded by the British Empire in 1788, the Association for Promoting the Discovery of the Interior Parts of Africa, Britain's Royal Geographical Society came into existence only with the merging of this Africa Association and the Palestine Association in 1830.

By 1933, the Nazi leadership had broken up all of the German professional geographical societies and slated them for reorganization.[96] This reshaping of all mapping agencies (private and public) was complex and almost absurdly detailed. The development of these efforts is recounted here not simply to boggle the reader's mind but to illustrate the Third Reich's inclination to micromanage its bureaucracy and its private industry. These changes also help to show just how vital the Nazis understood geography and cartography to be to the new Reich and its expansion. The majority of the information regarding Nazi cartographic policy recounted here has been taken from a report prepared by the OSS's Division of Map Intelligence and Cartography in 1947.

On July 3, 1934, the Prussian minister of the interior Wilhelm Frick instituted a series of new regulations to govern every mapping agency in Nazi Germany. Among other stipulations, the law made clear that the "Reich is in control of all surveying," that the "Minister of the Interior will regulate the professional training of surveyors and the operation of private surveyors," and that the minister held the authority to regulate all land surveying, the administration of all land registers, the unification of measurements, and any taxation associated with map surveying and mapmaking.[97] This law was focused primarily on gaining regulatory control over Germany's chief mapping agency, the Reichsamt für Landesaufnahme (RfL, Reich Office of State Survey). The RfL had existed since the First World War and throughout the Weimar years had slowly transitioned from a cartographic institute focused purely on the military into a more general mapmaking center.[98] The new Nazi government believed that without centralizing control over spatial representations, it could not keep important maps up to date or accurately plan infrastructural projects. Moreover, the Reichsministerium des Innern (Ministry of Interior) justified the new law as necessary so as to best "utilize the German area fully for settlement."[99] Signed by both Frick and Adolf Hitler, the new legislation was quickly enacted and applied to all German *Länder* (federal states), with some exceptions in the southern states, which were allowed a bit of flexibility but were still subject to the jurisdiction of the minister of the interior and the RfL. Bavaria and Württemberg, in particular, maintained their own autonomously funded state mapping agencies and produced maps that were generally considered to be more reliable than those produced by the other German states.[100]

Comprehensive implementation of spatial centralization was not, however, immediate. Some of these reforms, as the OSS report on these policies noted, would have taken "decades to complete even in peacetime." Even those parts of the law that could have been quickly implemented nationally were first experimented with in Westphalia and the Rhineland under close supervision.[101] The early centralized political control of maps was often problematic, with Nazi department heads disagreeing over minute details such as the color of particular nation-states on the world map. Frick, for example, believed that Germany should be depicted on European and world maps with the color red, whereas Nazi propaganda minister Joseph Goebbels wanted to reserve that color for the British Empire. This dispute forced geographers and cartographers (who were already, like most other social scientists, not particularly thrilled with methodological change) to relinquish their editorial decisions to political higher-ups, opting for adherence to orders rather than chance drawing a line or adding a color that had not been preapproved.[102]

By the end of May 1935, Frick had given the RfL "exclusive" rights over the production of Germany's most basic topographic maps: the 1:50,000 scale *Deutsche Karte* (German Map), the 1:100,000 scale *Karte des Deutschen Reiches* (Map of the German Empire), the 1:300,000 scale Übersichtskarte von Mitteleuropa (Survey Map of Central Europe), and the 1:1,000,000 scale Übersichtskarte (World Map). These maps would be drawn up by the RfL and produced by its state offices throughout the Reich. The RfL also made good use of the map agencies still open (but slowly losing their autonomy) in Bavaria and Württemberg, charging them with the maintenance and production of the 1:25,000 scale topographic map sets and the 1:5,000 scale map sets known as the *Deutsche Grund-karte und Katasterplankarte* (German Base Map and Cadastral Map).[103] Building this centralized and heavily regulated mapmaking infrastructure was important to the goals of the Nazis, who in September 1936 made it illegal for any private business firm to sell or even distribute maps of any kind that had not been preapproved by a Reich agency.[104]

Widespread regulations began to be more strictly imposed onto agencies throughout Germany in 1937. The new Deutsche Kartogra-phie Gesellschaft (German Cartography Association) was created for professional cartographers, a uniform set of symbols and measurements was established, and place-names became heavily regulated. There were still, however, some gestures toward cartographic diversity and interde-partmental conflict. The Latin script, for example, was the only style authorized to be used by the RfL even though the Reichsministerium für Volksaufklärung und Propaganda (Ministry of Public Enlightenment and Propaganda) and other German departments concerned with the dissemination of information had already banned it in favor of the German script type.[105] So whereas every other official publication released during the Third Reich boldly displayed German script, all maps maintained the Latin script. Moreover, although the use of symbols chosen by the RfL was made obligatory, the state of Bavaria was allowed to produce its maps with its own place marker for churches and its own method of drawing topographic contour lines.[106] No exceptions were made for place-names, however. By April 1937, every map in Germany was to apply German place-names to any area that had belonged to Germany before 1918. Cartographers could label a particular territory with its new, post–Versailles Treaty label, but the German name had to be published next to it in bold, while the foreign name was subjugated into parentheses. If there was room on the map for only one label, the German place-name was always to be given precedence. The rules were even more stringent concerning bodies of water, many of which bordered or ran through the German state. Any sea *near* Germany (that meant every sea surrounding Great Britain!) was to be designated by its German name. Rivers that ran through Germany could, at some point on the map, be labeled with a foreign name, but that name had to be in parentheses, and the German name had to be listed multiple times along the river's demarcation.[107]

Spatial totalitarianism continued to set in as the years drove on. In January 1938, a statute requiring all surveyors to take a loyalty oath to the state and join a state-sponsored professional organization was enacted. Surveyors could also no longer change their office addresses without permission from the Ministry of Interior; they could not open any new offices; and they were not supposed to turn down any work "for which [they were] considered competent."[108] The next month, as the eventual incorporation of Austria into the Third Reich drew closer, the Ministry of Interior ordered all private cartographers to remain in their current positions. Cartographers were effectively banned from changing jobs so that the Nazi government could easily pluck them from the private sector in case they needed them to serve in the Reich's mapmaking departments.[109]

On March 12, 1938, Nazi Germany annexed Austria in the Anschluss. Six days later and obviously anticipating future expansion, Wilhelm Frick, Adolf Hitler, and the Reich minister of finance Johann Ludwig von Krosigk signed the Gesetz über die Bildung der Hauptvermessungsabteilungen (Law Concerning the Organization of the Main Surveying Offices). Although each of the German *Länder* had had its own surveying office under the supervision of the RfL, these offices were now to be entirely defined and controlled directly by the minister of interior. Prior to the creation and consolidation of these offices, "there was no systematic collection of data on topographic changes" in the German *Länder*.[110] The law went into effect on April 1, 1938, and required the *Länder* to pay for part of the surveying operations undertaken by these *Hauptvermessungsabteilungen*.[111] The new districts of these offices were, however, not explicitly made clear until June 1938, when the Ministry of Interior established fourteen different mapping districts:[112]

1. The Province of East Prussia
2. The Province of Silesia
3. The State of Saxony
4. Berlin, the Potsdam "region" (*Regierungsbezirke*), and Frankfurt/Oder of the Province of Brandenburg
5. The Province of Pomerania, the Grenzmark region of the Province of West Prussia, and the Prenzlau "district" (*Kreis*)
6. The State of Mecklenburg, the Hanseatic City of Hamburg, and the Province of Schleswig-Holstein
7. The States of Oldenburg and Brunswick, the Hanseatic City of Bremen, the State of Schaumburg-Lippe, and the Province of Hanover (excluding the Osnabrück region)
8. The States of Thuringia and Anhalt, and the Province of Saxony
9. The State of Lippe and the Osnabrück region
10. The Rhine Province
11. The State of Hessen, the Province of Hessen-Nassau, the Saar Territory, and the Bavarian region of the Palatinate
12. The States of Württemberg and Baden, and the Sigmaringen region
13. The State of Bavaria (excluding the Palatinate)
14. The State of Austria

As the Third Reich seeped further into eastern Europe with the October 1938 acquisition of the Czech Sudetenland, more associations and more districts were required for effective occupation, planning, and territorial assimilation. In January 1939, the Reich created the Forschungsbeirat für Vermessungstechnik und Kartographie (Research Council for Surveying and Cartography) and divided it into three subdivisions: geodesy, surveying techniques, and cartography. Later, in 1941, it added a fourth branch on colonial cartography and surveying.[113] By February 1939, all laws concerning the manufacture and production of maps and other spatial representations were imposed on Austria and the Sudetenland. All mapping agencies that had existed prior to German occupation, perhaps most importantly the Austrian Cartographic Institute, were simply subsumed into the *Hauptvermessungsabteilungen*, and the Sudetenland was territorially split up and attached to its surrounding districts (specifically, districts 2, 3, 13, and 14).[114] After the invasion of Poland on September 1, 1939, the Ministry of Interior established a fifteenth district for Danzig and West Prussia and a sixteenth for the Wartheland. A special survey division was also set up in Krakow and made available to the governor general of Poland.[115]

By the spring of 1940, the sheer volume of maps (and their accompanying regulations) was forcing many German geographers to recognize the need for a more collective approach to the academic study of mapmaking during the Second World War. On February 6, 1940, maps containing any information that "might be detrimental to the common good" were banned, even if those maps had been published after January 1933. Restrictions were broadened to include not only sheet maps and maps in atlases but also "cartographic illustrations in books."[116] The importance of consolidating the study of geography became even more evident as Germany settled into its occupation of eastern Europe. New provisions governing the cartography of the "Eastern Areas" mirrored the German laws but often included the important disclaimer that all regulations were valid only for those geographers, surveyors, and mapmakers "of German blood."[117]

Two months after the invasion of Poland, one of Germany's more prominent geographers and a member of the *Zeitschrift für Geopolitik* editorial board, Erich Obst, sent a confidential newsletter to every geography department in Germany: "Bitte vertraulich behandeln! Nicht für die Öffentlichkeit bestimmt!" (Please treat confidentially! Not intended for the public!). For Obst, the war brought about exciting opportunities for each of the academic sciences. Geography, however, was particularly important to the war effort, and the academic geographers' cooperation with their military counterparts was seen as necessary. So Obst proposed the creation of a new umbrella organization that would help protect and promote all of the fragmented geography associations through the German Reich. This new organization—which Obst called the Deutsche Geographische Gesellschaft (German Geographical Association)—would publish its own journal and organize inexpensive lecture tours. For Obst, the war provided an impetus for consolidating what until the Third Reich had been an enormously fragmented academic discipline that had produced far too much written material under substandard scrutiny and had no uniform policies for dealing with international academic exchange.[118] By the end of 1941, the Deutsche Geographische Gesellschaft was established and encompassed the interests and participation of university professors, secondary-school geography teachers, and independent geographers. The new *Gesellschaft* was planned, in effect, to help organize the current geographical societies of Germany and help them cope with the territorial expansion of the Third Reich as it grew larger and larger.[119] It would, however, remain of marginal importance throughout the war and postwar years largely because it lacked the funding and institutional power of another geographic institute founded during the Second World War: the Abteilung für Landeskunde im Reichsamt für Landesaufnahme (AfL, Department of Regional Studies in the Reich Office of State Survey).

The AfL was the brainchild of Emil Meynen. Born in Cologne to Josef and Anna Meynen on October 22, 1902, Meynen had already by the age of twenty managed to become a research assistant in the Geography Department at the University of Cologne.[120] He was the ideological product of the pan-German movement and was attracted to institutions and professional colleagues who shared his interest in studying the German *Volk* both inside and outside the borders of the German nation-state. In the 1920s, Meynen joined Friedrich Metz's Stiftung für deutsche

Volks- und Kulturbodenforschung (Foundation for German Folk and Cultural Landscape Research) in Leipzig while continuing to work as a research assistant in Cologne and Berlin. His training and networking resulted in his acceptance to the London School of Economics in 1929 and in subsequent external grants that allowed him to travel abroad (even after the Great Depression) in his attempt to study how German culture adapted to new places.[121]

Meynen received a Rockefeller Foundation fellowship almost immediately after his acceptance to the London School of Economics. By January 1930, he had used the Rockefeller funds to travel to the United States in an effort to complete "a research study of the economic and ethnographic geography of the German settlement district in Pennsylvania."[122] He was fascinated by the Amish in particular because they seemed to have maintained semblances of their German-ness (such as language and cultural traditions) while living peacefully alongside other immigrant groups that more readily embraced Americanization.[123] His research was to culminate in a map of Amish congregations throughout Pennsylvania that would provide the histories and population growth of each settlement. Meynen also told the Rockefeller Foundation that he planned to create a bibliography of academic work on the Pennsylvania Dutch.[124] In fact, the Pennsylvania German Society helped Meynen find a publisher for his bibliography,[125] and one of his articles, "Das pennsylvaniendeutsche Bauernland" (The Farmland of the Pennsylvania-Dutch) was translated into English and published in the *Pennsylvania Magazine of History and Biography* in 1940.[126]

Meynen's work on the Amish was, however, one small part of a much larger project. He returned to Germany from the United States in 1933, and on April 15, 1935, he presented his habilitation thesis at the University of Cologne. His thesis was titled "Deutschland und das Deutsche Reich" and was published in 1937. Meynen would later characterize this work as running directly counter to the state's totalitarianism at the time. In fact, he claimed that the sale of the book was eventually banned by the Ministry of Propaganda.[127] There is no evidence that Meynen's book was ever banned, though, and several geographers and historians have pointed out the pan-German revisionism with which Meynen approached the

concept of the German nation in *Deutschland und das Deutsche Reich*.[128]
There is also no denying that he enjoyed a very prosperous career under
the Third Reich. From 1935 through October 1944, he served as director of the Geschäftstelle der Volksdeutschen Forschungsgemeinschaften
(Office of German Folk Research Organizations). This office has become
incredibly controversial in recent years, especially after research revealed
that it was eventually relocated next door to the offices of Group II C of
the SS-Reichssicherheitshauptamt, the Nazi Gestapo's section focusing
on Jews. The historian Michael Fahlbusch has claimed that locating the
Office of German Folk Research Organizations right next to the SS office
was not at all coincidental but rather necessary for Meynen and his geographers to be as effective as possible in legitimizing the exclusion of Jews
from the German *Volk*.[129] Perhaps the greatest confluence of these two
offices was made manifest in the Generalplan Ost, the Nazi plan for the
ethnic cleansing and German settlement of eastern European territories.
From 1939 to 1945, somewhere between 31 million and 45 million people
living under the Generalplan Ost were displaced. In this territorial expression of the Lebensraum concept, individuals who were excellent at solv-
ing spatial problems were called upon to assist Germany's expansion. The
Lublin District was in particular a territory pegged for experimentation by
the SS—experimentation implemented and planned by land-use experts
such as Konrad Meyer and geographers such as Walter Christaller.[130]

On February 17, 1936, Meynen married and a few months later was
appointed to a lectureship at the University of Berlin.[131] Although Meynen
claimed to have not joined the Nazi Party until 1938,[132] most historians
believe he had joined already in 1937.[133] By 1938, Meynen had also become
editor of the Publikationsstelle Ost (Publication Office East), one of the
primary points of information collection and dissemination of all things
concerned with policy toward the Soviet Union, Ukraine, and other areas
of eastern Europe.[134] Before the end of the war, Meynen would serve as
an adviser for central European affairs to the Ministry of Interior, would
head the Kommission für den historischen Atlas Europas (Commission
on the Historical Atlas of Europe), and would maintain a presence as one
of the most knowledgeable experts on German-speaking enclaves in eastern and southeastern Europe. Fahlbusch has argued that Meynen was

deeply entrenched in redrafting central and eastern Europe, helping not only to redraw Czechoslovakia after the Munich Agreement of 1938 but also consistently working to help resettle Germans into the eastern occupied territories and to re-Germanize (*Umvolkung*) the *Volk* living there.[135] At the very least, Meynen was in Poland during the fall of 1939 and almost certainly contributed in some way to its initial invasion and occupation. This was no secret—Albrecht Penck wrote to Meynen while Meynen was at the front, as did Meynen's students and colleagues at the University of Berlin.[136] Only in August 1940 was Meynen recalled from the eastern territories to resume his academic work.[137]

It should come as no surprise, then, that after his return from the front, Meynen was interested in the creation of a new central institution devoted to "regional studies." In October 1940, he submitted a formal report to the Ministry of Interior that carefully outlined the need for this new institution. It was quickly approved, although it was not given the autonomous status he had requested.[138] Instead, on April 1, 1941, the AfL was established in Berlin as a branch of the RfL and charged with undertaking research concerning all German regional studies.[139] Although the AfL was allowed to do a certain amount of its own research, it also was required to participate in the collection and dissemination of cartographic data (a process that was becoming slower and slower as the war dragged on), and it shared a fairly intimate relationship with the government and military institutions of the Third Reich during the Second World War.[140] From April 1941 on, the AfL would play a major role in the development and regulation of cartographic material produced for the Third Reich.

By the summer of 1941, the National Socialist government had come to realize that the Second World War was not going to be as short as it had hoped. The RfL was ordered to streamline the dissemination of maps. From May 1941 until the end of the war, maps would be made available to the public only through preapproved distributors in each of the *Hauptvermessungsabteilungen*.[141] In what was initially a somewhat spontaneous attempt to help organize and distribute the new edicts from the Nazi government, the changes in academic appointments, and a running list of German geographic publications, the AfL began publishing a newsletter, the *Berichte zur Deutschen Landeskunde* (Report on German Regional

Studies), in October 1941.[142] Within a year, the *Berichte* had become so authoritative and so helpful to the cartographers and geographers of the Nazi regime that the minister of interior issued a memorandum in August 1942 encouraging administrators of his various offices to subscribe to it.[143] The minister had good reason to do this—Meynen was more than happy to toe the Third Reich's line in his academic and public publications. For example, one of the AfL's first publications was a gazette assembled by Meynen and titled *Amtliche und private Ortsnamenverzeichnisse des Großdeutschen Reiches und der mittel- und osteuropäischen Nachbargebiete, 1910–1941* (Official and Private Gazetteers of the German Reich and the Central and Eastern Neighboring Area, 1910–1941). In its foreword, Meynen emphasized the importance of adhering to the Nazi regulations requiring German place-names to be used in all maps, even if those places were beyond the German frontier. In an effort to be as helpful as possible (apparently to both the Third Reich and its mapmakers), this publication included a place-name directory and a list of every gazetteer that portrayed the German Reich and its central/eastern neighboring areas from 1910 to 1941.[144] Also in 1942, Meynen published an article on Germans' land acquisition in the United States titled "Die Ausweitung des europäischen Lebensraumes in Nordamerika" (The Expansion of European Lebensraum in North America), which was popular enough to merit a second printing in 1943.[145] There is little evidence that Meynen was attracted to the Nazi Party because of antisemitism, but as these publications show, he was very willing to promote the Third Reich's understanding of the German nation and the expansion of Germanness into other parts of the world.

It was in 1942 that maps began to be heavily censored. Although place-names, borderlines, and other territorial semiotics had been regulated since the dawn of the Third Reich, it was only in the summer of 1942 that these regulations were extended to "all textual explanations of cartographic works . . . especially tourist guides and hiking manuals, even if no maps are attached."[146] In fact, by the end of 1942, all descriptive names on maps were ordered removed. All maps published after and all maps published prior to this point had to exclude any and all references to "gasworks, power plants, waterworks, chemical factories, blast furnaces, oil tanks, transmission stations, barracks, powder storage, and ammunition factories." Moreover, many rail lines and public roads were also ordered off of the Reich's maps.[147]

By 1943, of course, things were not going well for the Axis powers. Allied bombing raids were devastating many of Germany's urban centers, and geographers were not immune from the destruction. On November 22, 1943, Emil Meynen's home in Berlin burned to the ground. Although his family survived intact, his entire personal library was obliterated.[148] Meynen quickly sent his family off to live with his mother-in-law in East Prussia and moved what little remained of his cartographic collection to the AfL offices. Unfortunately for Meynen, Allied bombs hit the AfL headquarters in Berlin a few days later, on December 4, and many of its holdings were also destroyed. This "terrorist attack" (*Terrorangriff*), as Meynen called it, forced the AfL to take refuge in the small town of Worbis, Thuringia.[149] Because of his work on various projects and in various offices of the Third Reich, Meynen did not follow the AfL until mid-March 1945.[150]

As the Second World War grew worse for Nazi Germany and the Third Reich grew more desperate, attempts to control cartographic material reflected mounting levels of institutional distress. On February 20, 1944, individuals and organizations that were not "official agencies, schools, armed forces, organizations of the Nazi Party, and the Red Cross" were banned from acquiring maps at a scale of 1:300,000 or larger.[151] Although this ban strangely did not require Germans to hand over any maps they had already previously purchased or obtained, the new restriction was logistically problematic. On February 21, 1944, millions of Germans showed up at their local train stations only to find that all the rail maps had been taken down and were no longer available for distribution. The Ministry of Interior was then forced to quickly redraft the regulation, allowing for railway stations (and tourist guides) to produce maps at a scale of 1:300,000, but only "provided they are sketchy and schematic, have no scales, and show no industrial plants."[152]

By the end of 1944, the inevitability of Nazi defeat became increasingly evident to Germany's functionaries. The eastern front had shifted from deep into the Soviet Union back to the territory of East Prussia.

Geography organizations within the German military—such as the German navy's Marine Geographie (Mar-Geo) Unit and the German army's Forschungsstaffel (Research) Unit and Militärische Geographie (Mil-Geo) Unit—eventually disbanded as the war drew to a close. A small team of Mar-Geo mapmakers, in an effort to keep compiling and disseminating war material, moved out to Kronach, Bavaria, in February 1945. By March 16, the Mar-Geo's relocated headquarters had been bombed, and the unit was dissolved by "wireless order."[153] German academic associations and government branches, however, were forced to figure out ways in which to make conciliatory gestures toward an oncoming enemy while maintaining their most valuable cartographic material. Many, such as the Geographisches Institut (Geographical Institute) at the University of Bonn—where Carl Troll was professor at the time—chose to flee. The Geographical Institute moved from Bonn to the small Bavarian town of Scheinfeld in the late winter of 1944. Scheinfeld was in no small part chosen among the many other small German towns because Troll's mother lived there.[154] Other organizations did, however, sometimes disband. The RfL—that massive mapping institution under which the AfL operated—was dissolved after the German surrender on May 8, 1945, along with nearly every other government agency and institution.[155] The AfL, though, was still holed up in Worbis. Meynen, who had not heard from his family in months,[156] was stuck along with the majority of his staff in a territorial limbo at the end of the war. Where they would end up exactly was no longer a decision they could make on their own. Their future place, both literally and in service to a future German government, would be dictated to them by an Allied occupational power.

Allied Plans for German Maps

When the war ended, Emil Meynen and his staff became important agents of cartographic change in Germany for two reasons: because territorial disagreements among the Allied powers resulted in a contentious and unreliable initial map of postwar Germany and because the United States had only just begun to develop a useful set of world maps. Even after Allied powers' dependence on maps during the First World War, the

United States had failed to organize any semblance of "systematic map collecting" or cataloging. Captured maps from the Central powers were largely discarded or allowed to be clumsily stored in various unidentified libraries throughout the world. Even if the US military had cared to begin building a major cartographic archive after the Great War, most of the participants' maps were limited to areas of "relatively static trench warfare" and were fairly useless more than twenty years after the enactment of the Treaty of Versailles.[157] Shortly before and certainly after the US Congress declared war against the Axis powers in December 1941, a state of cartographic panic enveloped all branches of the US military as they realized that they needed to begin deploying troops into various theaters for which they "had virtually no maps."[158]

In an attempt to avoid this chaos during future military endeavors, the US Army Map Service dubbed forty-five public-college libraries "map depositories." The service began sending tens of thousands of discarded maps to these depositories in the fall of 1945, mandating their storage and allowing for their destruction only by expressed permission. The University of Florida, just to give one example, was slated to receive 50,000 maps within the span of just three years through this Army Map Service depository program.[159] Because of the Army Map Service's insistence that wartime maps be stored at public-college libraries throughout the United States, the US government and military would never again be so cartographically unprepared for conflict.

So desperate, though, was the American military for material during the first few months of 1942 that Major General William J. Donovan, director of the OSS (the institutional predecessor to the US Central Intelligence Agency) made a nationwide appeal for maps on the radio.[160] In fact, the American military regularly requested irrelevant maps from public libraries simply because its officers misunderstood the "sources of supply or the nature of the material."[161] The lack of available information on the maps of foreign nation-states prompted the rushed publication of several books on the topic. *Foreign Maps* by Everett C. Olson and Agnes Whitmarsh, for example, offered a collection of the major mapmaking nation-states' cartographic systems in one publication. Despite "the urgent wartime need for [its] information," however, the book was not published until 1944.[162]

Needless to say, then, those few individuals who did have experience with foreign maps and who were called upon by the US government for their cartographic expertise quickly became vital to the war effort.

One geographer whose importance to the war (and postwar) effort has been recognized by geographers and historians alike was Richard Hartshorne (1899–1992). Hartshorne received his doctorate at the University of Chicago in 1924 and landed a faculty post at the University of Minnesota through 1940. In the summer of 1941, he was asked to help establish and head the OSS's Geography Division and would eventually also become acting director of the OSS Research and Analysis Branch. He was not the first geographer asked to help with this new top-secret undertaking (that honor belonged to Preston James, who served as chief of the Latin American Section, Division of Special Information, and who had recommended Hartshorne), but his organizational skills and talent for managing his staff made him among the most influential.[163]

While working as a professor of geography at the University of Minnesota, Hartshorne became interested in the boundaries of central Europe and eventually, in the late 1930s, traveled abroad in an effort to learn more about them. He initially went to Nazi-occupied Vienna (and later, after he could "no longer stand it in Germany," to Zurich) but was disappointed when he had "almost no chance to look at" the boundaries themselves. In Hartshorne's own words, "they were too 'hot.'" He was forced to return to the United States in early 1939, much earlier than he wanted, because of the looming Nazi invasion of Poland.[164] After his return, Hartshorne published an essay in 1940 titled "Suggestions for a More Stable Settlement of European Boundary Problems." In this essay, he argued that ideas of abstract "justice" could not adequately be applied to the European map—there were just too many nations and ethnicities with legitimate claims to large swaths of disputed territory. Already thinking about potentially redrawing Europe after the Second World War—a war the United States had not even entered yet—Hartshorne immediately rejected calls for a return to the imperial boundaries that existed prior to the First World War. In a bit of an ideological departure from the post–First World War days of Isaiah Bowman and the *Black Book*, Hartshorne readily admitted that after the new world war, no reasonable European would see national sovereignty as a means through which to attain the solidification of national borders or international security. He instead prophetically advocated for a Europe in which nation-states would give up some sovereignty in exchange for some security, a Europe in which it would be "less critical just where the boundaries [were] located."[165]

For postwar planners such as Hartshorne, the placement of boundaries looked to be a sizeable obstacle in reestablishing European political and economic stability. Between 1939 and 1943, the combined aggression and expansion of Hitler's Third Reich and Stalin's Soviet Union had resulted in the territorial displacement of 30 million Europeans.[166] This created a huge problem for Allied geographers, who by 1941–42 were actively trying to figure out how to solve the problem of European territorial restructuring after the war. The most urgent concern was what to do with Germany. Prior to the war, Hartshorne had warned against splitting Germany into separate states because little "faith could be placed in an arbitrary division forced upon Germany that no major group within Germany would support."[167] President Franklin Roosevelt's secretary of state, Cordell Hull, also warned that any new division of Germany would create more problems than it would solve. But Roosevelt and two of his closest policy advisers, Undersecretary of State Sumner Welles and Secretary of the Treasury Henry Morgenthau, genuinely wanted to dismember what had become Europe's chief aggressor state. Almost immediately after the entry of the United States into the Second World War, then, the Roosevelt administration began planning postwar territorial changes for the Continent. Roosevelt himself realized what an important undertaking this was. Before being sworn in as president of the United States in 1933, he had served as an active member of the Council of the American Geographical Society from 1921 to 1932. As assistant secretary of the navy from 1913 to 1920, he had undoubtedly taken an interest in Europe's remapping after the First World War.[168] Now as commander in chief during the Second World War, he would play a primary role in literally shaping the territorial trajectory of the twentieth century.

Germany's initial postwar zonal mapping was more the result of miscommunication and unclear expectations than of careful planning. In April 1943, British general Frederick Morgan was made chief of staff to the supreme Allied commander (a strange post considering there was no appointed commander quite yet) and charged with planning Operation Overlord, the largest amphibious military invasion in the history of the world. Although there was little chance that Germany would collapse before the invasion (which was scheduled for 1944), Morgan believed that he needed to prepare for the possible occupation of Germany by Allied forces. In an emergency plan code-named Operation Rankin, Morgan and his staff worked out where into Germany each member of the Allied powers would send its respective troops. Because he was simultaneously planning Operation Overlord, Morgan counted on using the British and American troops being mobilized on the British Isles for this potential occupation. Operation Rankin required British troops to push into northwestern Germany while the Americans moved into southwestern Germany. The Soviets had consistently refused to cooperate adequately with Allied Command, so Morgan's staff ignored eastern Germany (including Berlin) because they assumed that they had no authority over the Soviet military.[169]

One month later British state secretary of war Anthony Eden, pitched the Rankin plan to the British War Cabinet. In effect, Germany would be split into three zones of occupation. Several members of the cabinet were unconvinced, and the issue was sent to the British military's Armistice and Post-war Committee (chaired by Deputy Prime Minister Clement Attlee). The committee soon agreed with Eden and Morgan but further added the suggestion that Berlin be divided between the Allied powers as well. The three zones, as drafted by the committee, included a British "Northwest Zone" made up of Hanover, Hessen-Nassau, the Rhine Province, Schleswig-Holstein, and Westphalia; an American "Southern Zone" made up of Baden, Bavaria, Hessen-Darmstadt, Westmark (the Saar and Palatinate), and Württemberg; and a Soviet "Eastern Zone" made up of everything else except East Prussia (which, the committee assumed, would be ceded to Poland) and Berlin.[170] This plan was never entirely adopted, but it served as a launching point for territorial negotiations. The committee's suggestion to divide Berlin was, of course, taken up by the Allies, as was the committee's demarcation of the western border of the Soviet Union's zone of occupation. Moreover, the committee's attempt to create zones by using already established *Länder* became part and parcel of Allied postwar planning. On August 23, 1943, the Combined Chiefs of Staff accepted the Rankin plan at the First Quebec Conference, along with the plans for Operation Overlord.[171]

Although President Roosevelt had been at the First Quebec Conference, he was not present for the adoption of the Rankin plan. He was also absent when in October 1943 Cordell Hull presented Anthony Eden and Soviet minister of foreign affairs Vyacheslav Molotov with his own plan for an Allied occupation, which encouraged the creation of an "Inter-Allied Control Commission" and was intentionally vague about the territorial demarcations of an occupied Germany. Historian William M. Franklin claims convincingly that Hull's plan was purposely filled with ambiguity because he did not want to "encourage Roosevelt's inclination toward dismemberment" and was concerned about turning the proposed zones into "lines of permanent cleavage."[172] Nevertheless, within a month Roosevelt was clearly aware of the Rankin plan and used it regularly as a great example of how to split up Germany into smaller sovereign states. Although he maintained this position throughout 1943, the number of little Germanys he wanted swung back and forth. He told the US Joint Chiefs of Staff at one point that "practically speaking there should be three German states after the war, possibly five," but then at the Tehran Conference (November 28–December 1, 1943) he proposed five states, with an additional two internationalized regions, and finally at the Yalta Conference (February 4–11, 1945) proposed somewhere between five and seven.[173]

Indeed, Roosevelt had his own idea of how the occupation zones of Germany should be drawn and who exactly should occupy what. At a meeting in November 1943, he haphazardly drew lines on a National Geographic Society map that just happened to be sitting nearby.[174] He split Germany into two, tracing the division from the city of Stettin southwest through Berlin and Leipzig and then along Germany's border with Czechoslovakia, Austria, Switzerland, France, Belgium, and the Netherlands in 1937. He further divided this western section of Germany into a northern half and a southern half, with a border drawn from Wiesbaden west to Bayreuth. From that moment on, there would be a serious disconnect between Roosevelt's often ambiguous and ever-shifting understanding of German space and the pragmatic approaches taken by the

State Department and OSS Geography Division staffs. As recounted by the assistant chief of the State Department's Division on Territorial Studies at the time, Philip E. Mosley, the State Department also had to cope with the War Department's unrealistic expectations. According to Mosley, the War Department constantly insisted that postwar zones of occupation were of no concern to anyone besides the military—it was a "military matter" that would be decided "at the proper time" and at the "military level."[175] The State Department was concerned, however, at the military's clumsy braying. The War Department's plan for zonal occupation was simply to let the chips fall as they might—the United States would occupy whatever territories its troops were in at the time of German defeat. The American military was not alone in adopting this position, and in late 1943 a member of the British Foreign Office also proposed avoiding altogether the creation of zones. Allied troops were instead simply to be dispersed throughout the nation-state, intermingled and forced to rely on cooperation with one another.[176] This plan was never adopted. Neither the United States nor the Soviet Union was willing to risk leaving troops potentially isolated from the centralized logistical and military support the establishment of zones offered.

By 1944, the abstract lines being planned and tentatively drawn by Allied cartographers began to solidify and become more concrete. At this time, more than 200 geographers had been recruited by US government departments and agencies and were working on making new maps not only of Germany but of territories in Asia and Africa as well. This engagement with the world (an engagement that included the American public through newspaper maps, burgeoning map libraries, and fresh textbooks) stood in stark contrast to the State Department's narrow European focus on the small geography unit during the First World War.[177] But, of course, it was the territorial problems of Germany that spilled the most ink, and the proposals came hard and fast in 1944 as the war began winding down in favor of the soon-to-be Allied victors. Catchwords such as *denazification* and *reconstruction* began appearing in nearly every Allied report.[178] Figuring out exactly who would be denazifying whom and who would be rebuilding what was becoming more and more urgent as the year wore on.

On January 14, 1944, the British submitted their preliminary official maps of the planned occupation at the first formal meeting of the European Advisory Committee (EAC) in London.[179] The map depicted a return to Germany's boundaries of 1937 (which came as a surprise to no one) and divided that territory into three zones of occupation mirroring the Rankin plan. Despite the initial lines drawn by Roosevelt, this division was surprisingly equitable. The British would occupy all of northwestern Germany (Brunswick, Hesse-Nassau, the Rhine region, and everything north of it), while the Americans would control the Saar, the Bavarian Palatinate (west of the Rhine River), Hesse-Darmstadt, Württemberg, Baden, and Bavaria. The Soviets, according to this British proposal, would occupy Mecklenburg-Pomerania, Brandenburg, Saxony-Anhalt, Thuringia, and everything eastward, with the exceptions of East Prussia, which would become part of a new Poland, and Berlin, which was to be jointly occupied. In effect, the Soviets would control what Allied geographers had agreed was 40 percent of Germany's territory, 36 percent of its population, and 33 percent of its resources.[180] This proposal received mixed reactions. The Soviets were thrilled, despite not receiving more territory and resources to counter their disproportionate losses during the war. According to the British proposal at the EAC meeting, the American and British troops that had plunged into eastern Germany would be forced to relinquish control of that territory to the Soviet Union.[181] The Americans, however, refused to adopt the plan. Roosevelt, after hearing about it, personally intervened and demanded that the United States be granted the northwestern zone Britain had allotted itself. The United States would still be fighting a war in East Asia after Germany's defeat, and Roosevelt wanted easy access to the North Sea for the redeployment of troops. Moreover, he did not believe that it was the job of the United States to take up the "postwar burden of reconstituting France, Italy, and the Balkans"—which, he felt, were effectively British problems. Britain, he believed, should swap zones with the United States and maintain the southern German zone along with Austria.[182]

On February 18, 1944, the Soviet Union submitted its own draft of a postwar Germany. This map was very similar to the British proposal in several ways (and these characteristics immediately became the least controversial): Berlin was still shared by the Allies, and the western border between the Soviet Union's zone and the American/British zones remained unchanged. Austria, however, was split up between the three powers rather than being occupied solely by the United States. Moreover, East Prussia was clearly demarcated within the Soviet Union's zonal borders (a move that surprised few, considering the Soviet Union had cut ties to the London-based Polish government in exile by 1943).[183] This proposal—which seemed to accept the most fundamental boundary lines of the earlier British proposal—appeared, according to Philip Mosley, as "a sign of a moderate and conciliatory approach to the problem of how to deal with postwar Germany."[184] Everyone on the EAC believed the big territorial issues were settled. It would not be the Soviet Union, then, that forced the issue. Rather, it would be the continual refusal by an unnecessarily stubborn and erratic American president.

After being informed that the Soviets had submitted a territorial proposal to the EAC, Roosevelt quickly jotted a note to Acting Secretary of State Edward Stettinius Jr.: "What are the zones in the British and Russian drafts and what is the zone we are proposing? I must know this in order that it conform with what I decided on months ago."[185] Stettinius rushed this impromptu query along to the State Department. The State Department had no idea what to do. What was Roosevelt talking about? The Tehran Conference? His National Geographic Society map? Which of the multiple territorial proposals—the five-state plan, the seven-state plan, the three-state plan—did Roosevelt want them to draft? The only thing Roosevelt had consistently made clear was his opposition to occupying the southern zone of the British proposal.[186] A few days later, on February 25, the State Department received a zonal plan from the War Department. It was a mess: it proposed the United States receive an enormous northwest zone of Germany (51 percent of its population and 46 percent of its territory), but it had nothing about Berlin, and the boundary lines it proposed "cut crudely across geographic features and administrative boundaries . . . not actually [even] meet[ing] the German–Czech frontier."[187] Mosley describes the proposal as having "penciled lines radiating north, west and south from Berlin," a plan that ceded only 22 percent of German territory to the Soviets and was therefore certain to be met with hostility if actually proposed to the other Allies. The State Department demanded that the military mapmakers at the War Department explain this plan, but they could not. They readily admitted that the plan had not been negotiated but had come directly from the president.[188]

The State Department eventually convinced Roosevelt to adopt the zonal lines drawn by the British and Soviet EAC delegations.[189] Throughout the first half of 1944, then, the lines were solidified, but Roosevelt refused to give up on the possibility of occupying Northwest Germany. Maps dealt with in negotiations marked eastern Germany under the occupation of the Soviet Union but were forced to leave the other two zones unlabeled. Both Churchill and Roosevelt refused to entertain the idea of occupying the southern zone. Only in July was this "deadlock" broken, when General Dwight D. Eisenhower—after successfully invading the beaches of Normandy on June 6—made clear his intention to follow the Rankin plan and protect the southern flank of the British troops as they moved into Northwest Germany. Roosevelt never intervened with Eisenhower's decision and at the Second Quebec Conference in September 1944 eventually caved and accepted the southern zone of Germany for American occupation. He did, however, require certain changes: the Saar and Palatinate would be transferred to the British northwestern zone in exchange for the state of Hesse-Nassau. He also only agreed after being promised the small states of Bremen and Bremerhaven, which would supply the United States with access to the North Sea. Roosevelt also refused to occupy Austria alone.[190]

On February 6, 1945, despite protest from Roosevelt, France was granted a zone of occupation in Germany and a sector of Berlin, derived from the American and British zones.[191] The French were allowed to control the Rhineland-Palatinate and the Hessen territories west of the Rhine River. The French delegation—particularly at the Yalta Conference on February 11—initially asked also for control of Baden, Württemberg, Hesse-Kassel, and Hesse-Nassau so that the French could have direct access to the Soviet Union. Baden and the southwestern half of Württemberg (renamed Württemberg-Hohenzollern) were granted to the French, but their request for northern Württemberg, Hesse-Kassel, and Hesse-Nassau was denied because this demarcation would cut off the American

and British zones from one another.[192] At the Yalta Conference, the Cur-
zon Line was also established as Poland's new eastern border, a decision
accompanied by many an empty promise regarding the demarcation of its
eventual western frontier.[193]

President Roosevelt died on April 12, 1945, leaving his vice president,
Harry Truman, in charge of planning and reconstructing a postwar continent. As Germany went through the final death throes of the Second
World War, and as Allied forces marched deeper and deeper into German territory, Churchill proposed to his new counterpart that it might
be advantageous to postpone the occupational zonal plan and to maintain the presence of American and British troops in East Germany as a
kind of bargaining chip with the Soviet Union.[194] Truman refused, but not
because he had any empathy for the Soviets. In fact, by the end of April
the Allies would not only win the war in Europe but also begin work on
redrafting a German map that would reflect US values at the expense of
the Soviet Union. The future of German space, as the Americans understood it, would need to be drawn by Germans if that space were to have
any real meaningful authority. Most of those Germans, having worked
out of Berlin by the end of the war, were scattered throughout the future
Soviet zone. Finding them, finding their maps and mapping equipment,
and convincing them to draw a new, post-Lebensraum state would be a
fascinating yet overlooked chapter in Germany's history. The Allies could
"denazify" German space, but they knew it would take the genuine cooperation of German mapmakers if their new postwar orientation was to be
an integral part of Germany's democratic "reeducation."

3

Rebuilding Germany's Geography

An Occupation

"To dwell" as a transitive verb . . . it has to do with fashioning a shell for ourselves.
—Walter Benjamin, *The Arcades Project*

History's greatest geographic adventures are lines of flight.
—Gilles Deleuze and Félix Guattari, *On the Line*

On the fifth of December 1948, a young German named Theodor typed a letter to his teacher, Mr. Schmidt. In broken English, Theodor thanked his teacher for a recently received care package and praised the American military's "gentleness" as a postwar occupying force.[1] In the town of Kelsterbach, Theodor's home stood just within the Hesse region of Germany and, as of 1945, the American zone of occupation. Attached to the letter was a hand-drawn map depicting two intersecting streets lined by three rectangles meant to represent houses. Slightly to the northeast of the houses sits a fourth rectangle with an arrow pointing to it. Above the arrow is written "KURT SCHMIDT." This map is simple; its assertion is obvious: here is where Mr. Schmidt lives. It was drawn to show someone how to get somewhere. Indeed, this is *what maps do*: they offer propositions.[2] There is no scale and no legend affixed to Theodor's rendering of space. Nor can his map accurately operate within any mathematical projections. Yet the map, as is the case with all maps, makes a claim. In a sense, the map is unique—a subjective and abstract proposition of real, lived space. It is the place of Mr. Schmidt according to Theodor. This map is unique in another sense as well: it is a representation of late 1940s German space as autonomously produced by a German. Whereas the vast majority of surviving German maps from this period in history were created by agents of the Allied powers, Theodor's map—as blatantly unscientific as it is—stands as a stark reminder that Germans could and did map their own spaces. However, as an occupational force, the Allied victors had a vested interest in controlling the reconstruction and remapping of German space. From the earliest days of the Second World War, the creation and maintenance of a carefully plotted German spatial identity were a priority for the Allied military and, throughout the postwar era, became a serious point of contention between the Germans and their Allied occupiers. German territory also quickly became a point of contention among the Allied powers themselves. Cartography, then, was not simply an academic exercise or a wartime strategic necessity; it was the medium through which national identity and national territory could be most effectively linked and then seared into the imaginations of the conquered and the conquerors alike.

Nazi Germany's surrender to the Allied powers in May 1945 only complicated the territorial disputes that had plagued wartime meetings between the United States, Great Britain, and the Soviet Union. In fact, it escalated the urgency of laying down solid and specific borders around the German zones of occupation soon to be established. On June 5, 1945, the central German government was entirely dissolved and submitted to complete Allied control.[3] That very same day the United States and Britain formally turned over to the Soviet Union the territories of Saxony, Thuringia, and Mecklenburg, territories that they had invaded and occupied during the war. In response, the Soviet Union assured the British and American governments that they would be allotted regions of Berlin for occupation, according to the Allies' earlier territorial agreements.[4] (Figure 2 shows the final zonal demarcations after the war.) This all seems very amicable, but both the Western Allies and the Soviets were working desperately to undermine the geopolitical importance of their counterparts' territorial holdings.

It is generally accepted that those individuals forced to flee Nazi Germany during the Third Reich "were the greatest collection of transplanted intellect, talent, and scholarship the world has ever seen."[5] Similarly, the immediate postwar years saw the (often forced) exportation of German

Occupied Germany, 1945–49

2. *Occupied Germany, 1945–49*, scale not given, in John Gimbel, *The American Occupation of Germany: Politics and Military, 1945–1949* (Stanford, CA: Stanford Univ. Press, 1968), xvi. Copyright © 1968 by the Board of Trustees of the Leland Stanford Jr. University. All rights reserved. Used by permission of the publisher, Stanford University Press, sup.org.

intellectuals and scientists to their respective Allied occupiers.[6] Even while the Allies prepared to finalize some of their territorial agreements at the upcoming Potsdam Conference, July 17–August 2, 1945, each rushed to secure any and all potentially important individuals its military had come into contact with. Historians have largely overlooked one of these attempts—Operation Dustbin—despite its important outcome for the German zonal area controlled by the United States.

Three weeks before the Potsdam Conference began, the OSS recruited Captain Lloyd D. Black and Lieutenant Thomas R. Smith to help participate in Operation Dustbin. A joint venture between the OSS and British intelligence, Dustbin focused on obtaining scientific information by securing the scientific institutes of universities and the various agencies of the now defunct German government.[7] Dustbin was a subsection of Operation Paperclip and a counterpart of the more politically oriented Operation Ashcan. Dustbin and Ashcan were presumably named for their potential ability to "sweep up" after the German defeat in 1945.[8] Germans vetted for denazification through Operation Paperclip were sent either to Dustbin if they had important technical knowledge or expertise or both or to Ashcan if they were high-profile Nazi politicians.

Geographers were a prime commodity targeted by Operation Dustbin for denazification—many had been killed in the war, had fled Germany altogether, or were still in captivity.[9] Black and Smith were assigned to locate and interrogate prominent German geographers for Dustbin, and both were enthusiastic about this new assignment. Black had been a high school teacher before joining the war effort and was deeply interested in the sociopolitical causes of population transfers (as evidenced in the dissertation he wrote for the University of Michigan in 1940, "The Peopling of the Middle Willamette Valley, Oregon"). Smith was the son of prominent geographer J. Russell Smith and, prior to receiving his PhD in economics from Columbia University in 1943, had traveled the world with his father throughout the 1920s, spending a great deal of time in Europe. The importance of their affiliation with the American military cannot be overstated. Unlike in the cartographic redrafting of Europe after the First World War, the civilian academics of the OSS Research and Analysis Branch who had planned for a new postwar Europe were by October

1945 either allowed to go back to their universities or absorbed by the State and War Departments.[10] By the end of the year, the OSS had been significantly downsized, and the Research and Analysis Branch no longer existed. In 1945, then, Black and Smith were jointly charged with finding Emil Meynen and the Abteilung für Landeskunde and then with quickly moving the institution out of the soon-to-be Soviet zone of occupation into the American zone. The OSS was aware that the AfL had been moved from Berlin to Worbis in northwestern Thuringia, and it badly wanted access to its staff, its equipment, and its maps. In the eyes of the American intelligence community, acquiring excellent German geographers and cartographers would make the mapping of an occupied Germany all the easier and could potentially hinder the Soviets' mapmaking capabilities (a hope that would turn out to be prophetic).[11]

On June 28, nearly a month after the United States had formally ceded the German state of Thuringia to the Soviet Union, Black and Smith drove into the small town of Worbis. They had already contacted Meynen, collected the names of his staff, and picked up many of their immediate family members. Time, however, was not on their side. Upon their arrival at the make-shift headquarters, they ordered the AfL staff to grab whatever the staff believed to be of importance (Smith supervised this selection of material), load these items into an equipment truck, and then jam themselves into the passenger truck that already held some of their family members.[12] Meynen and thirty-four of his staff members had been chosen for export—quite the squeeze. From all accounts, it was a terrible and rushed experience. All furniture was left behind, a great deal of outdated and unimportant cartographic material was abandoned, and it rained the entire day.[13] As the AfL staff would later recount, Black and Smith had retrieved them in the nick of time. The Soviets had already lined the roads in and out of Worbis with red banners, just as they had at many towns and cities prior to formal liberation announced by means of a marching parade.[14]

The AfL staff were headed for Scheinfeld, the Bavarian town where Carl Troll's Geographical Institute at the University of Bonn had found refuge during the war. The American military had initially promised that the AfL would be housed in Scheinfeld's Schwarzenberg Castle, the very building where Troll had managed to keep his own staff and materials safe from harm. After Meynen and his staff arrived, however, the military reneged and housed them in an abandoned restaurant and hotel named the Hotel Krone.[15] The AfL employees were now—whether they liked it or not—employees of the US military government and were paid on a temporary monthly basis, a much nicer financial arrangement than what most Germans experienced in the initial months after the end of the war.[16] Their employment was, however, vital to the reconstruction of both Germany itself and German identity. As in most postwar stories of individual German subsistence, the work these geographers were required to do for their respective occupation power was the justification for their economic well-being, from which the means of survival and (in rare cases) personal economic prosperity could be bargained.

After all, the postwar situation was bleak. Many of Germany's most critical problems were spatial in nature and required the attention of geographers and cartographers familiar with German infrastructure, land-use planning, and urban development. One of the most pressing issues during the Second World War had been the problem of displaced persons, a population estimated to have been nearly 30 million.[17] By September 1945, the number of displaced persons still hovered around 1.8 million.[18] Through the summer of 1945, more than 450,000 German expellees rushed back into the German *Land* of Saxony, sometimes sitting on the engines and coal cars of overloaded trains packed to the brim with freshly homeless faces—German colonists who now faced the consequences of the Third Reich's expansionist policies and attempts to expropriate parts of eastern Europe. By 1948, 5 million people had passed through Bohemia, 2 million of them settling in Saxony.[19] Finding housing for these individuals, the first step toward political normalization and a return to a peaceful Europe, was a priority for the Allied powers. The AfL—although housed in Bavaria—was almost immediately charged with helping to solve this transzonal problem, and although it may have been the most involved and independent of the agencies assisting in this effort, it was certainly not the only one.

After the German surrender, all geographical and cartographical societies in all zones were banned and forced to apply for reestablishment.[20]

Of course, this did not mean all work by geographers and cartographers immediately halted or that coordination between individuals did not pick back up after the war. In fact, the Allies encouraged coordination. Black and Smith, the OSS operatives responsible for retrieving geographers in Operation Dustbin, were permitted to appoint zonal supervisors of spatial reconstruction. Each important *Land* in the American zone was given a geographer-representative: Wilhelm Credner for northern Bavaria, Emil Meynen for southern Bavaria, Gerhard Bartsch for Hesse, and Heinrich Schmitthenner (who, like Meynen, had been evacuated from eastern Germany by the American military[21]) for Baden-Württemberg. Moreover, Smith and Black appointed chairs for the Allied powers' zones: Walter Behrmann was placed in charge of the Soviet zone, Hermann Lautensach of the British zone, and Carl Troll of the American and French zones. Finally, Emil Meynen was made general coordinator and became responsible for the bulk of cartographic and geographic material produced by this group.[22] By August 1945, Meynen had already begun work on a 1:1,000,000 scale map of Germany (a project he had begun with many of these same colleagues in 1942), and by the fall of that year this core group appointed by Black and Smith helped establish the Zentralausschuß für deutsche Landeskunde (Central Committee for German Regional Studies).[23]

The United States did not recruit all notable geographers, however. In fact, Operation Dustbin was executed in order to obtain very specific individuals (such as Meynen and Schmitthenner) and resources (such as the AfL holdings). For example, Rudolf Reinhard, director of the Deutsches Institut für Länderkunde (German Institute for Regional Studies) in Leipzig, seems to have been much less involved in the National Socialist government than either Meynen or Schmitthenner and yet was not targeted by the American OSS.[24] As a resident of Saxony, Reinhard and his institute were functioning under American occupation during the final months of war in Europe. During that short time, the US Army frequented the institute and regularly borrowed maps and other literature. Already by May 12, 1945, the American and British occupation forces had confiscated more than 12,000 maps from the institute, along with nearly 200 cases of books, 4 cases of atlases, and 7 cases of archive material.[25] In his many requests for institutional reparations after the war (bombing

raids had destroyed much of the institute's equipment, but most of its cartographic material had been housed in the nearby town of Glauchau),
Reinhard repeatedly referred to the use of his holdings by the American
military as evidence of the institute's postwar importance.[26] He drafted
for the Americans a list of where he had hidden maps and geographic
data during the war: a castle at Glauchau, a castle in Podelwitz, and a
castle near the town of Oschatz (where the Soviets had apparently found
the material and confiscated it, much to Reinhard's chagrin).[27] Nevertheless, when the American military pulled out of eastern Germany and took
the AfL staff with it, Reinhard was left behind. After a brief period of
internment,[28] he reopened the institute under the auspices of the Soviet
Union and worked (often begrudgingly) alongside the Soviet occupation.
While the Anglo-Americans, then, were interested in exporting certain
geographers and their material, it seems that in at least some cases the
personnel could be abandoned if the cartographic material had already
been attained.

Creating new material, though, became the AfL's job. By consistently
securing contracts with the American occupiers, the AfL became the
leading producer and disseminator of cartographic material in the trizo-
nal area after the Second World War. No other geographers or geography
institutes had the AfL's relative financial security. As discussed at length
in this chapter, even reopened geography departments at state universities
were forced to rely on shaky government funding, whereas the AfL had a
direct financial connection to the American military (a connection that
continued after the creation of West Germany in 1949).[29] On December
1, 1945, the AfL was formally absorbed as an agency of the US military
government, with, according to Captain Black, "a mandate to initiate and
coordinate geographical research in Germany."[30] Meynen would report to
the US State Department's Division of Map Intelligence and Cartography.
Although the AfL would be required to prioritize work for the occupation,
a certain level of autonomy was allowed, and the staff could work on their
own projects if time permitted. Perhaps the most important work that
came from this ability to draw unauthorized cartographies was the *Landkreis Scheinfeld*, a comprehensive atlas of the town and district of Scheinfeld eventually published in 1950. The *Landkreis Scheinfeld* helped to lay

the foundation for a uniform approach to small-scale geographic study. By 1959, Meynen's institute had published thirty-two volumes of this *Land-kreis* series, each volume carefully chronicling the space of a distinct German geographic district.[31] One of the first projects given to the AfL by the American military government, however, was the compilation of a report on the situation of German maps and mapmakers after the war. Meynen's staff was also immediately given the task of rewriting Germany's place-name index so as to reflect the country's 1937 boundaries.[32] By December 1945, the AfL had been hired by the US military government to draft a new map of Germany according to those 1937 borders that would be ready for publication by the following March. Although clearly a determination made for political purposes, the understandable imposition of these boundary lines on German space was veiled in scientific rhetoric. *This* map would be entirely disinterested, a "purely geographically oriented spatial structure" ("eine rein geographisch ausgerichtete Raumgliederung")![33] Of course, this was not the case and had never been the case. Each of various publishing houses lobbied Meynen to choose its "ground map" of regional divisions for this project.[34] The map had to go through a screening process and needed to receive the approval of the American occupation authorities before it could be published, but, as both the American supervisors and their German mapmakers consistently testified, this new map was somehow both apolitical and a cartographic rebuking of German aggressiveness and expansionism under the Third Reich.

But the truth was that everything about reconstructing postwar Germany was political. In an effort to genuinely denazify and redemocratize German territory, rebuilding education (in particular geographic education) was a serious concern for the Allies after the war. At the Potsdam Conference, the victorious nation-states made it clear that "German education shall be so controlled as to completely eliminate Nazi and militarist doctrines and to make possible the successful development of democratic ideas."[35] Some of the Third Reich's most virulently antidemocratic and militaristic educational tools had been spatial doctrines: Lebensraum, *Geopolitik,* and the Generalplan Ost. To truly denazify Germany, the Allies had first to denazify the way Germans thought about space. The most obvious way to accomplish this goal in the immediate postwar years was by reforming German education and inundating the German public with maps depicting the freshly truncated German state.

Displacing the Spatial Imagination of National Socialism

As already discussed in the previous chapter, the modern academic study of space found its origins in nineteenth-century German universities. Although the incorporation of geography and cartography into the universities of other nation-states helped to solidify the importance of those subjects on an international level, the Germans remained at the avant-garde of spatial studies up through the Second World War. The prominence of German faculty members and the relatively unusual reverence the German public had for its professors were not lost on the Allied occupiers (just as it had not been lost on the Nazis).[36] As the Allies strove to "reeducate" many of Europe's most intelligent and educated minds, they worked hard to target specific disciplines for revision at both the secondary and post-secondary school levels. Subjects such as history, geography, and biology were seen as particularly vital to redemocratization.[37] The denazification of educational materials was a process undertaken differently by each of the occupation powers, but common themes certainly existed and were often couched in references to territory and space. In German textbooks and school maps after the war, postcolonialism, globalization, and transnationalism were emphasized at the expense of ethnocentric territorial aggrandizement.[38] Although these changes and the project of "reeducation" were slow to start (and certainly did not attract much attention from the *military* administrations charged with governing the defeated Germany),[39] the emerging Cold War—a war of ideologies in which Germany would serve as "ground zero"—eventually prompted enormous financial and personnel investments from the United States, Great Britain, France, and the Soviet Union.[40]

In the American zone of occupation, for example, General Lucius Clay, a deputy to General Dwight Eisenhower and by 1947 military governor of the American zone, allotted only roughly one percent of the military occupation's budget to education.[41] In fact, at the time of the German surrender, the United States had only ten trained education officers for a zone with a population of almost 20 million.[42] The American occupation administration was initially interested only in reopening university medical facilities and actively exploiting the Germans' achievements in the American zone to the advantage of US businesses. On August 25, 1945, President Truman issued Executive Order 9604, effectively opening up "all information concerning scientific, industrial and technological processes, inventions, methods, devices, improvements, and advances" to the American public. As one businessman put it, flying into Germany after August 1945 was "just like going out on a hunting trip into unexplored territory." With nearly 5,000 American applicants approved for travel to Germany for the sole purpose of obtaining and disseminating the trade secrets of German businesses (and often the scientific processes responsible for industrial/technological development), university research in the American zone—particularly in the sciences, geography being no exception—came to a standstill.[43] Only in the summer of 1947, after General Clay determined that Executive Order 9604 was hampering research and thereby hampering Germany's economic recovery, did the United States stop allowing its business interests to prey on German research institutes and universities.[44]

The predatory inclination of American capitalism, however, was the last thing on the minds of many German university faculty members. In January 1946, the Allied Control Council released Directive No. 24. Although the Allied powers had made several threats concerning German denazification in the lead-up to the Third Reich's defeat, Directive No. 24 was the first to offer specific details as to how this process would occur and exactly what professions would be forced to undergo it.[45] Professors were, of course, included, and from the fall of 1946 to the spring of 1947 around 15 percent of them were fired.[46] Even before the directive was issued in January 1946, several professors had been dismissed from their posts. A few of them had been geographers. Wolfgang Panzer, for example, was forced out of his position at Heidelberg University in November 1945 for his service as a high-profile cartographer for the Third Reich from 1934 to 1939.[47] Most geographers, however, were recognized as having joined the Nazi Party for the sake of opportunity—not to have joined would have been an obstacle to further research. Yet whereas many of the natural scientists enjoyed relatively relaxed denazification proceedings, especially if they were considered valuable to the occupation or to the American occupiers, many geographers were in the strange position of having helped justify the aggressive spatial planks of the Nazi political platform.[48] The Americans called upon these same geographers, before the creation of the geographers' own new state in 1949, to help revise the territorial narratives they had so carefully crafted during the Third Reich. This transition from (at the very least) passive bystanders—and benefactors—of the Third Reich's destructive spatial policies to active participants in redrawing a truncated and more peaceful Germany was a messy enterprise.

The US military occupation wasted little time in its attempt to remake the German education system in its own image. By September 1946, a ten-member commission created by the American Council on Education recommended changing the time spent in elementary school from four years to six years, establishing educational exchanges, and using "improved teaching aids and library facilities."[49] Implementing these changes was particularly problematic because by the end of 1946 roughly 20,000 (of 28,000) general-education teachers in the American zone had been fired as a result of Directive No. 24.[50] Moreover, between 1945 and 1947 "a considerable number of students had no books, pencils, paper, or other aids to learning."[51] During this period, those subjects prioritized for educational dissemination were often broadcast from radio towers in the form of the US occupation's *Schulfunk*, educational program. Even though radios were few and far between throughout the American zone of occupation, the lack of teachers and lack of course material for regular schooling made these broadcasts necessary and often popular. Geography was one of the earliest segments taught in this format, alongside English, music, animal science, and economics. Teaching students how their particular space coexisted next to that of various other nation-states was seen as an important step toward democratization (see figure 3).[52] These sentiments were also clear in the planning of textbooks within the American zone, although producing these textbooks was a slow business. Already by December 1946, American education specialists had begun demanding the de-emphasis of borders on German maps, preferring rather to stress

3. A German student studying geography in the American zone of occupation, *Heute*, Apr. 13, 1949, MS 069, Boxes 1–3, Univ. of Nebraska Library and Archive, Lincoln.

the common "connection between all people and nations" ("Vor dem Kinde soll das Bild der ganzen Welt und der Zusammenhang aller Menschen und Völker erstehen").[53]

In the immediate aftermath of the war, because of a lack of resources, occupying powers simply reprinted pre-Nazi geography textbooks. The American zone initially produced a series of small, thirty-page pamphlets for geography courses under their control, which lacked any kind of mapped Germany (or any maps, for that matter). Rather, this series (published by Belser in Stuttgart on June 12, 1947) was simply a collection of excerpts from poems and travelogues dealing with specific areas. The pamphlets covered topics such as the Swabian Alps, upper Swabia, and the Neckarland. One of the American zone's most important geography textbook publications was the *Geographie Weltkunde Lehr- und Arbeits-buch für deutsche Schulen* series, written by Ernst Karl and Franz Schnei-der. In the earliest volumes of this series, from 1949 through 1952, no national maps of Germany were included. Eventually, in 1953, the West Germans published a volume that specifically focused on German geog-raphy. They even went so far as to include linguistic maps of German speakers throughout central Europe (see figure 4, but note that this map was only ever used in a historical context after the Second World War). In this same volume's national map of Germany (see figure 5), the 1937 borders were again included, with the easternmost territories labeled as being "under foreign administration." In this map, then, the textbook showed a Germany that was simultaneously preserved in its 1937 form but temporarily divided. This same cartographic proposition was reiter-ated in 1958, albeit in more detail (see figure 6), when the authors of this volume changed from Karl and Schneider to Gustav Kreuzer and Eduard Müller-Temme. The text itself also delved more deeply into the problems of Germany's division. While the Karl and Schneider version of this book made clear Germany's "natural predisposition" to link Europe together through trade, Kreuzer and Müller-Temme emphasized how Germany's political divisions could cause its economy to collapse, thereby launching the continent of Europe into disaster. "Therefore," they wrote, "it is the fateful mission of the German people to realize their reunification as an economic and political community for the benefit of the European com-munity of nations and for all humanity."[54]

As the 1950s dragged on, West German mapmakers struggled with how to represent the division between East Germany and West Germany. *Deutschland, die Mitte Europas,* volume 5 of Heinrich Barten's textbook series *Länder und Völker Erdkundliches Unterrichtswerk,* is an excellent example of this problem. In the 1951 edition of this volume (see figure 7), originally published by Ernst Klett, Barten depicted a national Germany with its 1937 boundaries but with representations of several different types

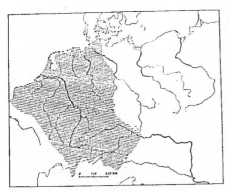 

Deutsches Sprachgebiet im
9. Jahrhundert
(vereinfacht nach Mackensen,
Helbok u. a.)

Deutsches Sprachgebiet im
15. Jahrhundert
(vereinfacht nach Mackensen,
Helbok u. a.)

4. *Deutsches Sprachgebiet im 9. Jahrhundert (vereinfacht nach Mackensen, Helbok u.a.)* and *Deutsches Sprachgebiet im 15. Jahrhundert (vereinfacht nach Mackensen, Helbok u.a.)*, scale 1:20,000,000, in Ernst Karl and Franz Schneider, *Geographie Weltkunde Lehr- und Arbeitsbuch für deutsche Schulen: Deutschland, eine geographische Zusammenschau* (Baden: Badenia, 1953), 8.

of German expellees, including those living in the "Ostzone" (who are depicted as ghostlike, seemingly ephemeral figures) and Germans living outside of Germany in the Sudetenland. This characterization changed abruptly in the 1954 edition (see figure 8). Barten replaced the 1951 map with a new map, showing no distinction between Germans and certainly no Germans outside of Germany. In the new edition, the "Ostzone" was now clearly depicted as something separate from the West (with the exception of Berlin), but the people themselves were portrayed as being the same. The 1956 edition (see figure 9) eliminated the cartographic distinction between East and West. It should be noted that by this point Germany was represented as an "island" apart from Europe—a trend of the period. The 1937 boundaries have also been dropped. This 1956 version of Germany made no more territorial claims to those lands east of the Oder-Neisse boundary line. Although the East/West distinction was not clearly marked, other "island maps" of West Germany—in this very same

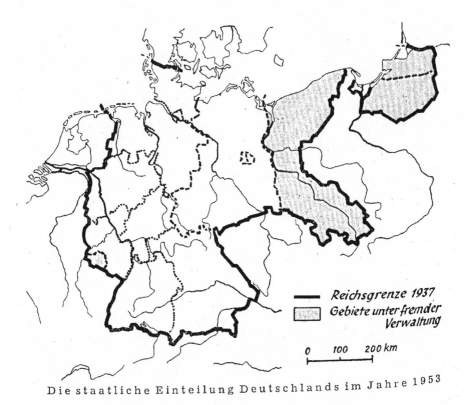

Die staatliche Einteilung Deutschlands im Jahre 1953

5. *Die Staatliche Einteilung Deutschlands im Jahre 1953*, scale 1:20,000,000, in Ernst Karl and Franz Schneider, *Geographische Weltkunde Lehr- und Arbeitsbuch für deutsche Schulen: Deutschland, eine geographische Zusammenschau* (Baden: Badenia, 1953), 64.

edition!—were being produced. In these representations, East Germany was often left off the map entirely.

Attempts at reshaping the spatial narrative of Germany were not exclusive to formal education. Printed material—magazines, journals, and newspapers—published and disseminated by the US military government were often heavily peppered with depictions of the postwar German state. Take, for example, *Heute*, a German-language magazine distributed biweekly by the American military government from 1946 to 1951. Sometimes—usually to accent articles on intrazonal political or economic developments—*Heute* presented the American zone itself as an island, seemingly ripped

6. *Die Verwaltungseinteilung Deutschlands (in den Grenzen von 1937) Stand vom Jahre 1957,* scale 1:20,000,000, in Gustav Kreuzer and Eduard Müller-Temme, *Geographische Weltkunde Lehr- und Arbeitsbuch für deutsche Schulen: Deutschland in Europa* (Baden: Badenia, 1958), 16.

out of Germany's territory. As the relationship between zones changed, so did their respective representations on the pages of *Heute*. After the Bizonal Agreement of May 1947, "island mapping" of the American zone was still used, but the American zone was often combined with the British zone. Even in depictions of the German nation-state, American maps in *Heute* reflected the western Allies' desire to keep "their" zones of occupation cartographically distinguished from the Soviet zone.[55] In figure 10, for example, the borders of the German *Länder* are clearly marked, but

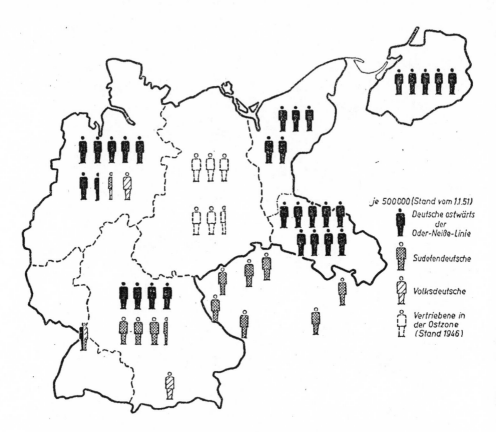

je 500000 (Stand vom 1.1.51)

Deutsche ostwärts
der
Oder-Neiße-Linie

Sudetendeutsche

Volksdeutsche

Vertriebene in
der Ostzone
(Stand 1946)

7. Untitled map of German population distribution, scale not given, in Heinrich Barten, ed., *Länder und Völker Erdkundliches Unterrichtswerk*, vol. 5: *Deutschland, die Mitte Europas* (Stuttgart: Ernst Klett, 1951), 39.

only for those states subsisting under the watchful eye of the Western powers are capitals identified and text-box elaboration given in this proposition drawn in 1949.

Just as important—or so it seems when one considers the frequency of these mapped narratives—were depictions of Germany as part of a greater Europe and greater world community. The isolationist "island mapping" of Germany was by 1949 regularly expanded to depict transnational institutions such as the North Atlantic Treaty Organization (NATO). Illustrators would sometimes converge maps with graphs, but—again by 1949 in an American military publication—these maps typically emphasized the

8. Untitled map of German population distribution, scale not given, in Heinrich Barten, ed., *Länder und Völker Erdkundliches Unterrichtswerk*, vol. 5: *Deutschland, die Mitte Europas* (Stuttgart: Ernst Klett, 1954), 39.

9. *Verteilung der Heimatvertriebenen auf die deutschen Länder 1952*, scale not given, in Heinrich Barten, ed., *Länder und Völker Erdkundliches Unterrichtswerk*, vol. 5: *Deutschland, die Mitte Europas* (Stuttgart: Ernst Klett, 1956), 47.

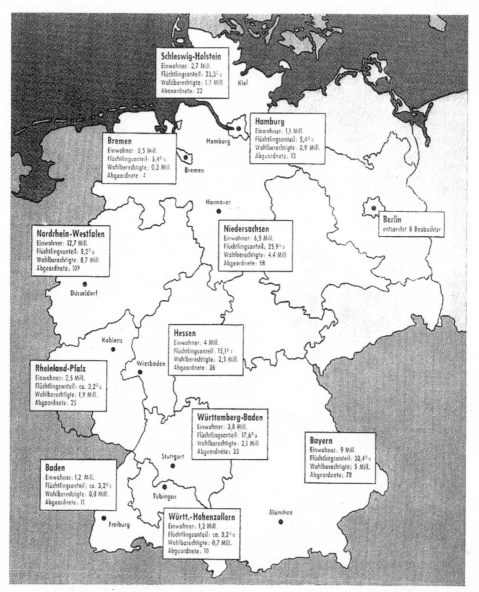

10. Untitled map displaying information about German states, scale not given, in "Wer die Wahl hat-," *Heute*, July 20, 1949, MS 069, Boxes 1–3, Univ. of Nebraska Library and Archive, Lincoln.

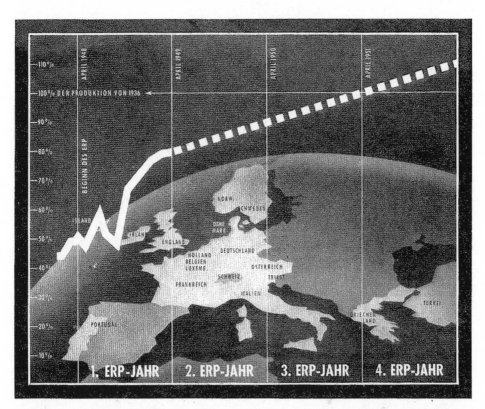

11. Untitled map displaying productivity growth in Europe, scale not given, in Erich Haase, "Das ERP feiert Geburtstag," *Heute*, Mar. 30, 1949, MS 069, Boxes 1–3, Univ. of Nebraska Library and Archive, Lincoln.

importance of transnational economic unity. In figure 11, for example, the projected influx of European productivity (as compared to levels in 1936) was superimposed onto a map highlighting nation-states receiving aid from the European Recovery Program (ERP). In those initial postwar years, the United States quickly recognized the usefulness of maps for establishing not only new German boundaries but also Germany's new role within an economically integrated European continent.

The British had begun the process of reeducation in their northwestern zone of Germany at a much quicker and more intense pace than their American colleagues. The British were also less determined than the Americans to create reform through a series of top-down decrees or by reshaping the German educational framework. British education policy in their zone of Germany was initially to revise textbooks and then simply to assist and advise.[56] By July 1945, the British Education Branch had already set up shop in the region of Westphalia under the directorship of Donald Riddy and with the explicit order to smoothly reopen schools and universities while simultaneously denazifying German curricula.[57] In December, the Education Branch established the German Textbook Committee, made up of educators, administrators, and clergy. As one might expect, this committee was much more effective at criticizing the Nazi textbooks than in creating its own denazified alternatives. Like the Americans, British educators initially simply reprinted pre-Nazi textbooks. For example, from 1945 to 1949 the British zone reproduced the 1931 edition of *Teubners Erdkundliches Unterrichtswerk für höhere Lehranstalten*, vol. 2: *Europa*, written by Robert Fox and published by B. G. Teubner.[58] It is notable that, despite the many maps of Germany in Fox's textbooks during the Third Reich and his use of maps to address the changing borders of Europe's neighbors in his earlier editions of this same volume, the British *chose* to remove those maps.

Textbooks published in the British zone of occupation would also often reuse the rhetorical tropes of earlier rabid nationalists and geopoliticians to fit new needs. For example, although the study of "military geography," the glorification of nationalism, and the propagation of National Socialist doctrine had been explicitly banned, one of the German Textbook Committee's proposed books—a cultural *Lesebuch* (reader)—introduced itself with the following foreword: "I am sitting before the map of Germany. Germany is the land of our dreams. Germany is the height of all glory! My school-mate Jürgen Wieben went to Hamburg once with his father; his boot had trod on ground where Denmark had no say. Jürgen Wieben's boot was a hallowed boot."[59] This scenario—or, rather, the mental image of Germany presented here—mirrors the Third Reich's spatial tropes but with a very different focus. Rather than incite frustration with what were, according to the Nazi cartographers, suffocating and unnatural borders, here Germany's territorial demarcation (largely a reflection of the 1937 demarcation) is presented as ideal. Political geography was, in fact, de-emphasized, much to the German geographers' chagrin. Navigation, map reading, and the importance of German assimilation outside of Germany (the study of the *Auslandsdeutsche*) were major sections of the geography curriculum in the British zone. Geographers throughout the world criticized the heavy omission of potentially harmful geographic material, and some British administrators recognized that they were presenting unnecessarily watered-down lessons to Germany's youth. One of these educational consultants recounted later that many of the Third Reich's textbooks contained much more interdisciplinary and "realistic" problems than the textbooks back in Britain. Those problems, however, had all been given a National Socialist tinge. From 1933 to 1945, whereas "[British children] seemed forever to have to cope with plumbers filling plugless baths with water," German children had been studying questions such as "If it takes 50,000 members of the *Wehrmacht* 3 days to conquer Holland [area of the country stated], how many days will it take 80,000 men to conquer England [area stated]?"[60] British revision of German textbooks had become, to many British administrators (and surely to many Germans as well), an attempt to replace the tragedy of Nazi expansionism with the farce of academic impracticality.

Britain, then, became the Western occupant most eager to hand control over education back to the Germans. In September 1946, the German Textbook Committee passed off the responsibility of reviewing Nazi textbooks for revision to textbook committees in each of the *Länder* occupied by Britain.[61] By January 1947, the British had given control of education back to the Germans through Ordinance No. 57 and shifted their focus to supervision and advisement.[62] In this same month, US general Lucius Clay announced the tightening of American control on its zone of occupation.[63] After this, it became increasingly clear to the various Allied powers and to the Germans that the United States had rhetorically understated the role it had initially meant to play in reconstructing Germany's education and that genuine reform would be done in 1947. Simply shipping educational consultants to the US zone in a lackadaisical effort to "advise" the restructuring of postwar German education had not worked well for the Americans. The British, French, and Soviets had dedicated much more time and money to education in the immediate postwar years than their American counterparts had. By mid-1947, the French had assigned

400 education officers to their zone of occupation, and the British had assigned 190. Each German university in the French zone had 4 officers assigned to it; the British also had at least one officer assigned to each of their occupied universities. The United States, in contrast, had assigned only 70 educational officers to its very large zone (*much* larger than the French zone). The Americans had appointed one education officer per four universities in the Hessen *Land* and only one per eight universities in Baden-Württemberg![64] These disparities were apparent not just at the university level. By the end of 1947, the French had published roughly 800 textbooks per 1,000 schoolchildren within its zone; the Soviets, 700 per 1,000 (although to be fair, the Soviets did control Leipzig, which at the time was one of the largest and most efficient centers of book publishing in Europe); and the British, 400 per 1,000. The United States, in contrast, had published a paltry 150 textbooks per 1,000 schoolchildren.[65] From the end of the war to the creation of the West German nation-state in 1949, the United States was by far the slowest producer of school and university textbooks.

But the United States recommitted itself to German education in 1948, with General Clay going so far as to claim that reeducation had become the American military's "most important goal."[66] Throughout that year, the American military spent $100,000 for nearly 200 American education specialists to travel to Germany and help with this effort.[67] These specialists produced all kinds of "paper plans," advocating everything from a "free, fully comprehensive secondary school system"[68] to Americanizing the German schoolyear calendar (which, rather than beginning in September, began in April).[69] By 1948, the American administrators had made clear their expectations that each *Länder* within the US zone was required to submit a plan detailing how it would begin incorporating the suggestions of these various educational consultants imported from the United States. Only the city of Bremen (which "had a City Assembly favorable to radical reform"[70]) ever actually got around to submitting a plan that was palatable to the American occupiers. Although Hesse did submit a plan, it demanded that higher-income families pay for public school—a requirement the US military government refused to endorse. Bavaria, too, submitted a plan, but this plan either willfully ignored the wishes of the

Americans or blatantly displayed Bavaria's refusal to comply with them. It maintained the traditional German two-track educational system and charged tuition for public-school attendance. Württemberg-Baden did not complete or submit a plan, continually asking for an extension instead.[71] By the time the American occupation forces had had an opportunity to look over and respond to these plans, the American military was already preparing to hand over the control of German education to the new West Germany. What one British educational consultant during this time called the Americans' "missionary zeal" in reforming German education had clearly backfired.[72]

German schools in the American zone, although never actually adopting any systemic reforms, did eventually adopt denazified textbooks. From July 1945 through March 1948, the US military government examined 2,509 textbooks for pro-Nazi material. It threw out 859 of these books, slated 567 for revision, and allowed 1,047 of them to be used without alteration. It found the most "nazified" disciplines during the Third Reich to be, unsurprisingly, history and geography.[73] Like the geography textbooks published in the British zone after the war, the new American textbooks employed terminology similar to that used during the Third Reich. *Teure Heimat, sei gegrüsst* (Greetings to You, Dear Homeland, 1948) by Josef Dietz, for example, still works within its first few pages to encourage nationalism, but it is an insular nationalism—a nationalism that appreciates what it has and does not long for territory it has lost: "Yes, our *Heimat* [homeland] is like a good mother. She cares for us from our cradle; shares sorrow and joy with us; and after death gathers us into her cool lap. This little book tells you about her, so that she shall grow ever closer to your heart."[74] By 1949, more than 600 new textbook titles— many of them focused on history and geography—had been incorporated into Germany's curriculum. By the fall of that year, when West Germany emerged from the Western Allies' occupation zones, the United States had managed to publish roughly 14 million copies of textbooks for the schoolchildren living within the lines of its occupation.[75] After denazification efforts, 28,000 new teachers had been hired, making up 70 percent of the profession's total population at the time.[76] These developments—textbooks and teachers—were the only successful marks the Americans made on German education, by and large. Most historians rightly attribute both these changes and the lack of changes to the American military government's tenacious obsession with denazification. However, the collaboration between the American military and German educators also brought about positive changes for the German people. Under the supervision of the American occupation government, Germans were often allowed to take the initiative and reestablish various organizations and institutions in an effort to normalize and legitimize academic and educational life under a foreign occupier.

German geographers were quick to recognize the American administrators' willingness to permit their reorganization after the war and to allow them to participate in the revision of geography education. In fact, the first formal meeting between academic geographers after the war took place in August 1947 under the leadership of Carl Troll and was encouraged by OSS operative Lloyd Black.[77] The meeting took place deep in the British zone of occupation, at the town of Lüdinghausen, but included representatives from each of the zones and focused on geography instruction.[78] The very next month this same group of geographers met with English-speaking colleagues at the town of Büren (again in the British zone but with representatives from each of the other zones) to discuss various approaches to incorporating geography into school curricula.[79] The American representative at these meetings, Wilhelm Credner, managed to convince the American occupation authorities to relicense the Verband der Hochschullehrer der Geographie (Association of German University Teachers of Geography) on November 14, 1947.[80] A list in English was kept of the roughly 120 lecture courses taught at German universities throughout 1947 and submitted to each of the four zonal governments.[81] By early 1948, German geographers had been successful in relicensing a slew of organizations that the Allied powers had abolished after the war: the Gesellschaft für Erdkunde zu Berlin (Berlin Geographical Society, originally established in 1828), the Geographische Gesellschaft Bremen (Bremen Geographical Society, 1876), the Verein für Geographie und Statistik zu Frankfurt/Main (Frankfurt/Main Association for Geography and Statistics, 1838), the Geographische Gesellschaft zu Hamburg (1873), the Geographische Gesellschaft Hannover (1878), the Gesellschaft für

Erdkunde zu Köln (1887), the Geographische Gesellschaft zu Lübeck (1882), the Geographische Gesellschaft zu Magdeburg (1927), and the Geographische Gesellschaft München (1869).[82]

In the fall of 1948, German geographers were permitted to hold their first postwar *Geographentagung* (geographers' conference) in Munich.[83] From September 26 through October 2, geographers from all over Germany came together (as they had since 1885) to share ideas, teaching methods, papers, and publications. At this meeting, Wilhelm Credner, Emil Meynen, and Kurt Brüning began discussing the creation of the Verband deutscher Berufsgeographen (Association of German Geography Professionals). Despite some reservations, Meynen was particularly fond of this idea and used the publishing power of the AfL to begin laying the groundwork for the new organization.[84] Meynen's influence in his position as both an academic and the director of the most well-funded geography institute in Germany was made clear in Credner's opening statement at the *Geographentagung*. Credner called for the AfL to work alongside other research centers in Germany. Collaborative efforts, Credner argued, were vital to the postwar maintenance of geographic institutions—many of which did not enjoy the consistent flow of work (or dollars) that the AfL had secured.[85] Although flattered, Meynen likely cringed at this reference to his work with the American occupation forces. He had certainly secured steady employment for many of his colleagues and for himself, of course. His cooperation with the Americans, however, had not always been pleasant.

Interrogation and Internment: The Denazification of the Abteilung für Landeskunde

As already noted, academic and educational denazification in the American zone was more rigid and prevalent than in the British, French, and Soviet zones. The Americans, after all, had evacuated a great many scientists from the eastern territories of Germany into its own southwestern zone. So although the British and French allowed questionable individuals to continue teaching, particularly in universities, the American military government had both the political will and the resources at its disposal to undertake long and arduous investigations of former Nazis.[86] Geographers were no exception. Emil Meynen, the director of the AfL and the individual who would become central to spatial reconstruction under American occupation, had welcomed the OSS operatives of Operation Dustbin with open arms and gone along with the evacuation of the AfL office from Thuringia to Bavaria. However, by the fall of 1946 he and several members of his staff were being interned at the Kranzberg Castle (Hermann Göring's headquarters during the Third Reich, north of Frankfurt) and were the targets of formal interrogations and investigations.[87] This small piece of postwar history reflects not only the suspicion with which the American military government approached liberated Germans who had helped to serve the Nazi regime but also just how inconsistent (at both the institutional and individual level) attitudes toward such agents really were.

As the Second World War in Europe came to a close in the spring of 1945, and as Meynen and the AfL rushed to Worbis in an attempt to avoid Allied bombing raids, the geographer Otto Schulz-Kampfhenkel hid some geographic material at a monastery in the Bavarian town of Ottobeuren. During the war, Schulz-Kampfhenkel had been a special geography consultant to the Reichsforschungsrat (Reich Research Council) and had also served as a lieutenant in the Luftwaffe (air force) and the SS. In April 1946, Meynen visited the monastery and retrieved this material by claiming, according to the monastery's abbot, that the information was needed for German universities. Instead, though, Meynen took the material back to the AfL in Scheinfeld without mentioning it to the military government.[88] As recounted in a British intelligence report, "The significant part of this move is that these documents deal chiefly with Russia and not with the geography of Germany which is Prof. Meynen's sole task at present."[89]

This lapse of judgment caught the attention of the US occupation administrators, and they began investigating Meynen and the postwar AfL. As it turned out, several questionable geographers were working for the AfL. Many of them had had loose or sometimes not so loose ties to the geography section of the Nazi military, the Forschungsstaffel zur besonderen Verwendung (Special Research Unit), and to Schulz-Kampfhenkel. Moreover, this investigation uncovered several other concerns for the Allied powers. In the summer of 1944, Meynen had collaborated with Schulz-Kampfhenkel on two different occasions, doing work for the Forschungsstaffel. Specific work included the "study of the appearance of different soils on aerial photographs" and the "improvement of methods of keys to the marks on maps."[90] The Allies also noted that Meynen had failed to prevent the Russians' capture of one of his archives in Stassfurt, a city within the Soviet zone of occupation, in the summer of 1946. This archive, according to the Allies, most likely contained "secret maps and aerial photographs . . . covering Russian, Balkan, North Italian and, possibly, [Oder-Neisse] line territory." In fact, the American military had retrieved an OSS report that Meynen had forwarded to a colleague in East Berlin detailing the holdings of this archive after its removal.[91] Perceiving Meynen's actions to have been subversive attempts to undermine the American occupation, the Allies arrested him in August 1946 and, along with Albert Speer's staff and several officials employed by the chemical and pharmaceutical company I. G. Farben, took him to Kranzberg for interrogation.[92] As soon as Meynen was arrested, he explained that he was working for the American intelligence community but had no written evidence to back up that claim. As Meynen recounted the incident, the officers who came to arrest him had never heard of the AfL and therefore believed he was lying.[93]

The exact date of Meynen's arrest and the exact length of his internment are difficult to determine. It is clear, however, that from July 1946 to May 1947 Erich Otremba—not Meynen—was running the AfL.[94] Otremba, who was formally denazified in September 1946, had once served as a member of the Wehrmacht's Forschungsstaffel, and Lloyd Black had invited him to join the AfL in the fall of 1945. He quickly agreed and became a full-time employee in January 1946.[95] Although under investigation until September, Otremba was allowed to continue his work with only intermittent interruption by the denazification process.[96]

The denazification reports that describe the exchanges between Emil Meynen and the Allied officers make clear the strange position of both parties. The Allies wanted Meynen's cooperation, and Meynen, believing himself to have been extremely accommodating since the Allied invasion of Thuringia, remained indignant toward his interlocutors throughout several of these interrogation sessions. Moreover, during this internment

Meynen was heavily questioned about Germany's various geographic institutes and the hiding places of cartographic material, yet the Allied officers continued to approach Meynen with a great deal of distrust. These exchanges make it clear that some members of the Allied occupation felt that Meynen and his organization had not been properly vetted, despite their employment to help remap the German state almost immediately after the war.

The projection of Meynen here, through his reports to the interrogators and through the reports by the Allied officers themselves, is fascinating. He defended German geography (and many geographers and institutions) as a "purely objective" enterprise that took no "political initiative" during the Second World War. The only exceptions to this claim—an argument he realized would fall on sympathetic ears—were the involvement of geographers in helping to establish a scientific basis "for the defense of the German borderlands and the quest for colonies [particularly in Africa]."[97] The Allied interrogators, Major Edmund Tilley (of British Intelligence) and a Mr. Bailey of the US State Department, asked Meynen about the geographical influence of Karl Haushofer (who had died in March 1946) and Friedrich Ratzel. Meynen's response did not stray far from the truth: Haushofer's influence was limited. He did not enjoy the same kind of darling-academic status that earlier German geographers (such as Humboldt, Hettner, Ratzel, and Albrecht Penck) had enjoyed. Ratzel and the postwar demonization of his Lebensraum concept were also, according to Meynen, trumped up by the Allies. Meynen claimed that prior to the invasions of the Czech Sudetenland and Poland, German geographers read Ratzel's Lebensraum only as the application of "biological metaphor to human geography." Only after the Third Reich's foreign policy became more aggressive did geographers also begin working to scientifically justify that approach with appeals to Lebensraum. In fact, when asked why German geographers failed to object to the National Socialist regime's expansionist policies, Meynen went so far as to justify their silence as a response to the "rather sensitive boundary lines and borderlands" drawn at the Paris Peace Conference after the First World War. Even before 1933, he argued, university geographers "had only one opinion" on controversial territories such as the Saar and the Polish corridor.[98] These opinions, as any geographer at the time knew, were not restricted to the Germans. As mentioned in the previous chapter, many Anglo-American geographers sympathized with German territorial frustration during the interwar years and had adopted the practice of justifying foreign policy with appeals to geopolitics before, during, and after the Second World War.[99]

Many of Meynen's statements, then, reflect reality: Haushofer's influence had been overestimated, many German geographers' imperialist writings were no more ethnocentric or expansionist than those of their American or British or French counterparts, and the territorial secessions forced onto the German state after the First World War (as well as the justification for those changes—national self-determination and cultural competition) had helped to popularize Pan-Germanism and jump-start conversations about the importance of maintaining German-speaking lands. But many of Meynen's responses were also self-serving. He was, in effect, telling the Allies what they wanted to hear: his work and his mapmaking colleagues' work had always been "scientific" and had never been "political." He presented his own work on Lebensraum (which, as mentioned in the previous chapter, included an article about the potential for German territorial growth into North America) as uninterested in expansionism.[100]

To put his Allied captors even more at ease, Meynen, while formally being interned, continued to collaborate with his former AfL employees, who were—of course—all working in Scheinfeld at the Krone Hotel. With the help of Gottfried Pfeifer, Erich Otremba, and Siegfried Schneider (who had been denazified in the fall of 1945 and had been a student of Meynen's), Meynen drafted a nearly exhaustive list of hidden cartographic material and equipment. This list included not only the collections of major geographic and cartographic agencies such as the AfL, the RfL, and the Abteilung Kartographie (Cartography Department) but also some really obscure material. Discarded Norwegian sea charts and outdated aerial photographs of European coastlines were among some of the seemingly least-important collections but were cataloged for the occupation authorities nonetheless.[101] The list also included, among other agencies, the Geographical Institute at the University of Würzburg, the library of the Reichskolonialbund (Reich Colonial League), the Geographical

Institute of the German University at Prague, and the Forschungsdienst Berlin (Berlin's Research Department). All of these institutions, according to the list compiled by Meynen and his colleagues, hid material during and after the war to protect it from war damage.[102]

Meynen's efforts to convince the Allied officers of his loyalty took a leap backward when in January 1947 his wife attempted to send him a package. The package contained nothing more than a pair of shoes but was wrapped in an old newspaper published during the Third Reich. When the package was intercepted by the occupation authorities at Scheinfeld (Frau Meynen presumably did not know where exactly her husband was being interned, Kranzberg), Meynen was reprimanded for receiving pro-Nazi materials. He quickly wrote a (surprisingly restrained) response to the Scheinfeld government explaining that his wife had sent him the shoes because she had heard that there was a good shoe repairman in Scheinfeld. The newspaper wrapping was left over from the evacuation out of Worbis in the summer of 1945, which, he claimed, was why the slogans printed on it were pro-Nazi! Meynen noted that this "shoe-package affair" ranked as one of the more "humorous incidents of [Operation] Dustbin," but it nevertheless grated on his patience. He wrote in ever-improving English,

> Until my detainment I worked willingly and sincerely for the American Authorities and was firmly convinced that I was enjoying their confidence. Therefore I was the more surprised that I was arrested like a criminal and jailed. When I called attention to my collaboration with the Military Government and State Department, I was quite perturbed to receive the answer of the officer in charge: "We will find out about your business."[103]

In fact, Meynen's involvement with the occupation government was questioned multiple times, despite his numerous meetings and subsequent correspondence with Captain Black throughout 1945 and 1946. Even more puzzling was the clear disregard the interrogators, Tilley and Bailey, had for Meynen's concrete evidence. Otremba took a letter written by Black to the Kranzberg denazification headquarters, and it was immediately "seized away" without any perceivable investigation.[104] It would also seem that an easy way to verify Meynen's collaboration with the American government would have been to check the financial records of the AfL, an institute funded primarily by the occupation forces at Scheinfeld. In fact, throughout the duration of Meynen's detention, his wife, Editha, had been frantically contacting all English-speaking geographers she had access to and begging them to intervene on her husband's behalf.[105] These attempts at speeding up Meynen's denazification were apparently not convincing because the length of his detention suggests that it was a painfully slow conversion. It is difficult to see this drawn-out process as unintended, particularly considering that Tilley and Bailey now had at their disposal one of Germany's most prized geographers and an occupation tool worth utilizing.

By the end of January 1947, Meynen had been forced to continue providing his detainers with cartographic information. He drafted lists of aerial photographs obtained or produced during the war, lists of every research circle and institution remotely related to spatial policy, and lists of what happened to those groups and institutions after the demise of the Third Reich.[106] He signed an oath declaring that neither he nor his staff members ever "expressed thoughts of future plans relating to Forschungsgruppe[n] [Research Groups] or [the] Forschungsstaffel," and he continued to justify the AfL's existence.[107] When asked why, even after the collapse of the Third Reich and the Allied order to dissolve all Reich institutions, he had refused to close down the AfL, he responded by claiming that he had been left without instruction from his German superiors. Perhaps more importantly than this lack of direction, Meynen argued that the AfL, although "founded during the war," "had its aims in peaceful work." As a hub of geographic and cartographic information, it was in a position to ensure the protection of that material for "either the future German or military government of the occupancy."[108]

By the end of May 1947, Meynen was finally released "without prejudice."[109] His unauthorized actions were confirmed to be attempts at compliance with the instructions left to him by Lloyd Black (whom he would soon write after his release, lamenting the long detention with the old German saying "Wer Unglück hat, braucht für den Spott nicht zu sorgen"—"The laugh is always on the loser").[110] By July, he had sent the Bayerisch Staatsministerium für Unterricht und Kultus (Bavarian State Ministry for Education and Culture) proof of his denazification with letters signed by both Erich Otremba (who had filled in for him during his detention) and his former adversary Mr. Bailey.[111] On July 14, Meynen was reappointed director of the institute he had initially founded under the auspices of the Nazi regime.[112] Denazification, however, had taken a toll not simply on Emil Meynen but also on the discipline and structure of German geography itself.

During Meynen's nearly year-long detention, American denazification had changed the structural hierarchy of academic and professional geography. In March 1947, the RfL—having outlived its usefulness to the Allies—was formally dissolved.[113] The AfL, which had up until that point been one branch under the RfL's research umbrella, was now forced to declare a kind of independence. This formal detachment from the oversight of a larger German organization opened up some intriguing possibilities. On March 5, 1947, Gottfried Pfeifer, Wilhelm Credner, Mr. Bailey, and representatives from the military government's Legal Division and the Bavarian Ministry of Education and Culture met to discuss the potential reestablishment of the Abteilung für Landeskunde (that is, *Department* of Regional Studies) as the Amt für Landeskunde (*Office* of Regional Studies).[114] This new classification would provide Meynen's institution with an unprecedented level of autonomy and to some extent the ability to transcend zonal boundaries and work with other Allied-approved autonomous agencies without an intermediary research organization of supervisors.[115]

From *Abteilung* to *Amt*: Emil Meynen's New Independence

On April 1, 1947, the new Amt für Landeskunde was formally created, becoming the premier independent geographic agency in postwar Germany.[116] Although it would technically work at the behest of the Bavarian Ministry of Education and Culture, it was also granted the leeway to undertake "interzonal" (überzonale) tasks and allocated an initial monthly budget of 10,000 Reichsmark (RM).[117] For Meynen and his staff, these changes were welcome. After the dissolution of the RfL on March 1, the employees of the AfL did not receive any salary yet continued to complete map work that had been contracted by the American occupation forces. In fact, one of the primary reasons the Bavarian government agreed to incorporate the new office into its occupation framework was that the American authorities had wanted "to keep the Amt für Landeskunde fit for work."[118] The day after its institutional reconstruction, John P. Bradford, chief of the Governmental Structures Branch, Office of Military Government for Bavaria, released a memo to all occupation authorities operating in Bavaria. The memo made clear that the new AfL was to be allowed an "independent character" and perfectly clear that it "is now and has been working for the American authorities."[119] Although that work would evolve throughout the postwar decades, the AfL's initial tasks were hugely important to the American military government.

During his internment, Meynen spent some time drafting proposals of various ways the AfL and the Americans could work to ensure that their cooperative efforts would be mutually beneficial. He offered, for example, to keep records of new German geographical and cartographical publications and maps. The AfL could also forward all new maps "issued by private and official German agencies" directly to the US State Department. Changes in place-names and in German administrative boundaries, argued Meynen, could be monitored by his institution on behalf of the American occupation. His ability to read the situations in which he found himself—his particular brand of genius—and his constant attempts to exploit those situations to his own advantage can perhaps be seen best in how he eventually fulfilled these promises to the Americans. Not only would the AfL discreetly pass on information to the US State Department well after the Federal Republic of Germany was established, but it would work to produce maps, not simply disseminate them, in order to further the interests and maintain the favor of its postwar occupier.[120]

When on April 1, 1947, the AfL became an independent office under the supervision of the Bavarian military government, it was explicitly charged with the promotion of "regional geographical research work on Germany in cooperation with university geographers and other regional research agencies" as well as with the promotion of "regional geography as a basic research of economic development and administration."[121] In order to achieve these goals and with the understanding that it was to funnel as much information and data to the State Department as possible, the AfL immediately went to work on several projects. The first was a place-name directory of Europe. Although the directory would be written in German, it would be based on the 1:1,000,000 scale international map of the world (begun by Albrecht Penck more than fifty years earlier), and all place-names would be presented in the language of the nation-state to which they belonged. This approach was a stark contrast to the approach taken in the expansionist place-name directories of the Third Reich, which, not two or three years earlier, had been replacing all European place-names with their German equivalents. The State Department also requested the AfL to compile a list of all linguistic and ethnographic maps published in western Europe between 1845 and 1945 as well as all "cartographical information" related to the Oder-Neisse boundary line.[122] These requests are no surprise. In order to reestablish Germany in its truncated postwar form, the seemingly scientific justification for its new lines through geographic study and cartographic presentation was understood as an imperative undertaking.

The American military government quickly adopted Meynen's offer to monitor and send reports to the State Department. Observing the changing academic and institutional trends as well as the shifting lines of German maps was an integral task to understanding and working to control German perception(s) of space. How the State Department received this information was clever and unsurprisingly exploited both the arrogance and the confusion of postwar German geographers.

Wilhelm Credner had started Germany's first postwar geography newsletter, *Rundschreiben*, in February 1946.[123] The *Rundschreiben* began as an instrument through which literally to reorient the geography profession after the Second World War. In its second issue, Credner attempted to disseminate the addresses of the members of German geography's intellectual class. He found thirty-nine geographers in the British zone (including luminaries such as Carl Troll and Kurt Brüning), fifteen in the Russian zone, ten in the French zone, and forty in the American zone (including, of course, himself, along with Meynen, Otremba, and other

AfL staff members).[124] Credner's publication was, however, narrow in its scope and self-published. Emil Meynen knew he could do better.

During the Third Reich, Meynen's AfL had produced a newsletter titled *Berichte zur Deutschen Landeskunde* (Report on German Regional Studies), which had been distributed to all German universities free of charge. With the financial backing of the American-controlled Bavarian state, Meynen reinstituted the *Berichte* and once again made it available to many academic geographers at no cost. Although the circular did benefit the German geographic community by bringing attention to new publications, lecture series, and academic appointments, Meynen used it as an easy way to compile information for the State Department. Worried about their postwar lives and eager to maintain their integrity as members of a larger national and international community, geographers were more than willing to provide Meynen with all sorts of personal and professional information: new maps, new books, new articles, new hires, new fellowships, and so on. Much of this information was published (often on the blank backs of old maps!), and nearly all of it was forwarded to the US State Department.[125]

From April through October 1947, the AfL also worked on projects deemed more "scientific" by the US government. Already in the early stages of production was the book that would eventually become one of the first regional geographies published after the Second World War, the *Landkreis Scheinfeld*, in 1950. As previously mentioned in this chapter, the *Landkreis Scheinfeld* was initially an AfL side project but would become the seminal piece of German studies developed by the AfL in the immediate postwar years. A comprehensive geography of the Scheinfeld district, it was meant to serve as an example for other geographic institutions throughout Germany. The AfL was also charged with producing a 1:500,000 scale "map on the natural landscape divisions of Germany" and a 1:200,000 scale national topographic map.[126] More important to the occupation administration, though, were cartographic projects aimed at alleviating postwar problems: a comparative study of war damage done to German cities, a map of German refugees who had resettled in Bavaria, and an updated map of Germany's regional districts.[127] These issues took precedence over any studies unrelated to the occupation. As noted in the AfL's annual report for 1948–49, all AfL personnel were "engaged [primarily] in projects of the occupying power."[128]

Institutional independence did not always bring with it positive experiences. The AfL underwent particularly difficult months from January 1948 until the creation of the Federal Republic of Germany in May 1949. As the Allied occupation forces worked to reinstall some kind of sovereign German government, the AfL's financial stability (along with that of many other government-funded institutions) was continually threatened. Meynen's tenacious opportunism—his ability to sell his maps and data as vitally important to the postwar construction of a new German state— became the primary source of revenue for the office he had managed to create under the Third Reich, to move out from under the Soviets immediately after the war, and to maintain under the Americans well into the early stages of the Cold War.

On January 12, 1948, the Bavarian military government announced that new austerity measures required a round of deep government-spending cuts. The Bavarian administrators saw the Amt für Landeskunde, which by this point was being allotted 12,000 RM a month, as an unnecessary expense and so liquidated its government funding.[129] American intelligence agencies and the State Department, however, were frustrated with this decision. The AfL had offered them a great deal of help, providing military-oriented geographic descriptions of the German landscape (something a few of the AfL staff had mastered while working for the Third Reich's Mil-Geo unit), answering questions concerning boundary lines and place-name spellings, and by January 1948 completing the first postwar 1:200,000 scale comprehensive topographic survey of the new and diminished postwar German territory.[130] When the AfL's government funding was eliminated, Meynen immediately began contacting US State Department officials in an effort to expand the AfL's work for the occupation powers to make up for the lost revenue.[131] He was successful in securing "extra allowances," in convincing the State Department to intervene on the AfL's behalf and to stop the Bavarian government from recovering the AfL's furniture and equipment, and in keeping his organization afloat for a few months while he figured out what to do next. From January to

May 1948, Meynen understood that the money he was receiving directly from the State Department was a "transitory solution," but he was thrilled to have the support regardless. In his own words, he made clear at the time that "there is still no German government and therefore no German agency which would support my work on regional geography."[132] In an effort to make the mutual dependence of Meynen and the Allied occupation concrete and explicit, the AfL applied for incorporation into the British–American bizonal administration on May 5, 1948.[133]

Government contracting might have been the primary means through which the AfL secured funding, but it was not the only way. As early as 1945, Meynen and other German geographers had begun lobbying their colleagues in other nation-states to consider exchanging Cooperative for Assistance and Relief Everywhere (CARE) packages or other food packages for sought-after and nearly impossible to get ahold of German geographic publications. German map distribution and the distribution of most maps from western and central Europe had been halted after the outbreak of the war in 1939, yet the importance of many German publications had not diminished.[134] In November 1947, for example, a geographer from New Zealand named D. W. McKenzie wrote to Meynen asking if "it might be possible for us to obtain from you geographical material concerning Germany and Central Europe. . . . We might be able to effect an exchange of your materials if we can send you food parcels—containing particularly fats."[135] When months later Meynen requested cash in exchange for the material, McKenzie grimly responded that no New Zealand bank would exchange his money for Reichsmarks. "I am afraid," McKenzie wrote, "that we shall have to fall back upon the age-old system of barter!"[136]

Out of this postwar condition, bartering networks were created that, although usually direct—that is, in exchange for publications the individual receiving them would put in an order to CARE on behalf of the individual sending the publications—could also be complex. One hub of a food-for-publications exchange was the American Geographical Society (AGS), which occasionally found "buyers" for German geographers looking to "sell" material from their libraries for CARE packages. The AGS librarian, Nordis Felland, would receive the book, map, or atlas from the scholar and forward the material to the American university that had ordered it, and then the university would send Felland a cash payment, which she would forward to CARE.[137] In early 1948, Emil Meynen began publishing in English a *Rundbrief* (newsletter) titled *Neuigkeiten* (New Updates) with basic contact information for both German geographers and international geographers interested in making these exchanges.[138] This new publication also featured the agencies one could contact to receive official maps of Germany (four in the American zone, four in the British zone, three in the French zone, and five in the Soviet zone).[139] Although the Allied powers neither discouraged nor encouraged initial exchanges between German geographers and their colleagues around the world, by late 1949 the Allies were working hard to facilitate these exchanges and construct a consistent and fluid passing of geographic information between the Federal Republic and any democratic nation-state willing to participate.

Receiving food from abroad served as an important nutritional subsidy for the families of many German geographers, and, as discussed in the next chapter, the reinstitution of publication exchanges (that is, publications for publications) after the war was enthusiastically welcomed by German and non-German academics alike. Finding consistent funding for geographic institutions, however, remained elusive. Indeed, by December 1948 Meynen wrote to a colleague that the immediate postwar concerns about finding cartographic materials and paper for letters or publications had finally been eclipsed by the problem of financing. The introduction of the Deutsche Mark (DM) in June 1948 had "stripped off all former resources."[140] Months after applying for incorporation into the combined Bizone of the American and British military governments, the AfL had received no response and was still relying on contractual arrangements with intelligence agencies and the US State Department.[141] In July 1948, the American occupation forces moved the AfL from the Krone Hotel in Scheinfeld to a housing project within the southeastern Bavarian city of Landshut.[142] From his new office in Landshut, Meynen produced a stream of letters to the Bizone administration touting the importance of the work the AfL had been doing for American military intelligence and the State Department. Well into the summer of 1949, he continued to send Lloyd Black geographic information about German military organizations, which Black would, in fact, attempt to publish in the *Annals of the Association of American Geographers*.[143] By April 1949, Black was directing all military and academic inquiries regarding German geography to Emil Meynen.[144] However, the Americans continued to refuse to establish an autonomous budget for the AfL. The bizonal territorial arrangement between the British and American occupation forces had technically always been a violation of the Potsdam Agreement and was on its way to dissolution.[145] Although a new and quasi-sovereign West German state would be established in the summer of 1949, the spatial delineations of that state (and the extent to which Germans would be allowed to draft and publish representations of that space) were still contentious.

From the Potsdam Conference of 1945 to the adoption of the Constitution of the Federal Republic of Germany in August 1949, the exact boundaries of Germany remained problematic. The territory of West Germany was stipulated in the Grundgesetz für die Bundesrepublik Deutschland (Basic Law for the Federal Republic of Germany) of May 1949, approved by the Allied occupation, but various *Länder* (in particular Baden, Württemberg-Baden, and Württemberg-Hohenzollern) continually requested "boundary modifications."[146] From June 1948 to May 1949, the Soviets imposed a blockade on West Berlin. As historians so love to say, the Cold War was "heating up," and its hot glow was being fueled by territorial considerations. How those considerations were affected by the growing international conflict between Western democracies and Eastern Communist states (not to mention how the German geographers living on both sides of this infamous Iron Curtain were affected) is the subject of the next chapter.

4

The End of Occupation?

We have met at a great hour in the earth's history. It is obvious that
the people of the world face sober problems, but it is equally certain
that we face thrilling opportunities. Let us not despair or look backward, this is a moment for courage and constructive action.
    —George B. Cressey, quoted in John K. Wright,
        "The Sixteenth International Geographical
        Congress: Lisbon, 1949"

The encouraging and hopeful words spoken in the opening of the Sixteenth International Geographical Union Congress personified the
excitement of the group of men gathered from twenty-nine countries, all
seated in Lisbon's Portuguese National Assembly hall, on April 8, 1949.
The speaker was not, however, any kind of legislator or government func-
tionary but rather an American geographer from Syracuse University and
new vice president elect of the International Geographical Union (IGU),
George B. Cressey. In fact, Cressey's address served as a prophetic assump-
tion of the new postwar geopolitical reality and the role of the geographers
who would be called upon to shape it. The men he was addressing, seated
at the desks of statesmen in a building designed for statecraft, were mapmakers of the highest order. Each was a delegate sent by his respective
nation-state, and each recognized postwar Europe as a land of territorial
opportunity. They believed it would be geographers who, just like after
the First World War, would be once again called upon to help reestablish
the new Europe. At this same meeting, the American cartographer John
K. Wright, who was also chair of the IGU's Committee of Cartography,
remarked that "since modern war is the most powerful of all stimulants to
human mobility, it is not surprising that the mightiest of wars has brought

about a cartographic revolution."[1] Indeed, nothing short of a cartographic revolution could mend the broken boundary lines of Europe.

As earlier chapters have made clear, the territory of Germany enjoyed a central role in this remapping project. The participation by actual Germans in this project was, however, often limited. At the IGU Congress in 1949, for example, there was only one German present to hear Cressey's words: Hermann Lautensach.[2] Germany had been expelled from the IGU during the Second World War and would not be readmitted as an official member state again until the Seventeenth IGU Congress in 1952 in Washington, DC (and most of the German delegates would be from West Germany).[3] By August 1951, Marshall Plan agents from the United States were pushing hard for West German participation in the new Cartography and Photogrammetry Program of the Organization for European Economic Cooperation. The Germans, however, had neither the capital nor the time to rebuild their industrial mapmaking plants. Moreover, they were concerned that participating in the centralization of western European cartography would make it more and more difficult to efficiently create and effectively distribute goods for both the German and European markets.[4]

The Germans, though, were to be counted on as an obvious means of disseminating material produced by their discipline's international Congress. As was so often the case, foreign geographers turned to Emil Meynen, director of the Amt für Landeskunde, for information concerning their German colleagues. Since the end of the war, Meynen had been consistently collecting and publicizing the addresses, appointments, and accomplishments of German geographers—simultaneously as a newsletter of academic interest and as a report for his supervisors in the American occupation government. He was the obvious choice, then, for the IGU to contact when attempting to distribute its newsletter to German academicians (including those Germans living in the new Communist East Germany). The IGU's secretary-general, George H. T. Kimble, sent 250 copies of the organization's newsletter to Meynen in September 1950, thanking him for his willingness to send them out and promising that the IGU's Executive Committee was "anxious to assist German geographers in every possible way."[5] Such sentiments seemed genuine, and the IGU set aside a large amount of travel funds to help encourage a significant

German delegation to attend the IGU Congress in Washington, DC, in 1952.[6] These funds would prove instrumental in attracting a large contingent of twelve Germans from the Federal Republic of Germany (FRG) to the United States.

Strangely, even after the formal territorial split between the German Democratic Republic (GDR) and the FRG, geographers both in Germany and abroad continued to refer to the states together as "Germany"—even as late as the IGU Congress in 1952. The delegation sent to Washington, DC, included the usual West German collaborators, such as Emil Meynen, Hermann Lautensach, Gottfried Pfeifer, and Carl Troll, but it also included Germans from the East such as Ernst Blume of Magdeburg. All were listed in the Congress's proceedings under the member state name "Germany" (keep in mind that place-names were something taken very seriously by the world's leading geographers).[7] Such naming suggests that although Soviet and American politicians were beginning to engage in the Cold War, most German academics (at least in the discipline of geography) were still hopeful for unification and more interested in the state of their maps and materials than in who lived behind which side of the new Iron Curtain. The state of German geographical study seemed more urgent than which government was facilitating or reconstructing that study. Indeed, Edwin Fels expressed this sentiment in his report to the IGU on the Berlin Geographical Society, the same society that had counted Alexander von Humboldt, Carl Ritter, and Albrecht Penck among its early members. The society in 1952, he explained,

> works in a city which now geographically—I am sorry to say—is perhaps the most noteworthy and interesting capital in the world. . . . The house of the Society has been destroyed. The famous library is in Eastern hands. The fortune is lost. . . . In spite of these vicissitudes the Society has been rebuilding since 1948. We have already more than 600 members . . . [and are exchanging publications with] 260 societies all over the world.[8]

This seemingly near-universal sense of camaraderie, however, would not last beyond this meeting in 1952. Some of the Germans who had delivered papers at the IGU Congress and then traveled the United States together afterward, visiting the country's major libraries and its academic hubs of Russian/Soviet studies,[9] would turn against each other in just a few short years.

Before this shift in attitude can be discussed, however, it is important to emphasize the territorial problems that plagued the formal split between the German East and the German West. Immediately after the Second World War, the lack of communication and subsequent tension between Allied zones of occupation became problematic. As more and more displaced persons and refugees swarmed into the postwar German state proper, the possibility of emigration from Germany into the territory of one of the occupying powers quickly sprang to the minds of many Europeans. Geography often served as the only factor determining whether a family or individual could emigrate and, if they could, where they were allowed to immigrate to. As one American consulate staffer noted,

> It is one thing to say to a man in Hamburg that he can not go to America although his friend in Frankfurt can; it is quite another thing to say to a man in Berlin-Wilmersdorf that he cannot go to America while his friend and neighbor one-half or one-fourth or one-eighth of a mile away in Berlin-Schoeneberg can. And it is near tragedy to say, as has actually occurred in several instances, that one family on the south side of a street may qualify, while their friends and neighbors on the north side of the street, which happens to be the British sector, may not.[10]

By September 1945, the US military had split its respective occupation zone—which consisted largely of southern German states—into three provisional *Länder* (excluding Berlin): one encompassing nearly the entire state of Bavaria according to its preoccupation administrative boundaries and the other two incorporating sections of Württemberg-Baden, Hesse, and Bremen with little regard for "traditional administrative lines."[11] By March 1946, however, the US State Department had established six consular districts meant to make resettlement within Germany and emigration from Germany more efficient in accordance with President Truman's Directive 225 of December 22, 1945, which emphasized the importance of allowing European displaced persons to apply for immigration to the United States. The new consulate offices were based in Berlin, Hamburg, Bremen, Frankfurt, Stuttgart, and Munich, which, in theory, allowed for the expanded ability of the United States to cope with territorially sensitive issues (i.e., resettlement and emigration).[12]

The fluid nature of these provisional administrative boundaries, however, often resulted in confusion for the administrators and frustration for those individuals living within lines that everyone recognized as artificial. For example, one particularly problematic section of Germany was the "Bremen Enclave," a small slice of land smack in the middle of the British occupation zone. As mentioned in chapter 2, the United States had requested control of Bremen because the city-state acted as a convenient port on the Weser River, which flowed into the North Sea, giving the American military a foothold in northern Germany. Prior to January 10, 1946, the American-occupied Bremen Enclave consisted not only of Bremen but also of three surrounding districts: Osterholtz, Wesermarsch, and Wesermünde. After January 10, the administrative authority over these three districts was transferred to the British military government and subsequently became subject to British resettlement and immigration policies. However, many individuals living in the Osterholtz, Wesermarsch, and Wesermünde districts appealed to the US consulate in Frankfurt (which was responsible for the Bremen Enclave until the territorial reorganization in March 1946) for immigration to the United States on the basis that they had been occupied by the American military government when the Truman directive was issued in December 1945. After all, it was typical American military policy to accept the registrations and visas from "qualified displaced persons and persecutees who resided in the American zones of occupation prior to December 22, 1945."[13] The consul general in Frankfurt apparently did not know the territorial history of the Bremen Enclave and requested from his superiors information on the actual boundaries of American-occupied Bremen. He was told to concern himself only with those persons living within the new American Bremen Enclave and that individuals living in the three districts that in December 1945 had been under American occupation were no longer eligible to be considered for immigration to the United States, despite what the immigration policy might have been elsewhere in Germany. A map was, of course, sent to the consul general, clearly delineating the four sections of the old Bremen Enclave to serve as a refresher course for cartographic memory and to make clear exactly what territories were no longer under American control (figure 12).[14]

By the spring of 1947, the immediacy of establishing administrative control over Germany had waned. Having etched into the German map their respective occupation zones, the four Allied powers sent

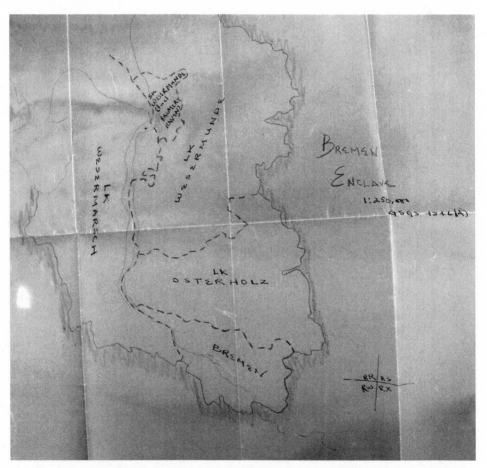

12. General Staff, Geographical Section, *Bremen Enclave*, scale 1:250,000, 1946, GSGS 4346(A), Record Group 84, Stack 350, 58/11/05, Box 2, National Archives and Records Administration, Washington, DC.

foreign-policy representatives to form the appropriately named Control Council and to hold a series of meetings in which they were charged with rebuilding "a Europe better than it replaces."[15] Furthermore, they were commissioned to "establish a precise definition of the administrative and territorial division of Germany as of May 1, 1947, indicating boundaries of lands and provinces."[16] Such a task would not be easy, especially when the council members were required only to solidify cartographic propositions of Germany that had been approved by all four Allied powers.

On March 15, 1947, the Control Council met for the first time with position papers in hand. From the outset, it was clear that problems were going to arise—even before the mapping could begin. The delegation from the Soviet Union began their statement by railing against what they perceived to be the conceptual basis behind territorial reallocation by the British. According to the Soviets, Great Britain had made it clear during an Allied meeting in November 1946 that "the territorial frontiers of the Lands in the British Zone were determined in such a way that the Lands should not be very small and consequently could not be swallowed by the future central government." The Soviet delegates found this attitude wholly unacceptable. In their eyes, the British were attempting to "pre-determine the future structure of the State of Germany in the direction of federalization." How, asked the Soviets, could reterritorialization even begin to take place if the British were already trying to rig the eventual political environment in a way favorable to their own ideology?[17] Yet the French released a statement not one week later supporting the British position and emphasizing the necessity of a German territory that would encourage decentralization and "local responsibility."[18] Somewhat surprisingly, however, the United States agreed with the Soviet delegation that Germany should eventually be free to determine its own political environment and that all amendments to the German map had to be met with unanimous consent.[19] Having not really resolved the competing sentiments among the Allied powers regarding German reterritorialization, the Control Council trudged on to more tangible problems.

One such concern was the Polish–German border. It had already been established at the Potsdam Conference of July–August 1945 that Poland would gain a considerable amount of eastern German territory. What still needed to be worked out was "how and where to draw the final line so as to avoid unnecessary and unjustified economic upset and to minimize inescapable irredentist pressure in Germany."[20] The Allies projected that some 66 million people would be residing in Germany by 1950, and they were concerned about squeezing them all into a smaller nation-state. At the same time, the Allies easily admitted that Poland needed to be compensated for what had happened to it during the Second World War and for its easternmost territory, which the Soviet government had permanently consumed. Thus, the council agreed to cede southern East Prussia and German Upper Silesia to Poland, effectively granting Poland all German territory east of the Oder River.[21]

The French delegation was willing to go along with such cartographic addenda so long as the other powers supported the transfer of German territories that would be advantageous to them. The Saar territory (or, as it would be known after this date and until 1957, the Saar Protectorate) was ceded to France in April 1947, its large deposits of coal downplayed by the French, who claimed that such an act of reterritorialization was a humanitarian endeavor, depriving "Germany of a portion of her war potential."[22] In fact, if the French delegation were to be believed, France only ever acted out of the impulse to "offer to the world a genuine guarantee of security . . . guided by no spirit of private ambition."[23] Somehow, though, France could not help but benefit from playing world savior along with the Americans, British, and Soviets. It managed to gain substantial economic advantages in the Ruhr region and along the Rhine River, pushing for that territory's internationalization under the watchful eye of the French government.[24] Even when supporting the claims to territory by other Allied nation-states—such as Belgian settlement claims and the redrafting of Czechoslovakian borders to their 1938 boundaries—the French could not help but "say a few words about the Franco-German frontier," barraging their colleagues with tales of the many historical "vicissitudes" suffered by the French at the hands of the ever-aggressive Germans.[25] Such an attitude on the part of the French would create territorial problems later, allowing the Saar Protectorate to serve consistently as a potential "stumbling block to [the] establishment of a European Defense Community" throughout the early 1950s.[26]

The majority of the Control Council's work was completed by May 1, 1947, in accordance with its mandate. Talks lasted well into the fall of that year, but few things changed (including each nation-state's rhetoric). In November 1947, the Control Council officially concluded territorial talks, allocating any further remapping problems to each Allies' respective German deputy for study and report.[27] What followed would permanently divide Germany into two quasi-sovereign nation-states: the Berlin Blockade of 1948 and the subsequent year-long airlift (figures 13 and 14).[28] This is a familiar story, but how did the Americans, British, and French respond administratively to this permanent division? How did they utilize their influence in West Germany and the polarization of East European–West European politics to their advantage? What happened cartographically after the division?

After receiving official approval from the Allied occupiers earlier in the month, the West Germans adopted the Grundgesetz für die Bundesrepublik Deutschland (Basic Law for the Federal Republic of Germany) on May 23, 1949, simultaneously creating the FRG. Unlike the "founding documents" of many nation-states, the FRG's Basic Law explicitly defined its territorial holdings. The law's preamble, in fact, predicated the document's (and thereby the new republic's) legitimacy on the authority of "the German people in the Länder Baden, Bremen, Hamburg, Hesse, Lower Saxony, North-Rhine-Westphalia, Rhineland-Palatinate, Schleswig-Holstein, Württemberg-Baden and Württemberg-Hohenzollern." Moreover, claimed the preamble, "[the Basic Law] has also acted on behalf of those Germans to whom participation was denied. The entire German people," it evangelized, "are called upon to achieve by free self-determination, the unity and freedom of Germany."[29] As if arming itself with that bit of self-assurance was not quite enough, it went on in Article 23 to list again the *Länder* that would operate under its dictates and to predict that the law would "be put into force in other parts of Germany on their accession."[30] One telling difference between Article 23 and the preamble, however, was the inclusion of Greater Berlin. In fact, even in the initial drafts of the law during the summer of 1948, Greater Berlin had continuously been excluded as a territory to be directly governed by the FRG. Rather, Article 23 initially stated that

Administrative Districts of the DDR after 1952

13. *Administrative Districts of the DDR after 1952*, scale not given, in Arthur Hearnden, *Education in the Two Germanies* (Boulder, CO: Westview Press, 1974), 63.

"Greater Berlin has the right to send representatives to the Bundestag and the Bundesrat."[31] Understandably, after the nearly year-long Berlin Blockade from June 1948 to May 1949, the Allied powers decided to apply West Germany's new foundational document directly to the former capital.

Länder *of the Federal Republic after 1949 (Saarland added in 1957)*

14. *Länder of the Federal Republic after 1949 (Saarland Added in 1957)*, scale not given, in Arthur Hearnden, *Education in the Two Germanies* (Boulder, CO: Westview Press, 1974), 60.

The FRG's territory was not completely solidified yet, and the Basic Law made provisions for territorial shifts and changes. Realizing that some Germans found the postwar *Länder* too artificial, Article 29 laid out circumstances under which the German people themselves could reshape their map. Any territorial changes had to be mapped within one year of the ratification of the Basic Law. Changes could be made only by general referendum, and 10 percent of a *Land*'s voting population had to participate in the petition for a referendum. Any majority decision made by that referendum would be final so long as the change took into account "regional ties, historical and cultural connections, economic expediency and social structure."[32] One notable exception to Article 29 was permitted: the territorially contentious states Baden, Württemberg-Baden, and Württemberg-Hohenzollern. This exception was made owing to, in part, the size of these *Länder* and their complicated territorial origins. Baden and Württemberg-Hohenzollern had initially been subdivisions under French administrative control, whereas Württemberg-Baden had been occupied by the Americans. Article 118 of the Basic Law allowed these states, which had been considering a cartographic merger since early 1949, to operate outside of the Article 29 provisions and to hold a referendum later than one year after inclusion into the FRG. These three *Länder* held a referendum in 1951 (which the state of Baden rejected, but the more populous Württemberg states approved) and were united in 1952 as "Baden-Württemberg," the only state created after 1949 by popular German vote.[33]

By 1951, West Germany had clearly regained some semblance of sovereignty. The Bundestag (Federal Assembly) was elected in August 1949, and on July 9, 1951, President Truman called on the US Congress to terminate its state of war with Germany.[34] By October 1951, the Allies had seriously relaxed their commercial oversight of the country by means of an agreement signed between Allied foreign ministers in September 1950.[35] None of this, of course, meant that West Germany had been relieved of Allied military government control, but such quasi-independence lent itself to problematic circumstances—particularly in regard to mapmaking. The Allied administrators still saw cartography and geography as potentially subversive disciplines and heavily regulated them. In September 1949, shortly after the election of the FRG's first Bundestag, the Allied powers imposed Law No. 23 on the West German state, prohibiting the development of scientific research and application "to the extent to which it may be used for warlike ends or contribute to the establishment of war potential." Making unapproved maps, an undertaking considered to be "scientific," had the potential to result in life imprisonment or a 500,000 DM fine or both as well as the closing of any participating organization.[36] Aside from Emil Meynen's AfL, perhaps the only exceptions to strict regulatory control of mapmaking research and processes were educational institutions operating with the Allied powers' implicit approval—namely, universities.

Geography Education in the New Federal Republic

As mentioned in the previous chapter, all of the Allied powers attempted to redemocratize Germany through reforming its education system. Despite having approached the issue in very different ways, the British, the French, and the Americans spectacularly failed to transform German education into something new or into an emulation of their own education systems. Those *Länder* that had been favorable to reform—Hamburg, Schleswig-Holstein, and Bremen—had initially lengthened the years required for primary school from four to six after Germany's defeat. This change had the effect of adding two years of collective general education before a child's admission into the *Gymnasium* or *Mittelschule*, a "tracked" divergence that the Allied powers (in particular the Americans) found crudely undemocratic. By the mid-1950s, under pressure from the other German *Länder*, Schleswig-Holstein, Hamburg, and Bremen reverted back to the traditional system and encouraged students to move into the split tracks after only four years of primary school. This falling into line was caused by what one historian of education calls a "conspicuous lack of enthusiasm for any modifications of the established highly selective system."[37] This "lack of enthusiasm" was also felt by the Allied powers, who after years of attempting to impose structural changes had been consistently ridiculed or ignored (usually both) by the majority of the German states' education administrations. The Allies made sure to avoid mention of education at all in the Occupation Statute of Germany of April 1949, the document that dictated the relationship between the new West German government and the occupation authorities.[38] By 1950–51, the West Germans had managed to oust the last few remaining Allied education officers and were once again in the position of molding the minds of their own primary, secondary, and postsecondary students without the direct supervision of an American, a Brit, or a Frenchman.[39]

Although heavily regulated outside the gates of German universities, the discipline of geography was thriving after the founding of the FRG in 1949. By 1950, there were twenty-four geography department chairs among twenty-five universities (the University of Hamburg had two chairs!). During the 1949–50 academic year, those departments were training more than 1,600 students.[40] Professors who had been fired during denazification were slowly reincorporated back into academia with the help of the Hochschulverband (German Education Association).[41]

Meynen and the Marshall Plan

Aside from universities, the AfL continued to work with the implicit support of the Allied occupation powers. The collaboration between the AfL and in particular the American government only grew after West Germany was granted sovereignty. Meynen's own newsletter indicates that by the summer of 1949 his institution was receiving direct funds from the ERP. The Marshall Plan had dictated that ERP deposits be channeled through various West German government agencies in order to create maps and topographic studies, and the AfL, having been an early participant in Germany's postwar remapping, was an obvious funding choice.[42]

In October 1949, the AfL—which up until this point had been operating under the supervision of the American military government—was put under the direction of the new FRG Ministry of Interior. Despite this shift, the AfL's primary purpose was still to produce information for the Allied military. (In accordance with its continued reliance on English-speaking approval, the AfL continued to submit its annual reports in English; only in the summer of 1951 did its reports begin to be submitted once again in German.[43]) The combination of postwar work for the Allied forces and now in 1949 funding from the ERP allowed Meynen to maintain a staff of fifty-five employees, including nineteen geographers and eight cartographers.[44] No other mapmaking institution in Germany, even after the initial postwar years, had such consistent funds, staff, and influence. By 1950, the AfL had cataloged all German maps drafted since 1939 and all German literature concerning geography since 1910. The official geographical encyclopedia of Germany, the only sanctioned 1:500,000 scale maps of Germany's regional subdivisions, and the authoritative *Kreislandeskunden* (regional descriptions) were created, edited, and maintained under the publishing authority of the AfL. It is no wonder that, writing for the *Geographical Review*, Captain Lloyd Black announced that this institution represented "the greatest actual and potential force in German geography" of the postwar period.[45]

As is true regarding the authority of any geospatial institution, government support and recognition can only go so far. The lines of a map and the agencies that draw them are nothing but empty propositions—cartographic fantasies—if unrecognized by the international community of nation-states. Even those lines forced onto the globe through the violence of capitalism, military conquest, and colonialism serve only as markers of territorial resentment and frustration without (and often even with) international acknowledgment. A vital part of Emil Meynen's job, then, was to convince his academic colleagues abroad of the AfL's continued importance. Black's report to the *Geographical Review* could sing the AfL's praises for eternity, but it was Meynen who actually needed to perform.

As has already been noted in other chapters, one important way to maintain authority over Germany's maps was to collaborate carefully but enthusiastically with the Allied military government. Another way Meynen could hold on to status and cultivate important international ties and acceptance was to broaden and deepen his intellectual and academic network. The existence of such agreements as the informal maps-for-food agreement undertaken by Meynen with his international colleagues simply suggests that the world's geographers were desperate for geographical information regarding Germany after the Second World War. It does not necessarily follow that the AfL had established itself as the premier geographical institute in postwar Germany.

By late 1949, then, Meynen had begun to heavily promote the AfL. Equipped with the Allied powers' blessing and ERP funds and untethered to the politics of postwar universities, Meynen undertook a massive project of cartographic dissemination. Many libraries and geographical societies were still very interested in receiving German maps and cartobibliographies, and as time went on, most of these societies wanted to work with institutions rather than with individuals (relationships with individuals became much too complicated after the war). Chief among the institutions eager for German material was the Association of American Geographers (AAG), which in 1950 commissioned none other than Lloyd Black to bolster its postwar contacts with European geographers.[46] Black then made Meynen the AAG's chief contact in West Germany and was even able to convince the AAG to allocate the AfL some space for regular updates in its periodical, *The Professional Geographer*.[47]

As a gesture of gratitude, Meynen went out of his way to inform the AAG that there were too few English-language geographical periodicals in West Germany, despite the opportunity to disseminate them. He pointed to the new Amerika Häuser (America Houses) program as an easy way to promote the study of geographic materials.[48] The Amerika Häuser were fairly popular centers of American information and literature, especially among well-educated Germans. "The idea behind them," as one historian writes, was "to provide Germans with 'windows to the West' and to acquaint them with democratic ideas and classics that had been closed to them during the twelve years of Nazi propaganda and cultural isolation."[49] A few Amerika Häuser had been established as early as 1945, but by 1950 there were 27 large centers in West German cities and 135 "affiliated reading rooms in smaller towns." These spaces of rigidly unapologetic democratization and Americanization helped to lay the groundwork for later German–American exchange programs and cultural institutions.[50] It was Meynen who facilitated the inclusion of *The Professional Geographer*—a journal that focused largely on technical and applied geography—among the many periodicals collected at the Amerika Häuser.[51]

Meynen also spent a great deal of his own personal time working to broaden the influence of the Amt für Landeskunde during the FRG's early years. He drafted maps for books by prominent American geographers, helped leading geographical societies complete their research aids, and sent university instructors maps of Germany for their respective classrooms.[52] He broadened his collaboration with other domestic West German scientific academies, such as the Institut für Raumforschung (Institute for Spatial Research) and the Statistisches Bundesamt (Federal Office for Statistics). Most importantly, Meynen facilitated a smooth transition of the AfL's existing contracts with the Allied military government to the new FRG government. The AfL produced and disseminated a majority of the FRG's official maps: the 1:1,000,000 scale map of its new administrative boundaries, the 1:1,000,000 scale map of the first Bundestag election, the 1:300,000 scale map of new German municipal boundaries (in collaboration with the Institute for Spatial Research), the 1:1,000,000 scale utility map of West Germany, the 1:1,000,000 scale transit/highway map, among many, many others.[53] All of these maps were produced or production had begun on them within six months of the FRG's coming into existence.

The AfL flourished as a subsidiary of the FRG Ministry of Interior. But Meynen did not want to simply work as an instrument of a government agency; by 1950, he had made it clear to many of his colleagues that he wanted the AfL to become a federal office in its own right. Only during the Second World War, as an *Abteilung*, department, of the Third Reich's Zentralkommission für wissenschaftliche Landeskunde (Central Commission for Scientific Regional Studies), did Meynen's institution enjoy the economic security he believed it deserved. If the AfL could once again become an agency directly funded by the government, rather than through contractual agreements with the Ministry of Interior and the American military, its two largest contributors, Meynen believed it could better serve the German people and the discipline of geography as a whole.[54]

By 1950, though, something else had also been bothering Meynen about the AfL's position in the FRG's hierarchy of federal agencies and offices. Even after the formal split between East Germany and West

Germany in 1949, Meynen worked hard to consistently include those geographers who ended up on the other side of the Iron Curtain. Well into 1950, he continued to report news updates on his East German colleagues in the AfL's *Rundbrief.*[55] The AfL continued to draft and sell quadrangles of its 1:200,000 scale national map series of Germany that did not account for any division. Indeed, after hosting the "founding assembly" of the new Association of Professional Geographers, and after the thirty-eight founding members elected representatives from Westphalia, Bavaria, Berlin, Lower Saxony, Hamburg, and Schleswig-Holstein as well as electing Meynen vice chair and secretary, Meynen unsuccessfully attempted to organize an "advisory council" to represent the East.[56] He believed in the importance of collaborating with his German counterparts, and if it can be assumed that his earlier work on regional studies, the Pennsylvania-Dutch, and Lebensraum still influenced his geographic thought, he likely despised the "curtain" drawn between German scientists, academics, and intellectuals.

In February 1950, however, the Office of the Federal Minister of Interior ordered the AfL to discontinue all cooperation with East German geographers. Meynen was furious. Here, years after Allied "liberation," he found his institution in its most compromised position.[57] There is no evidence to suggest that even during the Berlin crisis of 1948–49, that moment in which the Cold War began to come into focus, the Western Allies had required Meynen to stop working with other Germans in the Soviet zone. But no more under the FRG's auspices—the East German geographers were to be deliberately disconnected from the academic goings-on of their West German counterparts. No longer were their appointments and lecture dates to be published in the *Rundbrief,* nor was the line dividing Germany to be overlooked or ignored. The AfL could still publish maps that included East Germany, but those maps had to be approved by the Ministry of Interior (a laborious process made easy only under the most exceptional of circumstances—for example, producing a map of all Protestant churches throughout Germany proposed by Meynen in the summer of 1951).[58] Although Meynen was never thrilled with these restrictions, and although he continued to occasionally work outside of them (especially in regard to correspondence), Meynen adopted his usual stance of adaptation. If there is one glaring continuity from the Emil Meynen of the Nazi *Abteilung* to the Emil Meynen of the West German *Amt*, it is surely his ability to manipulate the circumstances in which he found himself to the benefit of his research.

By the end of 1951, Meynen characterized the state of his discipline in fairly dark terms. It was a time, he argued in an essay titled "Die Situation," for critical reflection ("kritische Besinnung"). He complained that geographers in the East and West were unable to collaborate or cooperate on major research projects and that the Allied powers were restricting the FRG in its ability to map itself (especially in regard to aerial photography, as explored later in this chapter). The essay closed with an appeal to all governments and their geographers. The freedom to travel, begged Meynen, had to be emphasized in a time of tightening border restrictions and fence-laden boundary lines. He made clear that travel, perhaps more than any other activity, was essential to the study of geography: the more rigid the lines, the less opportunity for exploration.[59]

But geographic work continued nonetheless. By early 1952, the FRG had commissioned a new group of geographers to figure out the best way of representing agricultural resources and production. Germany's premier spatial institution, the AfL, consistently hosted this group's meetings, bringing together some of Germany's greatest spatial thinkers (Meynen, Otremba, Troll, Blume, Friedrich Hoffmann, Theodor Kraus, Lautensach, and Pfeifer among them).[60] But Meynen was under constant political pressure to make clear the importance of his institution's autonomy. There were rumors that the Ministry of Interior was considering a merger of the AfL and Kurt Brüning's Akademie für Raumforschung (Academy for Spatial Research) into one organization, the Institut für Raumforschung und Landeskunde (Institute for Spatial Research and Regional Studies). Meynen believed that such a merger, if undertaken in 1952, would inevitably create an internal institutional power struggle between himself and Brüning, so he ignored the rumors and focused on the spatial problems he was so adept at confronting. He also continually offered up the AfL as a space for high-profile academic meetings. Such gestures, he found, were always met with great applause ("grosser Beifall").[61]

Tightening the Borders or Turning Lines into Fences

Historians tend to gravitate toward names such as "Cold War" and "Iron Curtain" not simply because they are easy terms within which to position temporal bookends but also because the mental demarcation of Europe—and the ideological confrontation foaming along its edges—was a very real one, and it was experienced by very real people. The historian Larry Wolff aptly describes this geographic simplification of Europe: "The map of Europe," he writes, "with its many countries and cultures, was mentally marked with Churchill's iron curtain, an ideological bisection of the continent during the Cold War."[62] Churchill's "iron curtain" speech was delivered in March 1946, but by May 1952 the mental cartography of its rhetoric was beginning to turn into a spatial reality. Already by mid-1952, tens of thousands of Germans had fled the GDR since its creation in 1949 for an FRG that in 1949 had a homeless population of 8 million people (a population that, even as late as 1970, still had nearly 1 million residents living in "nonpermanent structures").[63] Politicians on both sides of Germany's dividing line thus wanted their borders to be more secure.

On May 26, 1952, the FRG joined the European Defense Community, a Western alliance between nation-states aimed at responsibly rearming West Germany without admitting it into NATO.[64] Although the French refused to ratify and recognize the European Defense Community, the FRG's willingness to sign on was not lost on the GDR. On the exact same day, the GDR issued an order titled Verordnung über Maßnahmen an der Demakationslinie zwischen der Deutschen Demokratischen Republik und den westlichen Besatzungszonen Deutschlands (Regulation of Measures on the Demarcation Line between the German Democratic Republic and the Western Occupied Zones of Germany), refusing, of course, to recognize the FRG as anything more than a collection of zones still occupied by the Allied powers. This new regulation made it clear that the space around the border—not simply the border itself—was to be monitored and controlled. A 5-kilometer *Sperrgebiet* (restricted area) zone was instituted along the entire East/West divide, as was a more heavily restricted *Schutzstreife* (protection strip) zone of 500 meters. All border passes were immediately invalidated, and, as the anthropologist Daphne Berdahl recounts, "thousands of border residents" were evacuated throughout the following month.[65] In July 1952, the five *Länder* that had initially been unified into the GDR were replaced with fourteen new and largely arbitrarily drawn districts (*Bezirke*).[66] By the end of the summer, a sand-filled, 10-meter control strip ran alongside a freshly built barbed-wire fence—the new and concrete tracing of Germany's internal border.[67]

5

Mapping and Selling the Two-State Solution

Sovereignty implies "space," and what is more it implies a space
against which violence, whether latent or overt, is directed—a space
established and constituted by violence.
　　　　—Henri Lefebvre, *The Production of Space*

Both the American and Soviet geographers understood the importance of
German space. As the historian Carolyn Eisenberg convincingly argues,
"The conflict between the United States and the Soviet Union was most
geographically expressed in the division of [Germany]."[1] This expression
was not a natural development. It was not, as the more simplistic Cold
War histories still maintain, the obvious consequence of irretrievably dis-
similar political ideologies. In fact, during the immediate postwar period,
the Soviet Union was not at all interested in permanently partitioning
Germany. The United States and its Western allies, anticipating the postwar economic crisis, were worried that without a clean break from its
Soviet counterpart no politicians or taxpayers outside of Germany would
be willing to invest in its redemocratization.[2] It was with this in mind that
the American, British, and French military governments consistently vio-
lated the treaties outlined at the Yalta and Potsdam Conferences, first by
merging their occupation zones in December 1946 and establishing the
Marshall Plan in July 1947 and then by implementing currency reform in
June 1948 and convening a new and separate West German Parliament in
September 1948.[3] Surely, the Soviet Union was no easy partner to cooperate with and worked to undermine the West just as much as the West
worked to undermine it. The historical evidence is very clear, though:
the United States helped to create the geopolitical problems of the Cold
War—especially in Germany—by consolidating its zones of occupation

with its allies and by eventually insisting on the creation of an autonomous West German state in 1949.

The territorially driven polarization that occurred in the aftermath of Germany's East/West divide was not confined to military personnel and foreign-policy officials. Geographers were all too often but unsurprisingly dragged into dubious geopolitical rhetoric. Early in 1950, for example, a Professor Zimon from a Soviet geography department accused American geographers working in Germany of acting "as spies [for the military] clearing the path for aggressors" and serving to create maps that could only be classified as "imperialist propaganda."[4] As explained in chapter 2, during previous European conflicts (specifically in the Franco-Prussian War of 1870–71) mapmakers had in fact posed as seemingly benign professionals or artists in order to perform acts of cartographic espionage. Zimon named Richard Hartshorne—the OSS operative and Geography Division chief who by the end of the war had begun teaching at the University of Wisconsin at Madison—as "the greatest theoretician among American geographers" and as one of the foremost proponents of a new "field of propaganda presenting geographical grounds for a new war."[5] These words were initially printed in a Soviet gazette but were quickly picked up by a Communist magazine in France. Their distribution in continental Europe and the subsequent attention they received from the American press forced Hartshorne to respond. His initial reaction was to dismiss Zimon as either a liar or an indoctrinated propagandist. "Zimon seemingly doesn't realize," Hartshorne wrote in 1950, "that in the United States little attention is paid to the 'theorist.' In brief, he overemphasizes my importance."[6]

It is undoubtedly true that the majority of American intellectuals lacked (and still lack) widespread cultural influence. Hartshorne, though, was not simply a "theoretician." He was an academic who, as outlined in chapter 2, had been integral to the planned redrawing of Europe and Germany after the Second World War. He was also an academic who was extremely familiar with the geography of the Soviet Union (so familiar, in fact, that throughout the 1950s the US Postal Service began intercepting and withholding mail sent to him—much of it geographic material—from the Soviet Union and other "unfriendly countries").[7] Zimon's characterization of Hartshorne, however fair or not, coincided with a shift in Hartshorne's own language concerning the Soviet Union. Whereas prior to 1950 Hartshorne, especially in his capacity as a professor of geography, had made few public comments regarding the Soviet Union, by 1951 he was lambasting the Soviets as a menace "more dangerous than the previous German threats" and warning of "Russia's [potential] acquisition of all western Europe."[8] He justified his concerns by appealing to the "Heartland Theory" propounded by British geographer Sir Halford Mackinder. The Heartland Theory, which Mackinder first proposed in 1904, claimed that if any one political unit were able to control both eastern Europe and central Europe, that government would have "the greatest defensive and offensive strength of any world unit."[9] That government would control an enormous coastline, the largest and very resource-rich territorial block of the European continent, and the majority of Europe's food production. For Hartshorne, Soviet control of East Germany and its satellite states in eastern Europe had the potential for realizing what Mackinder had predicted at the outset of the twentieth century. Although Hartshorne toyed with other potential "heartlands" and refused to be labeled a "disciple of Mackinder,"[10] he never fully dismissed Mackinder's theory or his own fear of a potentially undefeatable Soviet-ruled territorial superstate. (One of these "heartlands," proposed by J. Wreford Watson in 1958, was an "American Heartland," "the Great Lakes–Ohio–Mississippi–Missouri plains," and claimed that "he who rules the American heartland rules N. America. He who rules N. America rules the Pacific and the Atlantic. He who rules the Pacific and the Atlantic rules the World."[11])

Hartshorne's concerns can be easily segued into a larger discussion of growing Cold War distrust among geographers. It should again be emphasized, as this book has tried to do in chapters 3 and 4, that geographers on either side of the Iron Curtain did not immediately break off relations with each other after 1945 or even after 1949. There were different levels of cooperation, distrust, and fear depending on the institution and the individual. In the immediate aftermath of the Second World War, many Germans were initially less interested than their Allied occupiers in establishing a sharp territorial divide through their nation-state. Emil Meynen, for example, constantly complained about the Allies' obsession with "the unsolved Berlin-struggle" and "the antagonism of West and East."[12] This is not to say, of course, that all Germans agreed with Meynen's assessment of the borders he was being asked to draw. Kurt Brüning, director of the German Academy for Spatial Research, seriously disagreed with Meynen's attempts to map Germany after the war without making clear its partitions. According to Meynen, it seemed "impossible to solve the German problem by such limitations of research," but he admitted by early 1947 that even he was excluding the Soviet zone of occupation for lack of information.[13] Most of the maps produced by Meynen's Amt für Landeskunde, however, usually still portrayed a complete "Germany" as late as 1954, even if the East/West division was noted.

As with US–Soviet interaction, the relationships between East and West German geographers slowly deteriorated throughout the 1950s. Although this development was influenced by politics, it was also spurred on by academics' paranoia. The opportunistic politics of this transition are easy enough to explain: German politicians used the new fortified East/West "frontier" to their own advantage. Those municipalities running along the new intra-German border were particularly useful in political rhetoric. When the Soviet Union closed a power plant in the border town of Harbke, effectively shutting off power to portions of West Germany, the FRG staged an enormous ceremony around the laying of a new power plant's foundation on December 1, 1952. Jakob Kaiser, federal minister for all-German affairs, delivered the ceremonial address, in which he made clear to the residents of this new "borderland" that all of Germany shared their territorial anxiety:

> I do not wish to use big words. But it so happens that it is a national, a European task to create healthy conditions in this area, which is the threshold of the free world. . . . I can only say that anyone who makes investments at Düsseldorf, Cologne, Ludwigshafen or Munich is safe— if he is lucky—for about twelve hours longer than he who lives near the zonal boundary. Every German would therefore do well to overcome the fear of running a risk. . . . This frontier is a mockery of all law and dignity of nations. Let us therefore transform this sorely afflicted land along the zonal boundary into a bulwark of our resolve to reunify our

country. But not only German industry ought to make investments. The
entire free world, which professes its sympathy with the reunification of
our country, should also make its contribution.[14]

In one phenomenal speech, Kaiser hits all of the right notes: solidar-
ity among West Germans, the importance of German reunification, an
appeal to the rest of the sympathetic "free world," and the necessity of
utilizing contentious space for geopolitical gain. Here, Kaiser's words make
clear the intensity of Germany's spatial condition. The zonal boundary
between East and West is made out to be inherently valuable because of its
precariousness. To residents living along this border, *space* was not merely
an academic term or concept but an integral part of their everyday lives.

Contentious spaces needed clear maps. As the political rhetoric and
the military condition of both Germanys became more heated, geographers and cartographers were called upon to increasingly isolate themselves from their colleagues on the other side of the line. Collaborative
long-term international projects, such as the international map of the
world, were scrapped in favor of smaller, more accurate maps for military
use.[15] Although most western nation-states continued to actively send multiple conglomerates of institutions and academics to international geography conferences and congresses, East Germany was often purposely
excluded, and West Germany usually sent only one representative institution or exhibit or one of each (and the maps presented were almost always
compiled and edited by the AfL).[16]

In 1958, German geographers' unwillingness to continue to hold a
hard line for their respective politicians became problematic. It was in this
year that the GDR applied for official admittance into the IGU. Until this
point, East Germany had been completely shut out of the world's foremost
forum on mapmaking. When the IGU Congress had met in 1952 and
1956, only the FRG had been allowed to formally represent the German
nation-state.[17] The GDR's application in 1958 was somewhat scandalous
and prompted serious backlash from West German academics and politicians alike. One West German official in the Auswärtiges Amt (Foreign
Office) wrote to a geographer on the IGU Application Committee express-
ing his belief that the GDR would undoubtedly send spies to the IGU

meetings. Moreover, this official was concerned that East Germany would use any recognition from the IGU as an opportunity to assert national sovereignty.[18] Several other individuals complained to the IGU about the validity of the GDR's application, but the ad hoc Statute Committee reviewed the issue and concluded that "on the basis of the structures of the IGU . . . no objection can legitimately be raised against the application for membership of [East Germany]" and that "the application shall be channeled through the regular procedures for consideration and decision by the Xth General Assembly [of the International Geographical Congress]."[19] Indeed, owing to the IGU's appreciation for territorial demarcations and sites of spatial controversy, its bylaws made it clear that any territory recognized as sovereign or not was free to apply for membership. Whether to include or exclude the GDR geographers and cartographers would therefore be decided at the IGU Congress in Stockholm in 1960.

So in 1960, for the first time since the tightening of the intra-German border in 1952, East Germans were explicitly invited to the IGU's Congress.[20] The atmosphere was understandably tense. From August 6 through August 13, nearly 1,700 members from sixty-four nation-states attended lectures, participated in exhibitions and field trips, and met for sessions of the General Assembly. It was in one of these General Assembly meetings that the question of East Germany's admittance into the IGU was brought to the floor. The IGU members, after some discussion, elected to admit the GDR alongside Australia, Bulgaria, Guinea, Iran, Iraq, Malaya, Rumania, South Korea, Tunisia, and South Africa.[21] Among the aye votes were those from several West Germans.

The vote to include the GDR in the IGU infuriated the West German government. Within a few short weeks, Erich Otremba—who had been particularly supportive of the East German geographers—received several angry letters from the minister of interior's office. A member of that office lambasted Otremba for his decision to ignore what these letters argued was a very clear directive from Stockholm's German embassy to vote against the inclusion of East German geographers into the IGU. Otremba's problematic situation was compounded by an interview he gave to a German magazine in which he seemed to criticize the politicization of the vote.[22]

Another major theme of West German geographic development in the 1950s was a consistently more contentious relationship between German geographers and their Allied military supervisors, particularly in regards to aerial photography. German geographers were expected to maintain maps based on aerial photographs (and often to maintain maps for important flight corridors, especially those between West German cities and Berlin).[23] By the 1950s, aerial photography had become an indispensable aspect of producing large-scale topographic maps. Since the end of the war, German cartographers had been compiling and using aerial photographs in close cooperation with the Allied Civil Aviation Board. By 1953, the Bundesministerium für Verkehr (Ministry of Transport) created procedural guidelines "on the permission, supervision, and release" of aerial photographs that were to be adhered to by both the Allied powers and the West German government. After the Allied Civil Aviation Board was dissolved in May 1955, the West German government was still more than happy to work alongside the Allied powers in producing aerial photos so long as everyone followed the clear procedures laid out by the Ministry of Transport.[24] This worked out well, without any complaints from either side, until the British and Americans began to get nervous about Cold War tension and the possibility of aerial photographs falling into the hands of a hostile world power.

On November 30, 1955, the Supreme Headquarters of Allied Powers in Europe released a memo to the "National Military Representatives" of Germany explaining how important it was for aerial photographs to be given a certain level of protection.[25] Roughly two weeks earlier, the American and British forces promised that they were not interested in requiring their "blanket approval" to regulate "all conceivable activities" undertaken by West Germany's aerial photographs, but they did feel as though they needed to begin supervising the production and dissemination of aerial photographs taken around certain areas of Germany in which the Western Allies had a particular interest. Any such activities, the Allies again promised, "would be [of a] character of which [the] Germans would approve."[26] The Germans, however, did not approve.

Nor did the Germans become more receptive when in December 1955 a British delegate demanded that the German laws surrounding aerial photography become "more stringent . . . with a view to achieving stricter [Allied] control." These new restrictions would include the Western Allied forces' permission "before disposing of prints or negatives in any way" and approval of any sensitive topographical photographs that might be "of considerable strategic value to a potential enemy."[27] In effect, the British delegate was demanding that the German aerial photographers be constantly subject to Allied security clearance and supervision, even when working on the most mundane of activities.

In response, the Germans argued that to redraft their aerial photography laws would be a violation of their sovereignty. Moreover, they claimed, laws concerning the protection of aerial photography already existed under the Luftverkehrsgesetz (German Aviation Law) of 1953. On December 9, 1955, the Allied forces ordered that this law be evaluated.[28] The Allies found it acceptable, for the most part, and understood the Germans' desire to control their own maps. However, a compromise was reached on April 11, 1956, after months of negotiations, requiring the mutual exchange of cartographic information important to a "common defense" and allowing the United States to make its own map surveys of West Germany under German supervision, if the Germans so desired (unless, of course, the Allies wanted to make these maps in secret, in which case they were allowed to do so according to the new agreement).[29] This agreement was eventually amended, renamed, and ratified in July 1957 as the US–German Bilateral Administrative Agreement on Aerial Photography,[30] which required little more than that the West German Ministry of Transport send "copies of all applications for aerial photography licenses which the German authorities intend to approve" to the Allied forces for review. The Allies could at any time and for any reason veto a license.[31] The Allies also created the Central Inspection Zone between East and West Germany, which allowed for fly-over aerial photographs to be taken by the Soviet Union as well as the United States and United Kingdom as an act of mutual confidence in one another.[32] Although the Allied powers wanted West Germany to remilitarize to an extent (and to serve as the front line of the Cold War), aerial mapping became a contentious and confusing issue. The aerial photography agreements between West Germany and the Allies remained in effect until the ratification of the

Treaty on the Final Settlement with Respect to Germany of March 1991, which eliminated all restrictions on German sovereignty. If a nation-state must have control over its own mapping projects (including the mapping of its own territory) in order to be a sovereign state, then it can certainly be argued that West Germany never genuinely achieved the sovereignty it had hoped to deny its counterpart to the East. The seemingly small stakes of the East German geographers' application to an international academic union were amplified in part by a West German government obsessed with denying mapmaking legitimacy to the GDR while simultaneously mapping itself under the supervision of a foreign power.

Growing Academic Exchanges

Throughout the 1950s, it seemed as though the geographers of the FRG were frustrated with the politics of their situation (both academically and territorially). The postwar autonomy that many had hoped would develop after the creation of the FRG in 1949 had not materialized. In fact, as the ideological and economic divisions between Europe's Communist East and capitalist West deepened, many West German geographers and map-makers began to realize that their dependence on the Western powers (in particular the United States) was no longer a temporary circumstance. Rather than work toward reconciling differences between themselves and their colleagues in the GDR, they began to refocus on emphasizing their usefulness and value to the American military and the American public. High-quality production and international dissemination became the twin priorities of most high-profile geographers in the FRG. In order to gain legitimacy—for both their new nation-state and their respective institutions—German geographers needed to establish relationships with American societies and scholars. In doing so, they hoped that the maps they produced would be understood as not only desirable but also neces-sary for the redrafting of the FRG's territory and for the reinstatement of German geographers among the leading voices of their discipline.

By the end of the 1950s, West Germany was producing seventy-six scientific "geographical serials." This number made the FRG the world's most prolific producer of geography periodicals. The Soviet Union (with forty), the United States (twenty-five), and France (twenty-five) were the next three most-productive publishers. The West Germans were also, especially in their relationship with the United States, very enthusiastic about exchanging geographic information. By 1959, West Germany was receiving more single-copy exchanges of the *Annals of the Association of American Geographers* than any other foreign nation-state and had the third-highest number of international subscriptions (behind the Soviet Union and Britain).[33] In fact, the AAG had more active periodical exchanges with German institutions than with all North American, African, and Asian institutions combined (a fact not lost on the AAG's financial staff, who were constantly questioning the importance of so many exchanges with one nation-state).[34]

This heavy flow of information between the United States and West Germany was an arrangement that benefitted educators and government officials in both nation-states. Individual geographers and institutions on both sides of the Atlantic were desperate to maintain their libraries. Several prominent West Germans traveled to the United States to deliver guest lectures and to bring material back to their home institutions.[35] Emil Meynen and the AfL were consistently sending and receiving geographic material from the United States. Meynen's own personal contacts in the United States often requested up-to-date maps of Germany from the AfL.[36]

The most important relationship the AfL was able to maintain, however, was its postwar exchange program with the AAG. The latter provided the AfL with copies of *The Professional Geographer* and the *Annals of the Association of American Geographers*—two premier journals of English-language geography—in exchange for the *Berichte zur Deutschen Landeskunde* (Report on German Regional Studies). The AAG was a formidable ally—an institution that, as one staff member of the American embassy in the FRG wrote, many German professors "are anxious to exchange information with" and "particularly interested" in.[37]

Meynen had been able to secure as consistent an exchange with the AAG as was possible in the immediate postwar years, but as more and more German geography institutions were rebuilt and reorganized, the AAG was forced to reconsider its exchange policies. Increasing postage costs, the lack of storage space for materials received, and a lack of managerial oversight over the exchanges led the AAG ad hoc Exchanges Committee in 1954 to recommend ending the entire enterprise of swapping publications with foreign geographers.[38] Although the AAG's Executive Council refused to close the program completely, it did opt to slim down exchange operations. In an effort to determine which international relationships were most useful, the AAG polled its membership about which institutions to drop from the exchange program and which to keep.[39] Only those journals of "real significance or quality" and those to which "a paid subscription cannot be obtained" were to be approved for exchange, and they were to have their importance to the AAG continually reevaluated.[40] In the case of Meynen's organization (renamed, in 1953, the Bundesanstalt für Landeskunde), nearly every member voted to keep making exchanges with it, with one important exception being the AGS librarian Nordis Felland. Felland fiercely checked the "Disapprove" column next to the row for the West German institute, dryly writing in the margin that "they always want a lot!"[41]

From Amt für Landeskunde to Bundesanstalt für Landeskunde: Emil Meynen's Ascension

It is unsurprising that the AfL remained an important hub of geographic exchange throughout the 1950s. In fact, because of the importance of Meynen's institution, the political consolidation of space (and the contentiousness of that consolidation) in the Federal Republic of Germany was heavily reflected in the changes the AfL experienced during this decade. Meynen himself admitted that the organization's changing names "mirrored a troubled time" ("Spiegel einer unruhigen Zeit").[42] Within six years, his office had changed its name three times: from Abteilung für Landeskunde im Reichsamt für Landesaufnahme in the Third Reich in 1941 to the institutionally untethered Abteilung für Landeskunde after the German defeat in 1945 and then to Amt für Landeskunde in 1947. Those years, amid a flurry of cartographic chaos, saw Meynen's work function as the geographic instrument first of Nazi Germany, then of the Allied military government, and finally of the state of Bavaria. After considering whether to simply merge the AfL with the FRG's Institut für

Raumforschung (Institute for Spatial Research), the West German Parliament determined that the breadth of the AfL's work demanded that its autonomy be maintained.[43] Moreover, its work was so compelling that the Bundesrat questioned why the AfL was formally tied solely to the state of Bavaria.

On April 1, 1953, the Amt für Landeskunde changed hands once again and became an official administrative organ of the West German federal government, adopting the new name "Bundesanstalt für Landeskunde" (BfL, Federal Institute for Regional Studies).[44] Although the AfL had been continuously publishing geographic information relevant for the entire nation-state after 1949, it had been funded by the Bavarian state government until this point. It had still managed to produce several widely disseminated geographic projects, including prominent periodicals; the *Geographisches Taschenbuch* (Geographical Pocketbook); the *Berichte zur Deutschen Landeskunde*, a sweeping academic survey of German geographic thought; *Forschungen zur Deutschen Landeskunde, 1885–1953* (Research on German Regional Studies, 1885–1953), one of West Germany's most prominent map series; and the 1:300,000 scale *Gemeindegrenzenkarte* (Municipal Boundary Map) series, along with several other publications concerned with aerial photography, climate, and landforms.[45] Now, with the financial backing of the federal government, Meynen was able to broaden both his political and academic reach even further. The FRG had confirmed the importance of his cartographies, and in the wake of the FRG's tightening border with the GDR the new BfL was poised to serve as its primary mapmaking and map-studying agency.

None of this meant, of course, that the BfL stopped its work with the American military. In 1954, Meynen was regularly updating the Americans about the BfL's completion progress regarding "Militär-geographische Erhebungen der US-Armee" (Military-Geography Surveys of the US Army)—a series of German topographic maps that included soil, rock, and vegetation demarcations.[46] In fact, even though the ERP was officially terminated in 1951, American tax dollars (misidentified by Meynen as "ERP money") funded several of the BfL's projects from 1954 through at least 1958.[47] This seems to help explain the emphasis the BfL began to place on economic geography during the mid-1950s. On June 1, 1956, and under the direct supervision of Emil Meynen, the BfL published the *Geographische Landesaufnahme: Wirtschaftsräumliche Gliederung* map series (Geographic Topographic Surveys: Spatial-Economic Regionalization) in an effort to establish a unified economic framework within which to study German geography.[48] The hope was that by focusing on the productivity rates of the various *Länder*, the FRG could better allocate its (and American taxpayers') funds. By 1959, the BfL had identified nine different "economic zones" with which to standardize its economic geographies:[49]

1. Schleswig-Holstein (with special attention paid to Flensburg and Rendsburg)
2. Lower Saxony (Cuxhaven, Lüneburg, Enden, Oldenburg, Hildesheim, Hamelin, and Göttingen)
3. Westphalia (Paderborn and Siegen)
4. North Rhine (Bonn-Godesberg)[50]
5. Hesse (Fulda and Limburg)
6. Rhineland-Palatinate (Trier and Koblenz)
7. Saarland
8. Baden-Württemberg (Heilbronn, Ulm, and Konstanz)
9. Bavaria (Würzburg, Bamberg, Bayreuth, Inglostadt, Landshut, Passau, and Kempten)

In this same year, the FRG Bundesrat merged the BfL with the Akademie für Raumforschung, creating the unimaginatively named Bundesanstalt für Landeskunde und Raumforschung (Federal Institute for Regional Studies and Spatial Research).[51] Meynen adopted the shorter designation Institut für Landeskunde (Institute for Regional Studies) and moved his offices from the town of Remagen in the Rhineland-Palatinate, where it had been since 1952 after moving from the Bavarian town of Landshut in 1948, to the district of Bad Godesberg in North Rhine–Westphalia.[52]

The independent work of Emil Meynen's institute was more autonomous compared to that of other German geographical agencies and institutions after the Second World War. Only Kurt Brüning's academy in Hanover had, up until its merger with the BfL, maintained a similar situation, but its focus was much broader. Brüning, in fact, often called on his more cartographically inclined colleagues in the BfL to create maps for the academy. Most geographical societies and research centers were dependent on the budgets of universities or local governments. After Germany's defeat in the Second World War, geography education had been suffering (as already discussed in the previous two chapters). Although material, teachers, and textbooks became more available throughout the 1950s, the difficulty in teaching German students about the space around them became more complicated as the European cartographic polarization of the Cold War set in. German students were also not the only audience German mapmakers were worried about. Solidification of the intra-German Cold War boundaries and the perceived threat of potentially imminent military action understandably did not go unnoticed by the US government. The ERP had been officially terminated in 1951, but West Germans rightly believed that American policy makers, by promoting a particular territorial national narrative—invoking a kind of "shatter zone" *Sonderweg*—could more easily convince American voters that investing in West Germany was a vital piece of US national security. Indeed, the West Germans had to "sell" the new map imposed on them by an American occupation back to the Americans themselves.

From the Mind to the Map: Public-Relations Firms and the Embrace of Cartographic Inaccuracy

> What do advertising and cartography have in common? Without a doubt the best answer is their shared need to communicate a limited version of the truth. . . . Neither can meet its goal by telling or showing everything.
> —Mark Monmonier, *How to Lie with Maps*

Maps sell in two ways. Maps are, obviously enough, textual commodities that can be produced, reproduced, purchased, and sold. More than this, though, they are themselves propositional narratives.[53] In effect, then, they are commodities that can be bought or discarded and that sell a story that can be bought or discarded. This understanding of cartography has led to a great deal of scholarship on touristic mapping and how spaces and places are "sold" to potential customers.[54] Most of this literature, however, fails to examine how public-relations (PR) firms are deeply entrenched in the creation and diffusion of such maps (although it usually does harbor fairly staunch critiques of the shades of capitalism that facilitate such reproductions). As the 1950s drove on, the government of the Federal Republic of Germany began to rely on the emerging PR discipline both to create and to distribute its maps.

The concept of PR as a practice arose during the early twentieth century. Perhaps its most famous adherent was a nephew of Sigmund Freud named Edward Bernays (1891–1995). His book *Propaganda* (1928) attempted to combine psychoanalysis with marketing strategy so that a "new propaganda" could be undertaken by those individuals (or governments or corporations) who might seek to "create public acceptance for a particular idea or commodity."[55] During the Second World War, Bernays created a handbook for potential acolytes titled *Speak Up for Democracy!* (1940), in which he declared that democracy itself depended on his readers' abilities to incorporate a kind of PR strategy that would sell American democracy to those who might seek to sabotage it or those ignorant of its greatness.[56] He concluded his text with an urgent plea:

> Twenty years ago, the phrase "public relations" was unknown in its current sense. Today we know leadership is largely the result of effective planning, techniques, and methods. . . . Democracy depends upon you. . . . It is up to you. You will help decide whether Democracy is to live or die. You are the country's most important figure. You occupy the highest office in the land—American citizen. You determine our destiny. Now is the time to act. Speak up for Democracy![57]

In 1952, Bernays produced his book *Public Relations*, which sought to establish the origins of PR campaigns, the historical development of PR throughout the nineteenth and early twentieth centuries, and how one could "chart" individuals' "hidden urges" for the sake of making a sale.[58]

Such publications inspired the creation of many PR firms in the United States. Several of them, in fact, could not help but see the postwar era as one of immense opportunity, especially when the newly established state of West Germany decided that it needed to change the American public's opinion of German culture. Bernays emphasized public opinion as a "vital" part of "rearmament, economic mobilization, and national defense."[59] In the FRG, "several German officials observed that public opinion played an uncommonly large role in the formulation of American foreign policy, and thus reasoned that the manipulation of representations of Germans in the United States should constitute a major element of their broader plan to win American friendship."[60] Who better to undertake this task than an American PR firm—one that could "sidestep American fears about renewed German propaganda in the United States"?[61] It had been, after all, American PR firms that had first so successfully represented the interests of Germans in the 1930s, attempting to mitigate the "hostility being bred by Germany's racial and military policies": Carl Byoir & Associates, which had worked on behalf of tourism in the Third Reich, and Ivy Lee & T. J. Ross and Associates, which had represented I. G. Farben.[62]

American businesses and map publishers also already had plenty of experience working with their own government during the Second World War. The OSS had purchased some of the maps it used for intelligence operations from corporations such as the International Map Company, Inc.,[63] and Rand McNally & Co.[64] Such interactions were always done in secret, prompting the repetition of one addendum sentence at the end of each series of correspondence: "As is usual in this sort of work, these maps should not be stamped 'Office of Strategic Services.'"[65]

The American military had also begun to use PR during the Second World War. District engineers (who, prior to the establishment of the Army Map Service in 1942, controlled the bulk of US maps) had been among the first members of the military to be assigned a PR officer in May 1941 and were already told prior to the bombing of Pearl Harbor to avoid giving any information to foreign audiences without first consulting the War Department's Public Relations Division.[66] By September 21, 1942, the Public Relations Division had been reorganized into the seemingly more efficient and at the very least much more benign-sounding Office of Technical Information.[67] By 1944, this office was organizing several promotional events concerning cartography and geography, one of which—the Map Reproduction Train—was a well-planned parade of "ten truck-mounted units . . . [with] both lithographic and photographic . . . field mapping units." The train was demonstrated in front of the news press at Wisconsin's Camp McCoy on August 24, 1944.[68]

The American military's employment of PR firms and use of maps continued into the postwar period. Many of the ERP's publications incorporated maps to help illustrate the rebuilding of Europe's economy (see figures 15, 16, and 17) to more effectively disseminate material that would "develop [a] sense of common effort and mutual aid."[69] Note, however, that the United States is absent from much of this literature, particularly as a geographic presence. In figure 15, drawn in 1948, there is also no "Germany" per se but rather zones of occupation. Furthermore, this map is a US publication and discusses the importance of "direct help" in rebuilding European nation-states but avoids cartographically representing America in favor of emphasizing the importance of a Europe that would reestablish itself (even when such reestablishment was to be funded by a non-European power). Figure 16 also attempts to portray a cartographically reconstructed Europe without depicting the United States. Part of Europe's recovery, in fact, is the absence of the imposition of America on its continental map. Figure 17 is, however, a different example of the use of maps in respatializing postwar Europe. Rather than completely leaving out the United States, this map portrays (with arrows and ships) the movement of economic assistance from Washington, DC, to Europe. America has drawn itself not as an occupational force but as a source of economic recovery! None of these maps had any strictly scientific value, but each one counted on the reader to recognize the authority and objectivity of maps so as to establish the spatial immutability of various nation-states and the movement of economic resources to and from those nation-states.

While the West German government was looking to hire American PR firms, the United States was more than happy to encourage West German corporations such as Inter Nationes (which merged with the Goethe-Institut in 2001) to distribute its information in the US publication *Inter Nationes*, which had mastered the art of depicting a carefully constructed West Germany to non-German audiences. Since 1952, Inter Nationes was not interested in presenting to its foreign publics an "*official* image of Germany or even *the* image of Germany *per se*. The reason for this is quite

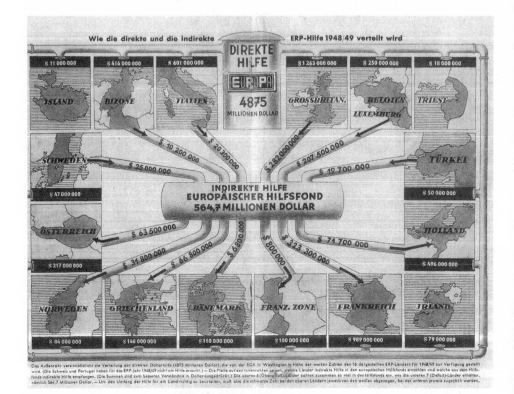

15. European Recovery Program, *Wie die direkte und die indirekte ERP-Hilfe 1948/49 verteilt wird*, scale not given, in *Sie Sollen es besser haben!*, 1948, Record Group 335, Stack 490 8/35/03–07, Box 19, National Archives and Records Administration, Washington, DC.

simple: such an image of Germany [did not and still does] not exist."[70] The territorially contentious history of the German nation-state, coupled with that state's expansionist foreign policy during the Third Reich, resulted in an inability to adequately articulate a static spatial narrative. In the absence of an official picture, the opportunity was left open for the West German government to cartographically propose a self-consciously drawn nation-state purposefully produced for mass consumption.

Several firms applied to represent the FRG's PR interests, and the freshly quasi-autonomous government was more than happy to entertain various "plans" for West Germany. John Maynahan & Associates, for

16. European Recovery Program, *Amerika Hilft Europa, Europa Hilft Sich Selbst*, 1948, cover page, Record Group 335, Stack 490 8/35/03–07, Box 19, National Archives and Records Administration, Washington, DC.

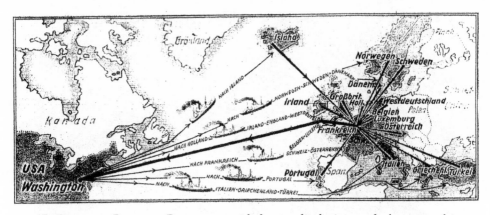

17. European Recovery Program, untitled map displaying trade between the United States and Europe, scale not given, in *Amerika Hilft Europa, Europa Hilft Sich Selbst*, 1948, Record Group 335, Stack 490 8/35/03–07, Box 19, National Archives and Records Administration, Washington, DC.

example, sent the government a fifteen-page strategy meant to prove that by choosing it "as public relations representative, [the government could] obtain the greatest effectiveness within the shortest possible space of time, with the least expenditure of money."[71] The Hamilton Wright Organization, Inc., which during the war had been forced to stop its activities in continental Europe,[72] promised to make Americans more "conscious" of the themes of German recovery and newfound appreciation for democracy by utilizing "large information media." It offered to work on behalf of the FRG government for six months at the price of $50,000 (roughly $452,000 in 2017 dollars).[73] Stephen Goerl Associates sent in its plan with an attached article from *Advertising Age* that was written for its client, the German Travel Association.[74] In fact, all of these plans and applications focused on getting prominent Americans to travel to Germany and write favorably about their experiences. The *New York Times, Fortune, Seventeen,* and *Cosmopolitan* were just a few of the publications that regularly showed up in the correspondence on this topic as being integral to American culture and therefore important to influence.

Yet by the time most of these applications reached the FRG, the government was already working with the Roy Bernard Company, Inc. This

American firm had signed a three-month, interim contract (which would later be continually extended) with the FRG government beginning on January 1, 1952, for which it would be paid $12,500 in advance, with another $12,125 to be paid for up-front printing costs (roughly $224,000 in 2017 dollars).[75] This contract specified that

> the Roy Bernard Co., Inc. shall represent the Federal Republic of Germany as public relations counsel in *all* matters falling within the general area of public relations that shall be considered by the Government of the Federal Republic of Germany conducive to the promotion of harmony, understanding, industrial and cultural intercourse and tourism between the Federal Republic of Germany and the United States.[76]

One such "matter" was the preparation of "finished art work for . . . literature, pamphlets, brochures and other materials."[77] As one can imagine, these materials included maps.

In a letter to the Press and Information Office of the FRG embassy to the United States, one of the founding members of the Roy Bernard Company, Bernard Gittelson, lamented in mid-1955 the sorry condition of German maps in the United States, most of which were "either too complicated or too old." In fact, "even [the] top [US] newspapers [carried] maps that were copyrighted in 1928 or 1933." Frustrated by this outdatedness, Gittelson began to describe how a new map of the FRG would help serve West German political and economic interests. As he went on to explain, the Roy Bernard Company had "been concerned with this map for almost four years," and the map had been one of "the first projects" it had recommended producing. From its conception, the company had envisioned it as a "simple map designed to do a very big public relations job, namely, to show the present size of the Federal Republic of Germany and how it has been divided and where the important areas are."[78] It would be a map created to provoke American sympathy and business. It would cost the FRG $300 (roughly $2,730 in 2017 dollars) to make the printing plates, but the payoff would be worth it.

By May 1956, Roy Bernard had made sure that more than 10,000 American schools and libraries received the map (figure 18). The first

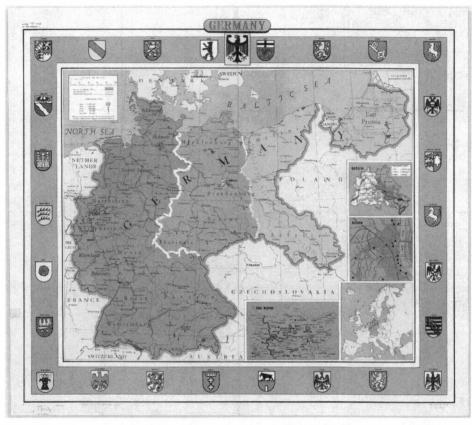

18. *Germany*, scale 1:1,500,000, World Wide Maps, Inc., 1956. Distributed by the Press and Information Office of the Federal Republic of Germany embassy in Washington, DC. Courtesy of the American Geographical Society Library.

edition sold out by June. It was one of the only maps produced since the collapse of the Third Reich to depict all of Germany's national territory in one single, easy-to-read sheet.[79] Moreover, the German press covered the map's dissemination as an objective rendering of a divided Germany— a map that made Germany's cartographic situation a bit more urgent to the typical American. After all, wrote one German newspaper, "es ist ein Unterschied, ob man von der Teilung Deutschlands gelegentlich hört, oder ob man sie sieht" (it makes a difference whether one happens to hear about the division of Germany or whether one sees it). Yet the paper also criticized the map for not somehow representing the expulsion of the Germans from the eastern territories and the Sudetenland. This omission, argued the journalist, left the map "unvollständig" (incomplete).[80]

Surrounding Roy Bernard's map are emblems of the German states, implying not only their existence but also their autonomy and importance—although none is as large and bold as the FRG crest. The most glaring symbols within the version of the map included in the newspaper article are the lines of division in Germany. This, of course, is what the FRG wanted to emphasize at the time, and it is what it paid Roy Bernard to produce. As the map's advocate from the company made clear to the FRG embassy Press Office, "This map is a public relations map. It is not intended for accurate geographical studies."[81] Such transparency was, of course, omitted from the map itself and from the news article covering the map's incorporation into American educational institutions. The accompanying press release from the Press Office also failed to mention the map's potential geographical inaccuracy but made sure to announce that "a divided Germany means a divided Europe. The reunification of Germany in freedom will make a vital contribution to the stability of Europe and the peace of the world."[82]

Roy Bernard had undertaken smaller mapping projects prior to 1955. In a letter written in August 1952 and marked "Confidential," Roy Bernard's employee Charles Campbell wrote to Georg von Lilienfeld of the Press Office to alleviate von Lilienfeld's fears that Roy Bernard was not doing enough to publicize a friendly Germany in the United States. As Campbell tried to make clear, "What is now beginning to appear in the pages of newspapers and magazines was put into the works months ago." After rattling off the various publications (*Esquire*, *Scholastic*, *Cosmopolitan*, *Fortune*, etc.) that would soon be printing editorials, pictures of the Bavarian Alps, and articles, he took a moment to mention that a "Facts on Germany" booklet had been sent off to the printer. On the back cover of the booklet was a map of Germany, which Campbell wanted to use as a barometer of cartographic public opinion. Herr von Lilienfeld had apparently been pestering him about "going ahead . . . [with] a schoolroom map," but Campbell had remained fairly apprehensive.[83] It is certainly possible that the information gained from the map's publication and subsequent reception was used in the four-year project that eventually ended up in schools and libraries across the United States. In a cordial effort to assuage any lingering doubts, Campbell ended his letter, "I have continued confidence in your understanding of this rather delicate business of molding public opinion. . . . There is much at stake."[84]

This cartographic urgency was often made explicit in maps that Roy Bernard considered for production. In 1952, a draft of a potential map was submitted along with a fictionalized narrative that proposed an alternate version of the Second World War's end: "The enemies' armies approached the [United] States from the north in a broad front. The defenders lacked everything. Losses increased . . . and the enemy was pitiless. . . . Things came to an end. . . . All states were occupied. The military and political leaders had fully surrendered. The victors met in Washington, D.C. and conferred about the future of a nation that lay crushed and powerless at their feet." In this inventive history, the United States was "quartered" into various fragments, one of which had been ceded back to Mexico, and the other four existed under the occupation forces of the Soviet Union, South America, South Africa, and Canada. The narrative continued in great detail, explaining to the reader how various zones were carved up, how New York City and Washington, DC, became "divided into four sectors under allied administration," and how US place-names were affected (perhaps most alarming to Americans at the time was the changing of the name "Seattle" to "Pacificgrad"). Self-described as an illustration "of the situation in Germany transferred to the territory of the United States," this story sought to render to an American audience the unimaginable humiliation, alienation, and suffering experienced under the very real circumstances a new postwar West German government was attempting to cope with.[85]

This account—aptly entitled "Democracy in Peril"—could not depend on the written word alone. In order to project more adequately the cartographically catastrophic effects of the Allied powers' redrafting of German territory, maps had to be included. The author provided two such maps to complement this unhappy fiction. The first (figure 19) provided the reader with a clear picture of what a fragmented America might look like. Although the boundaries and labels of the former states were clear, so

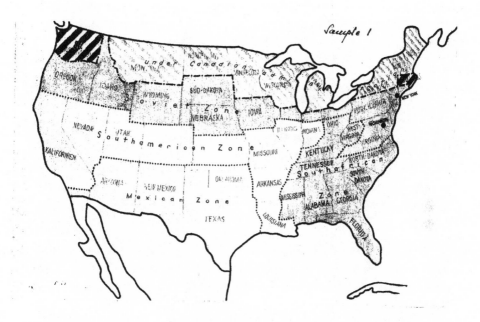

19. *Sample 1*, scale not given, 1952, B145/1277, Band I, Bundesarchiv, Koblenz, Germany.

too were the lines that divided them into occupied sectors. In the second map (figure 20), the states as an American audience might know them had been erased, leaving only the labels and boundaries of the occupied zones and two dots meant to signify New York City and Washington, DC—the two urban areas split between the four occupying powers. To add even further insult, the name "New York City" had been changed on this map to "Four Power City." Clearly, no cartographic referent in which Americans took great pride was safe from the geographic tyranny of their fictional foreign invaders.

The author of this American dystopia is unknown, but the practice of imposing European situations onto the map of the United States was not new (it was especially popular during the First World War, when American mapmakers were searching for ways to quickly and effectively provide the average citizen with a lesson in European geography). Dr. Richard

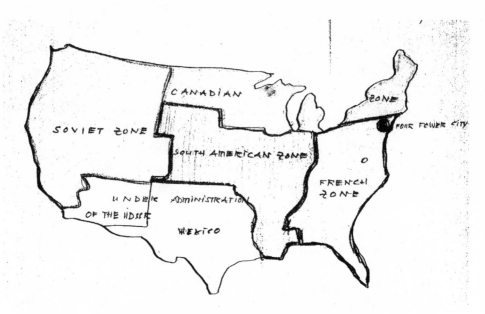

20. *Sample 2*, scale not given, 1952, B145/1277, Band I, Bundesarchiv, Koblenz, Germany.

Mönnig had submitted the project to Roy Bernard for approval and subsequent public dissemination into the psyche of postwar Americans. Dr. Mönnig was employed by the PR firm Inter Nationes. Located in Bonn, this firm occasionally worked in tandem with the American-based Roy Bernard Company. Roy Bernard had rejected this particular project as "unusable in the United States,"[86] but such collaboration between these two firms mirrors the mutually beneficial relationship between the West German government and several private PR enterprises (most notably, as already mentioned, the government's heavy dependence on Roy Bernard).[87]

West Germany was interested in utilizing the "science" of PR, among other reasons, to assert itself cartographically. Only by establishing its territorial place in the imaginations of its domestic citizenry and its foreign audience could West Germany fully recover from the Second World War. Only by legitimizing the FRG's territorial orientation could its freshly "imagined community"[88] rise from the abstract to the concrete—from the mind to the map.

The Roy Bernard Company worked with the FRG, filing quarterly reports, until 1961, when the FRG's American-based German Information Center took over owing to a growing wave of anti-German sentiment in America and Roy Bernard's inability to quickly and efficiently deal with it. The publication of Anne Frank's diary (1952) and its subsequent adaptation into a play (1955) and a movie (1959) as well as the Eichmann trial (1961) were difficult issues to affix a positive "spin" on.[89] Some investigative reporting done in 1960 by the American magazine *The Reporter* had discussed the Roy Bernard Company within a less-than-favorable evaluation of how foreign governments used private American enterprises to influence public opinion.[90] The FRG dumped Roy Bernard, and West Germany was back to mapping itself (although still under the watchful eye of the American occupation forces).

Having to cope with cartographic decision making, however, proved to be more strenuous than the government expected. The maps approved by the German Information Center, which chose "not to become directly involved in the dispute over German territories," "always included multiple boundary designations in the East."[91] This decision led to a serious lack in territorial uniformity—just as the GDR began cartographically solidifying its boundaries by using the technique of "island representation," a type of mapmaking that refused to acknowledge any mapped space outside of a nation-state's own borders. Such poor policy regarding the FRG's maps has led one geographer to claim that the 1960s and 1970s served as "the low point of the territorial script of the German nation in the FRG."[92]

But the genuine low point of Cold War–era German cartography began with the construction of the Berlin Wall on August 13, 1961. Only then did the abstract spatial posturing of Cold War rhetoricians combine with the radical fortification of an intranational border. Less than two weeks later, the wall's first casualty occurred when fifty-eight-year-old Ida Siekmann leaped from the third floor of a Berlin building on Bernauer Strasse, which stretched along the East/West divide. Although the building itself was in East German territory, the concrete in front of one of its sides was designated as part of France's West Berlin. Siekmann landed poorly (as had a forty-seven-year-old man who had jumped just days earlier and broken his leg[93]) and sustained serious internal injuries. Within a few hours, she died. Two days later, twenty-four-year-old Günter Litfin was shot trying to swim from East Berlin to West Berlin across a shipping canal that connected the Spree and Havel Rivers in the center of the city. By the time the wall fell in November 1989, 136 people had died trying to traverse it.[94] The manipulation of German space from the initial East/West split in 1949 erupted in "regular occurrences" of violence.[95]

The period from 1952 to 1961 saw a shift in cartographic renderings toward polarization. The most obvious mapped form of this polarization—the literal split between Germanys in 1949—could be sustained in West Germany only by creating a political culture willing to view its new eastern neighbor with suspicion.[96] Although generally ignored in most German histories of the period, this culture was in part shaped by the geographers of the Federal Republic. Many of these geographers, however, believed in the scientific authenticity of their maps, appreciated the contributions of their academic colleagues in the GDR, and were noticeably agitated by government intervention (especially foreign-government intervention) into their affairs. PR firms served as a useful medium through which to shape German space without compromising the legitimacy of geography as a discipline. Although Emil Meynen's Institut für Landeskunde had become the premier mapmaking center of West Germany, and although the maps it produced were some of the most desirable for his academic colleagues throughout the world (not to mention for the American military government), by 1961 simple and convincing cartographic narratives became preferable to accurate ones. Indeed, projections of German space to foreign audiences largely abandoned the dialectic model of academic discussion for the more cost-effective and politically beneficial model of corporate expedience.

6

Conclusion

Mapping Germany, Mapping Europe

Because maps are propositions you must accept responsibility for the realities you create.
　　　　　—John Krygier and Denis Wood, "Ce n'est pas le
　　　　　　　monde (This Is Not the World)"

The fluidity of German territory dictated the foreign policies of non-European powers toward Europe throughout the twentieth century. The construction of the Berlin Wall in 1961 established a concrete "iron curtain" between a capitalist West and a Communist East as well as a symbol of seemingly absolute cartographic divergence. But on November 9, 1989, the dismantling of the Berlin Wall began. Less than one year later, on October 3, 1990, the Federal Republic of Germany and the German Democratic Republic reunited as one German nation-state. The following year the Soviet Union imploded into a new European "shatter zone," free from imposed isolation but still plagued by the characterization of eastern European "Otherness."[1]

Reuniting Germany—particularly in regards to its geographic spaces—was not a smooth process. Almost immediately after reunification, a very public debate broke out regarding where the new Germany's *Reichshauptstadt*, capital city, would be located. Many saw Berlin as the natural choice. It had been Germany's initial capital, established in 1871 alongside the creation of the modern German nation-state. Berlin was also, however, the capital of Hitler's Third Reich, a city he desperately wanted to mold into "the centre of Europe and the world," a city that would "signify visually the power of the Nazis."[2] The alternative capital city proposed for the new Germany was Bonn. Bonn had been the capital of the FRG since the formal division of East Germany and West Germany in 1949. To many Germans, housing the new federal government in Bonn would be an indication of the nation-state's Western orientation and commitment to a new Europe and a democratic Germany. On June 20, 1991, the Bundestag voted between (as the choice was characterized at the time) "Bismarck's Berlin or Beethoven's Bonn" and chose Berlin by eighteen votes.[3] The contentiousness of the capital city quickly faded away as Germany made clear its intentions for Berlin to represent both the scars of its former national self and a new pluralistic, Europeanized, and multicultural state.

Germany's Europeanization, however, quickly became problematic. It was undeniable that, at least by 1990, German denazification had been hugely successful, but many of Europe's prominent leaders were wary of a unified German state that in the not-so-distant past had wreaked havoc throughout the Continent. Until reunification, East Germany had subsisted as a semiautonomous appendage of the Soviet Union, and West Germany had operated only under particular restrictions to its sovereignty (not the least of which, as pointed out in chapter 4, was an imposed supervision of its ability to map itself). In March 1991, with the ratification of the Treaty on the Final Settlement with Respect to Germany, all of these restrictions were eliminated. Although Europe's other powers had suspected the inevitability of reunification by 1989, several prominent politicians remained skeptical of Germany's promise to abandon any aggressive policy stances. French president François Mitterand worried that a new Germany would "result in [its] gaining more European influence than Hitler ever had."[4] British prime minister Margaret Thatcher also felt threatened by what she characterized as a nation-state that "had never found its true frontiers." On January 20, 1990, she complained to Mitterand that German reunification would result in the new nation-state's domination of Hungary, Poland, and Czechoslovakia, leaving only Romania and Bulgaria "for the rest of us."[5]

Here, then, we see the emergence of a post–Cold War understanding of Mitteleuropa. As the ideological and territorial East/West binary broke down, space seemed to open up for a new European "center." Once German reunification was realized, however, nationalist hopes of German domination quickly eroded. In fact, it seems as though Thatcher and Mitterand's concerns were largely unfounded. No new forms of pan-Germanism, aggressive militarism, or territorial accretion arose.[6] Only in 2006, prompted by the combination of Germany's hosting the soccer World Cup and a generation of Germans seemingly detached from the politics of both the Second World War and reunification, did Germans once again dare to display and promote their national symbols on a massive scale.[7] Yet Germany has grown significantly stronger. One could argue that in a cartographic sense Germany is today much less Europeanized than Europe is Germanized. Today it is Europe, not Germany, that grapples with finding (to quote Thatcher) "its true frontiers." For many post-Soviet states of "eastern Europe," inclusion into Europe's "center" now promises potential "membership in the European Union and participation in Western society."[8] The idea of Mitteleuropa has been displaced from its former conception as a region dominated by ethnic Germans and now serves as a proving ground for once-Communist nation-states looking to establish themselves as a part of "the new European order," often through maps meant to depict their states squarely in "the center of the continent."[9] Germany's territorial identity may now be stable, but Europe's internal boundaries and marginal frontiers dictate a great deal of political statecraft in the constantly redrawn mental and physical maps of the Western world.

The intertwined stories of postwar Germany and Emil Meynen are instructive examples of the vital role geography plays in the construction of a nation-state's political identity. But many of Meynen's professional experiences were not unique. Other geographers (perhaps most infamously Walter Christaller) advocated on behalf of Lebensraum during the Third Reich, went through denazification, and then assisted the postwar Allied occupation authorities. As this book has made clear, though, Meynen's professional fluidity—his career opportunism—kept his personal power and influence within Germany's academic community fairly consistent during the political transition from Nazi Germany to postwar-occupied Germany. Moreover, whether he was working for the Nazi regime or for the Allied occupation, his employer understood the usefulness of mapped space in molding national identity. Because of this understanding, Meynen was able to harness his professional relationships, his institute, and his well-established publications simultaneously to strengthen German geographical thought—which had been seriously damaged by its association with the Third Reich—and to satisfy the intelligence needs of the Allied powers (in particular the United States). For Emil Meynen and the Allied victors, geographic and cartographic study was more important than any ideology because it framed the space(s) of ideological debate. Whether working for Lebensraum or for the forces maintaining the occupation of Germany, the lives and careers of individuals seemed to have always played a secondary role to the security of the geographic-academic profession and the potential territorial realities it could construct.

Geography and cartography as academic disciplines changed drastically after the Second World War. Before the postwar occupation of Europe, the most prominent and influential American geographers were often fluent in French or German or both. The ideological trends of geographical thought (*Geopolitik*, Lebensraum, Heartland Theory, Central Place Theory, and so on) migrated to the United States from Europe. After the war, a significant intellectual shift occurred in which Anglophone geographers became the prominent voices of these disciplines. This shift continues to this day, with more and more influential Europeans publishing their work in English but their British, Canadian, and (to a larger extent) American colleagues failing to develop the foreign-language skills that were once central to their profession.[10] Yet as unique as this shift might seem, it was ultimately one development within a larger Anglicization of the relationships between territories and their national identities. Unlike the maps of earlier conflicts, the maps of the Second World War were massively and systematically disseminated so as to establish a particular and deeply interested rendering of the world picture.[11] Ensuring a geographic status quo required a tautological spatial narrative—the boundary lines existed because the boundary lines existed. Perpetuating a seemingly transparent cartography—that is, one that propagates the map itself but never the interests hidden within it—has become the fundamental approach to establishing spatial claims on the surface of the earth. It is tempting to dismiss these types of shifts in critical cartographic theory as ivory-tower musings, but the history of these ideas remade the political reality of Europe—and other parts of the world—after the Second World War.

Modern maps have transformed from individual cadastral maps to state-sponsored tax maps to marketed and mass-produced narratives, strategically placed into particular publications, libraries, schoolrooms, and Internet browsers for public consumption. Considering these trends of cartographic development helps to demystify the mapped spaces of the nation-state. As we have seen, Germany proves ripe for such an undertaking because of its unique cartographic history, the constant spatial (re)negotiations it has consistently grappled with, and the reproduction of its space by an occupying military force. Its purposefully manipulated remapping made clear the importance and possibility that both cartography and geography held in the twentieth century. Indeed, Germany's territorial malleability should not be forgotten in the twenty-first century, a time in which "western Europe" wrestles with the integration of what had been its "eastern" antithesis. In the age of Google, the illusion that maps are simply objective tools for corporate, government, and individual use has never been so strong. Yet the current challenges to the cultural and spatial identities of the European Union have the potential to call into question today's territorial status quo. Are the states of Turkey and Serbia so peripheral to the contemporary Mitteleuropa that they deserve exclusion? The history of Germany's remapping helps to clarify the importance of understanding the interests within these types of spatial representations (and within their complementary narratives of cartographic disinterest).

Nationalism, particularly in Europe, has waned significantly since its ideological heyday in the nineteenth century. The historian George Mosse has argued that in Europe "most national symbols, like national monuments, seem to have spent their force."[12] The mapped space of national territory, though, seems just as value laden today as it was 200 years ago. Even as Europe's nation-states cede sovereignty to the continent's transnational union, the postwar territorial status of those nation-states rarely changes. Whereas the first national maps of European states were established so as to invoke sovereign rule over particular areas, today's European maps—with their more easily traversable boundary lines and relaxed residency restrictions—suggest that sovereignty and territory do not necessarily have to complement one another. Economic "cooperation," as Mark Mazower asserts, may have "replaced competition" after the Second World War,[13] but competing claims for particular parcels of land continue to feed iso-lationist political rhetoric. In fact, it was nationalist sentiment established by spatial renderings of the nation-state that helped reestablish Europe after the war. Postwar Germany became a site of nationalist reconstruc-tion within a context of a new economic internationalism—arguably *the* model for a new Europe.[14] This book has offered evidence suggesting that maps and mapmakers played a large role in this reconstruction.

Ultimately, we are responsible for the worlds we create with maps. The history of Germany's territorial development undermines both the perceived objectivity of mapped space and the nationalist narratives built from within (or along the borders of) state and corporate cartographies. As we have seen with Germany's cartography after the Second World War, the control of space is in fact intimately tied to the control of a national identity. Unraveling this case study, I hope, encourages the investigation of space as a category of historical scholarship and makes clear the need for a deeper exploration of the realities constructed by the manipulation of spatial representations. Such undertakings will help to provide a more comprehensive understanding of the past and a more informed engage-ment with the spaces in which we find ourselves.

NOTES

BIBLIOGRAPHY

INDEX

Notes

Abbreviations

AGSL   American Geographical Society Library
AAG   American Association of Geographers
BArch   Bundesarchiv
Bd.   Band
FO   UK Foreign Office
LIfL   Leibniz-Institut für Länderkunde, Archiv für Geographie
NARA   National Archives and Records Administration
RG   Record Group
UFLA   University of Florida Library and Archive

1. Orientation

1. Michael Fahlbusch, "Emil Meynen," in *Handbuch der völkischen Wissenschaften: Personen–Institutionen–Forschungsprogramme–Stiftungen* (Munich: Saur, 2008), 427–28.

2. Ute Wardenga, "Emil Meynen—Annäherung an ein Leben," *Geographisches Taschenbuch* 23 (1995–96): 19–20.

3. Hans-Dietrich Schulz, "Fantasies of *Mitte*: *Mittellage* and *Mitteleuropa* in German Geographical Discussion in the 19th and 20th Centuries," *Political Geography Quarterly* 8, no. 4 (1989): 320.

4. Rainer Eisfeld, "Mitteleuropa in Historical and Contemporary Perspective," *German Politics and Society* 28 (Spring 1993): 39.

5. Henry Cord Meyer, *Mitteleuropa in German Thought and Action, 1815–1945* (The Hague: Martinus Nijhoff, 1955), 333–34.

6. David T. Murphy, "A Sum of the Most Wonderful Things: 'Raum,' Geopolitics, and the German Tradition of Environmental Determinism, 1900–1933," *History of European Ideas* 25, no. 5 (1999): 121–33.

7. Michael Stürmer, *Das ruhelose Reich: Deutschland, 1866–1918* (Berlin: Severin und Siedler, 1983).

8. Hans-Jürgen Puhle, "Die neue Ruhelosigkeit: Michael Stürmers nationalpolitischer Revisionismus," *Geschichte und Gesellschaft* 13, no. 3 (1987): 382–99. It should
come as no surprise to those familiar with the *Historikerstreit* that this publication—in my
view, one of the most scathing criticisms of Stürmer's academic work—comes in a journal
produced by the Bielefeld School. Bielefeld historians, committed to the new social history of the 1950s and 1960s, had little patience for nationalist renditions of their nation's
past (a practice too similar, they believed, to the type of historical approach promoted by
Nazism).

9. Richard J. Evans, "The New Nationalism and the Old History: Perspectives on
the West German *Historikerstreit*," *Journal of Modern History* 59, no. 4 (1987): 761–97.

10. Jürgen Kocka, "German History before Hitler: The Debate about the German
Sonderweg," *Journal of Contemporary History* 23, no. 1 (1988): 12.

11. Evans, "The New Nationalism," 785.

12. John K. Wright, "Highlights in American Cartography, 1939–1949," in *Comptes
rendus du Congrés International de Géographie: Lisbon 1949*, vol. 1 (Lisbon: Centro Tip.
Colonial, 1950), 299.

13. Mary Murphy, "History of the Army Map Service Map Collection," in *Federal
Government Map Collecting: A Brief History*, ed. Richard W. Stephenson (Washington,
DC: Special Libraries Association, 1969), 3.

14. In fact, one scholar has convincingly argued that "there were no maps before
1500" in the sense of the term *map* that we understand today (Denis Wood, *Rethinking
the Power of Maps* [New York: Guilford Press, 2010], 22). The function of the map as a site
of discourse and contention directly coincides with the production of the early-modern
state, an institution that necessarily depends on the authority we grant to the map.

15. One of the most promising combinations of history and space is the emerging
field of historical geographic information systems, which forces geographers to include
time in their analyses and historians to use space as a category of historical understanding. For more on this field, see Anne Kelly Knowles, *Placing History: How Maps, Spatial
Data, and GIS Are Changing Historical Scholarship* (Redlands, CA: ESRI Press, 2008).

16. Henri Lefebvre, *The Production of Space*, trans. Donald Nicholson-Smith (Malden, MA: Blackwell, 1991).

17. I am not the only one pointing out this lack of scholarship or the "strange aversion
to maps" historians seem to have. For another instance, see Helmut Walser Smith, *The
Continuities of German History: Nation, Religion, and Race across the Long Nineteenth
Century* (New York: Cambridge Univ. Press, 2008), 47.

18. Carla Hesse, *The Other Enlightenment: How French Women Became Modern*
(Princeton, NJ: Princeton Univ. Press, 2001), xii.

19. Ernest Gellner, *Nations and Nationalism* (1983), 2nd ed. (Malden, MA: Blackwell, 2006); Benedict Anderson, *Imagined Communities: Reflections on the Origin and
Spread of Nationalism* (1983), rev. ed. (New York: Verso, 2006).

20. Chenxi Tang, *The Geographic Imagination of Modernity: Geography, Literature, and Philosophy in German Romanticism* (Stanford, CA: Stanford Univ. Press, 2008), 137.

21. John Pickles, *A History of Spaces: Cartographic Reason, Mapping, and the Geocoded World* (New York: Routledge, 2004), 189.

2. Germany's Cartographic Collapse

1. H. Smith, *Continuities of German History*, 44, 41.

2. David Blackbourn, *History of Germany, 1780–1918: The Long Nineteenth Century*, 2nd ed. (Malden, MA: Blackwell, 2003), 10–11.

3. Rogers Brubaker, *Citizenship and Nationhood in France and Germany* (Cambridge, MA: Harvard Univ. Press, 1998), 57.

4. Thomas Nipperdey, *Germany from Napoleon to Bismarck*, trans. Daniel Nolan (Princeton, NJ: Princeton Univ. Press, 1996), 1.

5. Blackbourn, *History of Germany*, 47.

6. Nipperdey, *Germany from Napoleon to Bismarck*, 1.

7. Ibid.

8. Ibid., 3.

9. John Breuilly, "The German National Question and 1848," *History Today* 48, no. 5 (1998): 17.

10. Ibid., 16.

11. Brubaker, *Citizenship and Nationhood*, 69.

12. Wolfgang Schivelbusch, *The Railway Journey: The Industrialization of Time and Space in the 19th Century* (Berkeley: Univ. of California Press, 1986), 171–77.

13. Brubaker, *Citizenship and Nationhood*, 70–71.

14. Guntram Henrik Herb, *Under the Map of Germany: Nationalism and Propaganda, 1918–1945* (New York: Routledge, 1997), 9.

15. Todd Presner, "Remapping German-Jewish Studies: Benjamin, Cartography, Modernity," *German Quarterly* 82, no. 3 (2009): 303.

16. David Buisseret, "Monarchs, Ministers, and Maps in France before the Accession of Louis XIV," in *Monarchs, Ministers, and Maps: The Emergence of Cartography as a Tool of Government in Early Modern Europe*, ed. David Buisseret (Chicago: Univ. of Chicago Press, 1992), 120–21.

17. Michael Eliot Howard, *The Franco-Prussian War: The German Invasion of France, 1870–1871* (New York: Macmillan, 1961), 70.

18. Geoffrey Wawro, *The Franco-Prussian War: The German Conquest of France in 1870–1871* (New York: Cambridge Univ. Press, 2003), 47–48.

19. Schivelbusch, *Railway Journey*, 163.

20. Brubaker, *Citizenship and Nationhood*, 3–4.

21. Ibid., 12–13.

22. Blackbourn, *History of Germany*, 184.

23. Pieter M. Judson, *Guardians of the Nation: Activists on the Language Frontiers of Imperial Austria* (Cambridge, MA: Harvard Univ. Press, 2006), 14.

24. Nancy M. Wingfield, *Flag Wars and Stone Saints: How the Bohemian Lands Became Czech* (Cambridge, MA: Harvard Univ. Press, 2007), 9.

25. Judson, *Guardians of the Nation*, 13–14.

26. Tara Zahra, *Kidnapped Souls: National Indifference and the Battle for Children in the Bohemian Lands, 1900–1948* (Ithaca, NY: Cornell Univ. Press, 2011), 5–6.

27. Herb, *Under the Map of Germany*, 8.

28. Richard Hartshorne, "Political Organization of the Danube Region," attached to Stephen Jones to S. W. Boggs, June 2, 1942, Manuscript Collection 28, Box 8, Folder 24, American Geographical Society Library (AGSL), Univ. of Wisconsin, Milwaukee.

29. Neil Smith, *American Empire: Roosevelt's Geographer and the Prelude to Globalization* (Berkeley: Univ. of California Press, 2004).

30. Wesley Reisser, *The Black Book: Woodrow Wilson's Secret Plan for Peace* (New York: Lexington Books, 2012). Other accounts of this period can be found in Geoffrey Martin, *The Life and Thought of Isaiah Bowman* (Hamden, CT: Archon Books, 1980), and *Mark Jefferson, Geographer* (Ypsilanti: Eastern Michigan Univ. Press, 1968).

31. Zahra, *Kidnapped Souls*, 91.

32. Wingfield, *Flag Wars and Stone Saints*, 137, 141.

33. Annemarie H. Sammartino, *The Impossible Border: Germany and the East, 1914–1922* (Ithaca, NY: Cornell Univ. Press, 2010), 4–5.

34. Peter Gay, *Weimar Culture: The Outsider as Insider* (Westport, CT: Greenwood Press, 1981), 15.

35. Herb, *Under the Map of Germany*, 2.

36. Sammartino, *Impossible Border*, 5.

37. Veit Bachmann, "From Jackboots to Birkenstocks: The Civilianisation of German Geopolitics in the Twentieth Century," *Tijdschrift voor Economische en Sociale Geografie* 101, no. 3 (2009): 323–24.

38. David Thomas Murphy, *The Heroic Earth: Geopolitical Thought in Weimar Germany, 1918–1933* (Kent, OH: Kent State Univ. Press, 1997), 165.

39. Caitlin Murdock, *Changing Places: Society, Culture, and Territory in the Saxon-Bohemian Borderlands, 1870–1946* (Ann Arbor: Univ. of Michigan Press, 2010), 5.

40. Quoted in Sammartino, *Impossible Border*, 205.

41. Theodore S. Hamerow, *Restoration, Revolution, Reaction: Economics and Politics in Germany, 1815–1871* (Princeton, NJ: Princeton Univ. Press, 1958), vii.

42. Geoffrey Eley, *From Nazism to Unification* (Boston: Allen and Unwin, 1985), 12.

43. David Blackbourn and Geoff Eley, *The Peculiarities of German History: Bourgeois Society and Politics in Nineteenth-Century Germany* (New York: Oxford Univ. Press, 1984).

44. Max Otte, *A Rising Middle Power? German Foreign Policy in Transformation, 1989–1999* (New York: St. Martin's Press, 2000), 1.

45. Geoffrey Martin, *All Possible Worlds: A History of Geographical Ideas* (New York: Oxford Univ. Press, 2005), 7.

46. Ibid., 107.

47. Ibid., 120–24.

48. Ibid., 165.

49. "Geography-Teaching in Germany," *Science* 7, no. 161 (1886): 209–10.

50. Martin, *All Possible Worlds*, 178–79.

51. George Kiss, "Political Geography into Geopolitics: Recent Trends in Germany," *Geographical Review* 32, no. 4 (1942): 634.

52. D. Murphy, *Heroic Earth*, 7.

53. "Ratzel's 'Political Geography,'" *Geographical Journal* 13, no. 2 (1899): 171.

54. D. Murphy, *Heroic Earth*, 9.

55. Ibid.

56. The importance attached to the agrarian life was not an emphasis invented by Ratzel, nor was it the first time German thinkers had encountered such an idea. The French Physiocrats were the first group of intellectuals to promote the agrarian lifestyle as the more "natural" and beneficial alternative to urban society and worked to establish an economy fundamentally (and explicitly) dependent on agricultural production. For more on the Physiocrats' influence in Germany (although evidence does not suggest any overt links to Ratzel), see Kurt Braunreuther, "Über die Bedeutung der Physiokratischen Bewegung in Deutschland in der Zweiten Hälfte des 18. Jahrhunderts," *Wissenschaftliche Zeitschrift der Humboldt-Universität zu Berlin* 5, no. 1 (1955): 15–65.

57. Herb, *Under the Map of Germany*, 51.

58. Rudolf Kjellén, *Der Staat als Lebensform* (Leipzig: Hirzel, 1917). This book was originally published in Sweden in 1916 as *Staten som lifsform*. The publication issued in 1917 was the first German translation.

59. Andreas Dorpalen, *The World of General Haushofer: Geopolitics in Action* (New York: Farrar and Rinehart, 1942), 53.

60. Ibid., 52.

61. Herb, *Under the Map of Germany*, 78.

62. Ibid., 79.

63. Heinz Peter Brogiato, Dirk Hänsgen, Norman Henniges, Bruno Schelhaas, and Ute Wardenga, "'Ich kann sie nicht mehr gebrauchen, die Geographen, wie sie heute sind': Zur Gründungsgeschichte des DVAG," *Standort* 34 (2010): 74.

64. Jörg Hackmann, "German East or Polish West? Historiographical Discourse on the German–Polish Overlap between Confrontation and Reconciliation, 1772–2000," in *Disputed Territories and Shared Pasts: Overlapping National Histories in Modern Europe*, ed. Tibor Frank and Frank Hadler (New York: Palgrave Macmillan, 2011), 95–96.

65. In my citations of maps, I attempt to adhere as consistently as possible to the standards established in Christine Kollen, Wangyal Shawa, and Mary Larsgaard, *Cartographic Citations: A Style Guide*, 2nd ed. (Chicago: American Library Association, 2010).

66. Quoted in Hackmann, "German East or Polish West?" 95–96.

67. Ibid., 81.

68. Quoted in Dorpalen, *World of General Haushofer*, 95.

69. The most definitive repudiation of the early postwar belief that Haushofer served as some sort of chief Nazi geographer can be found in David Thomas Murphy, "Hitler's Geostrategist? The Myth of Karl Haushofer and the 'Institut für Geopolitik,'" *The Historian* 76, no. 1 (2014): 1–25. Geoffrey Martin has also expressed concern that Haushofer's "importance may have been exaggerated" (*All Possible Worlds*, 184).

70. D. Murphy, *Heroic Earth*, ix.

71. Wolfgang Natter, "Geopolitics in Germany, 1919–1945: Karl Haushofer and the *Zeitschrift für Geopolitik*," in *A Companion to Political Geography*, ed. John Agnew, Katharyne Mitchell, and Gerard Toal (Malden, MA: Blackwell, 2003), 193.

72. Ibid., 194–95, quoting Maull.

73. Kiss, "Political Geography into Geopolitics," 641.

74. Natter, "Geopolitics in Germany," 195.

75. Ibid., 190. Even Haushofer's student Rudolph Hess was no help to his former teacher in regard to this strained relationship.

76. Ibid., 198.

77. Mechtild Rössler, "'Area Research' and 'Spatial Planning' from the Weimar Republic to the German Federal Republic: Creating a Society with a Spatial Order under National Socialism," in *Science, Technology, and National Socialism*, ed. Monika Renneberg and Mark Walker (New York: Cambridge Univ. Press, 1994), 126–31.

78. Mechtild Rössler, "Geography and Area Planning under National Socialism," in *Science in the Third Reich*, ed. Margit Szöllösi-Janze (New York: Berg, 2001), 62.

79. Quoted in ibid., 63.

80. Gregory Paul Wegner, *Anti-Semitism and Schooling under the Third Reich* (New York: RoutledgeFalmer, 2002), 147.

81. Ibid., 147–56.

82. Rössler, "Geography and Area Planning under National Socialism," 63–65.

83. Natter, "Geopolitics in Germany," 190.

84. Many of the earliest American geographers studied under and regularly interacted with their German counterparts. For more detail on this relationship, see Geoffrey Martin, *American Geography and Geographers: Toward Geographical Science* (New York: Oxford Univ. Press, 2015), 27–38.

85. Herb, *Under the Map of Germany*, 94.

86. Karl W. Butzer, "Practicing Geography in a Totalitarian State: (Re)Casting Carl Troll as a Nazi Collaborator?" *Erde* 135, no. 2 (2004): 223.

87. Dan Stone, *Histories of the Holocaust* (New York: Oxford Univ. Press, 2010), 254–55; Herb, *Under the Map of Germany*, 94; Wegner, *Anti-Semitism and Schooling*, 151–52.

88. Butzer, "Practicing Geography in a Totalitarian State," 228.

89. Martin, *All Possible Worlds*, 183–84.

90. Ernst Plewe, "Heinrich Schmitthenner, 3.5.1887–18.2.1957," *Mitteilungen Universitätsbund Marburg* 2–3 (1957): 6.

91. Franz Tichy, "Leben und Werk Heinrich Schmitthenners," in *Heinrich Schmitthenner Gedächtnisschrift*, ed. Helmut Blume and Herbert Wilhelmy (Stuttgart: Steiner, 1987), 13; all translations are mine unless otherwise indicated.

92. Martin, *All Possible Worlds*, 184.

93. Steven P. Remy, *The Heidelberg Myth: The Nazification and Denazification of a German University* (Cambridge, MA: Harvard Univ. Press, 2002), 236–37.

94. Wolf Tietze, "A Politically Distorted Self-Portrait of German Geography," *GeoJournal* 57 (2002): 314.

95. Martin, *American Geography and Geographers*, 8.

96. "Interrogation of Dec. 10, 1946 with Major Tilley and Mr. Bailey; Summary of the Homework of Dec. 10, 1946—Geographical and Cartographical Institutions and Organizations, Status 1944," Dec. 17, 1946, Doc. 781-7/562, Leibniz-Institut für Länderkunde, Archiv für Geographie (LIfL), Leipzig, Germany.

97. Office of Strategic Services (OSS), Division of Map Intelligence and Cartography, *April 7, 1947 Report: Allan Evans (Director, Office of Intelligence Research) to Mr. C Hitchcock (American Geographical Society): "German Cartographic and Map Collecting Agencies: Controlling Laws and Regulatory Statutes"* (Washington, DC: OSS, Feb. 5, 1947), 2–3, 31–32.

98. For more on the history of the RfL, see Herbert Lang, *Deutschlands Vermessungs- und Kartenwesen Aspekte seiner Entwicklung seit der Reichsgründung 1871* (Dresden: Schütze, Engler, Weber, 2008).

99. OSS, *April 7, 1947 Report*, 32.

100. Mark Monmonier, "Mapping under the Third Reich: Nazi Restrictions on Map Content and Distribution," *Coordinates*, Series B, no. 2 (Jan. 2005): 3.

101. OSS, *April 7, 1947 Report*, 3.

102. Ibid., 19.

103. Ibid., 12, 33–34.

104. Ibid., 36–39.

105. Ibid., 14.

106. Ibid., 15.

107. Ibid., 18, 45–46.

108. Ibid., 23–24, 50.

109. Ibid., 22.

110. Ibid., 9.

111. Ibid., 52–53.

112. Ibid., 54–55.

113. Ibid., 29.

114. Ibid., 7.

115. Ibid., 8. *Hauptvermessungsabteilungen* I and II were also enlarged to include the provinces of East Prussia and the provinces of Upper Silesia, respectively.

116. Ibid., 65–66.

117. Ibid., 68.

118. Erich Obst, "Rundschreiben an die Geographischen Gesellschaften und die Inhaber der Lehrstühle für Geographie in Grossdeutschland," Nov. 1939, Doc. 335-26/1, LIfL.

119. "Interrogation of Dec. 10, 1946." Also see "Mitteilung über die Gründung der Deutschen Geographischen Gesellschaft!" Aug. 26, 1941, Doc. 335-25/7, LIfL.

120. Wardenga, "Emil Meynen," 18.

121. London School of Economics to Emil Meynen, May 31, 1929, Doc. 761-3/203, LIfL.

122. Rockefeller Foundation to Emil Meynen, Jan. 4, 1930, Doc. 761-3/258, LIfL.

123. Wardenga, "Emil Meynen," 33.

124. Emil Meynen to Rockefeller Foundation, May 1, 1930, Doc. 767-6/369, LIfL.

125. Tracy B. Kittredge to Emil Meynen, Dec. 17, 1934, Doc. 761-3/257, LIfL.

126. Julian P. Boyd to Emil Meynen, Jan. 19, 1940, Doc. 761-3/205, LIfL.

127. "Lebenslauf," Mar. 30, 1953, Doc. 818-2/94, LIfL.

128. Ute Wardenga, Norman Henniges, Heinz Peter Brogiato, and Bruno Schelhaas, *Der Verband deutscher Berufsgeographen, 1950–1979: Eine sozialgeschichtliche Studie zur Frühphase des DVAG* (Leipzig: Leibniz-Institut für Länderkunde, 2011), 16.

129. Michael Fahlbusch, "Emil Meynen," in *Handbuch der völkischen Wissenschaften: Personen-Institutionen-Forschungsprogramme-Stiftungen* (Munich: Saur, 2008), 425. For more on the Reichssicherheitshauptamt (Reich Security Main Office), see Michael Wildt, *An Uncompromising Generation: The Nazi Leadership of the Reich Security Main Office*, trans. Tom Pampert (Madison: Univ. of Wisconsin Press, 2009).

130. Piotr Madajczyk, "Generalplan Ost," in *Handbuch der völkischen Wissenschaften*, 188–92.

131. Fahlbusch, "Emil Meynen," 423.

132. Emil Meynen to Jan. O. M. Broek, Dec. 30, 1947, Doc. 761-5/460, LIfL.

133. Fahlbusch, "Emil Meynen," 424–25. Also see Wardenga et al., *Der Verband deutscher Berufsgeographen*, 16.

134. Wardenga et al., *Der Verband deutscher Berufsgeographen*, 16. Also see "Anlage zum Personalfragebogen," Sept. 17, 1946, Doc. 818-8/428, LIfL.

135. Fahlbusch, "Emil Meynen," 424–26.

136. Albrecht Penck to Emil Meynen, Oct. 22, 1939, Doc. 761-3/220, LIfL; various colleagues to Emil Meynen, Sept. 5, 1939, Doc. 761-3/256c, LIfL.

137. Ernst Correll to Emil Meynen, Apr. 23, 1949, Doc. 761-6/488, LIfL.

138. *Berichte zur Deutschen Landeskunde* 36 (1966), Doc. 816-3/49, LIfL.

139. OSS, *April 7, 1947 Report*, 6.

140. Ibid., 11. Also see Wardenga et al., *Der Verband deutscher Berufsgeographen*, 27.

141. OSS, *April 7, 1947 Report*, 78–80.

142. "Festschrift zum Dezennium des Amtes für Landeskunde: 1941–1951," 1951, Doc. 781-9/769, LIfL.

143. OSS, *April 7, 1947 Report*, 87.

144. Emil Meynen, *Amtliche und private Ortsnamenverzeichnisse des Großdeutschen Reiches und der mittel- und osteuropäischen Nachbargebiete, 1910–1941* (Leipzig: Hirzel, 1942).

145. Meynen to Broek, Dec. 30, 1947.

146. OSS, *April 7, 1947 Report*, 87.

147. Ibid., 15.

148. Meynen to Broek, Dec. 30, 1947.

149. "Bericht an den Vorsitzenden des Verwaltungsrates Herrn Oberbürgermeister Ministerpräsident Freyberg," Dec. 20, 1943, Doc. 581-1, LIfL. Also see Gottfried Pfeifer to Mr. De Graff, Feb. 24, 1947, Doc. 779-7/594, LIfL.

150. Meynen to Broek, Dec. 30, 1947.

151. OSS, *April 7, 1947 Report*, 21.

152. Ibid., 90.

153. Emil Meynen, "Geographical and Cartographical Institutions and Organizations, Remarks on Changes at the End of the War," Dec. 17, 1946, Doc. 781-7/575, LIfL.

154. Bruno Schelhaas and Ingrid Hönsch, "History of German Geography: Worldwide Reputation and Strategies of Nationalisation and Institutionalisation," in *Geography: Discipline, Profession, and Subject since 1870*, ed. Gary Dunbar (Norwell, MA: Kluwer Academic, 2001), 30–31.

155. Fahlbusch, "Emil Meynen," 426.

156. Meynen to Broek, Dec. 30, 1947.

157. M. Murphy, "History of the Army Map Service Map Collection," 1.

158. Alice Hudson, "The New York Public Library's Map Division Goes to War, 1941–1945," *Bulletin: Special Library Association, Geography and Map Division* 182 (Spring 1996): 2.

159. W. D. Milne to "Librarian, University of Florida," Sept. 19, 1945, Series 08a, Box 6, Univ. of Florida Library and Archive (UFLA), Gainesville. Also see Frank T. Nicoletti, "U.S. Army Topographic Command College Depository Program," *Bulletin: Special Library Association, Geography and Map Division* 86 (Dec. 1971): 7.

160. Leonard S. Wilson, "Lessons from the Experience of the Map Information Section, OSS," *Geographical Review* 39, no. 2 (1949): 302.

161. Ibid., 298, 307.

162. Everett C. Olson and Agnes Whitmarsh, *Foreign Maps* (New York: Harper and Brothers, 1944), xi.

163. For a more complete survey of the role geographers played in the Research and Analysis Branch of the OSS, see Trevor J. Barnes, "Geographical Intelligence: American Geographers and Research and Analysis in the Office of Strategic Services, 1941–1945," *Journal of Historical Geography* 32, no. 1 (2006): 149–68.

164. Richard Hartshorne to Elizabeth Platt, Nov. 5, 1939, Map Department Records, Box 2, Folder 37, AGSL.

165. Richard Hartshorne, "Suggestions for a More Stable Settlement of European Boundary Problems," Sept. 1940, Manuscript Collection 28, Box 8, Folder 24, AGSL.

166. Tony Judt, *Postwar: A History of Europe since 1945* (New York: Penguin, 2005), 23.

167. Hartshorne, "Suggestions for a More Stable Settlement."

168. Martin, *American Geography and Geographers*, 957.

169. William M. Franklin, "Zonal Boundaries and Access to Berlin," *World Politics* 16, no. 1 (1963): 5–7.

170. Ibid., 7–8.

171. Ibid.

172. Ibid., 3–4.

173. Ibid., 10.

174. For an image of this map, see Maurice Matloff, *Strategic Planning for Coalition Warfare, 1943–1944* (Washington, DC: Office of the Chief of Military History, US Department of the Army, 1959), 341.

175. Philip E. Mosley, "The Occupation of Germany: New Light on How the Zones Were Drawn," *Foreign Affairs* 28, no. 4 (1950): 587–88.

176. Ibid., 588–89.

177. Richard Hartshorne, "Geography," Jan. 1944, Manuscript Collection 28, Box 2, Folder 17, AGSL.

178. Kathleen Southwell Davis, "The Problem of Textbooks," in *The British in Germany: Educational Reconstruction after 1945*, ed. Arthur Hearnden (London: Hamish Hamilton, 1978), 108.

179. Franklin, "Zonal Boundaries," 13.

180. Mosley, "Occupation of Germany," 589–90.

181. Lothar Kettenacker, *Germany since 1945* (New York: Oxford Univ. Press, 1997), 9.

182. Mosley, "Occupation of Germany," 590; Franklin, "Zonal Boundaries," 14.

183. Franklin, "Zonal Boundaries," 13, 17; Zoltan Michael Szaz, *Germany's Eastern Frontier: The Problem of the Oder-Neisse Line* (Chicago: Regnery, 1960), 106–7.

184. Mosley, "Occupation of Germany," 591.

185. Quoted in Franklin, "Zonal Boundaries," 14.

186. Ibid.

187. Ibid., 17–18.

188. Mosley, "Occupation of Germany," 591.

189. Franklin, "Zonal Boundaries," 19.

190. Ibid.; Mosley, "Occupation of Germany," 596.

191. Franklin, "Zonal Boundaries," 23.

192. Mosley, "Occupation of Germany," 600.

193. "Report on the Crimea (Yalta) Conference, 4–11 February 1945," Feb. 11, 1945, in *Documents on Germany under Occupation, 1945–1954*, ed. Beate Ruhm von Oppen (New York: Oxford Univ. Press, 1955), 4–6.

194. Mosely, "Occupation of Germany," 602.

3. Rebuilding Germany's Geography

1. Theodor, *Studienrat KURT SCHMIDT*, map, no scale given, Kestlerbach, Hesse, Dec. 5, 1948, Record Group (RG) 355, Stack 490 8/35/03-07, Box 2, National Archives and Records Administration (NARA), Washington, DC.

2. John Krygier and Denis Wood, "Ce n'est pas le monde (This Is Not the World)," in *Rethinking Maps*, ed. Martin Dodge, Rob Kitchin, and Chris Perkins (New York: Routledge, 2009), 198–99.

3. "Neugliederung der Länder nach 1945," n.d., Doc. 770-8/1, LIfL.

4. Daphne Berdahl, *Where the World Ended: Re-unification and Identity in the German Borderland* (Berkeley: Univ. of California Press, 1999), 29.

5. Gay, *Weimar Culture*, xiv.

6. The most famous of these forced migrations—at least famous in the United States—was Operation Paperclip, which helped lay the groundwork for the American space program. For more on Operation Paperclip and other similar efforts, see John Gimbel, *Science, Technology, and Reparations: Exploitation and Plunder in Postwar Germany* (Stanford, CA: Stanford Univ. Press, 1990).

7. "Report on the Progress of German Government Agencies of Supplying Scientific Institutes with Materials Other Than Air Photographs," Jan. 10, 1947, Doc. 781-6/493, LIfL.

8. Jonathan Tucker, *War of Nerves: Chemical Warfare from World War I to al-Qaeda* (New York: Pantheon Books, 2006), 87.

9. Wardenga et al., *Der Verband deutscher Berufsgeographen*, 25.

10. "Phillip" to Richard Hartshorne, Sept. 30, 1945, Part II, Box 200, Folder II, American Association of Geographers (AAG), University of Wisconsin, Milwaukee.

11. Wardenga et al., *Der Verband deutscher Berufsgeographen*, 25.

12. *Festschrift zum Dezennium des Amtes für Landeskunde: 1941–1951*, Doc. 781-9/769, LIfL.

13. *Berichte zur Deutschen Landeskunde* 36 (1966), Doc. 816-3/49, LIfL.

14. Geo. H. Walker to Lt. Colonel CE, Chief, Military Branch, "Status of German Nationals Employed at Landshut," message, Feb. 27, 1950, Doc. 788-10/812, LIfL.

15. Gottfried Pfeifer to Mr. DeGraff, Feb. 24, 1947, Doc. 779-7/594, LIfL.

16. *Berichte zur Deutschen Landeskunde* 36 (1966), Doc. 816-3/49, LIfL.

17. Judt, *Postwar*, 23.

18. Mark Wyman, *DP: Europe's Displaced Persons, 1945–1951* (Philadelphia: Balch Institute Press, 1989), 37.

19. Murdock, *Changing Places*, 206–8.

20. Bruno Schelhaas, *Institutionelle Geographie auf dem Weg in die wissenschaftspolitische Systemspaltung: Die Geographische Gesellschaft der DDR bis zur III. Hochschul- und Akademie-reform, 1968/69* (Leipzig: Leibniz-Institut für Länderkunde, 2004), 32.

21. Gerhard Sandner, "Die unmittelbare Nachkriegszeit: Personelle, institutionelle und fachlichinhaltliche Aspekte 1945–1950," in *Kontinuität und Diskontinuität der deutschen Geographie in Umbruchphasen: Studien zur Geschichte der Geographie*, ed. Ute Wardenga and Ingrid Hönsch (Munster: Institut für Geographie der Westfalischen Wilhelm-Universität, 1995), 142.

22. Ibid., 144. Although the network was organized, no meeting of it took place until 1947 (Schelhaas, *Institutionelle Geographie*, 31).

23. *Berichte zur Deutschen Landeskunde* 36 (1966), Doc. 816-3/49, LIfL.

24. Rudolf Reinhard, "Lebenslauf," July 17, 1945, Doc. 590-50, LIfL.

25. "Deutsches Institut für Länderkunde," memo, Feb. 1, 1946, Doc. 587-36, LIfL.

26. Rudolf Reinhard to the Military Government, May 11, 1945, Doc. 587-36, LIfL.

27. Rudolf Reinhard to the Police-State Centre (Leipzig), May 16, 1945, Doc. 588-38/1, LIfL.

28. "Deutsches Insitut für Länderkunde," Jan. 2, 1946, Doc. 587-36, LIfL.

29. Wardenga et al., *Der Verband deutscher Berufsgeographen*, 28.

30. Lloyd D. Black, "Further Notes on German Geography," *Geographical Review* 37, no. 1 (1947): 148.

31. Emil Meynen to C. Schott, June 1, 1959, Doc. 825-3/449, LIfL.

32. "Aktenvermerk über die Aufgaben des Amtes für Landeskunde," Doc. 779-7/589, LIfL. Although Germany was perhaps the only nation-state forced to change its place-names, many other states also used place-names to help revise their postwar places. Czechoslovakia, for example, was quick to change German place-names into Czech ones. See Norman M. Naimark, *Fires of Hatred: Ethnic Cleansing in Twentieth-Century Europe* (Cambridge, MA: Harvard Univ. Press, 2001), 122.

33. Emil Meynen, "Karte der Landschaftsgliederung des Deutschen Reiches (1937)," Dec. 5, 1945, Doc. 779-8/617, LIfL.

34. Emil Meynen, "Interrogation of January 30, 1947: My Personal Thoughts and Aspirations in Doing My Task since Apr. 1945," Jan. 31, 1947, Doc. 781-6/448, LIfL.

35. Quoted in Arthur Hearnden, *Education in the Two Germanies* (Boulder, CO: Westview Press, 1974), 29.

36. Geoffrey Giles, *Students and National Socialism in Germany* (Princeton, NJ: Princeton Univ. Press, 1985), 7. As pointed out in chapter 2, geography (along with history) was one of the most heavily nazified school subjects. See Winfried Müller, *Schulpolitik in Bayern im Spannungsfeld von Kulturbürokratie und Besatzungsmacht, 1945–1949* (Munich: Oldenbourg, 1995), 255.

37. George Murray, "The Training of Teachers," in *The British in Germany*, ed. Hearnden, 137.

38. See Hanna Schissler and Yasemin Nuhoglu Soysal, eds., *The Nation, Europe, and the World: Textbooks and Curricula in Transition* (New York: Berghahn Books, 2005), and Charles B. Lansing, *From Nazism to Communism: German Schoolteachers under Two Dictatorships* (Cambridge, MA: Harvard Univ. Press, 2010), 130. The Morgenthau Plan of April 1945 (or Joint Chiefs of Staff Directive 1067) also made it clear that textbooks needed to be "free of Nazi and militaristic doctrine" ("JCS 1067," in *Documents on Germany under Occupation*, ed. von Oppen, 13–27). This is also made clear in the official report of the Potsdam Conference issued on August 2, 1945: "Report on the Tripartite Conference of Berlin (Potsdam) (2 Aug. 1945)," in *Documents on Germany under Occupation*, ed. von Oppen, 40.

39. James F. Tent, *Mission on the Rhine: Reeducation and Denazification in American-Occupied Germany* (Chicago: Univ. of Chicago Press, 1982), 9.

40. Lothar Kettenacker, "The Planning of 'Re-education' during the Second World War," in *The Political Re-education of Germany & Her Allies after World War II*, ed. Nicholas Pronay and Keith Wilson (Totowa, NJ: Barnes & Noble Books, 1985), 76.

41. Edward N. Peterson, *The American Occupation of Germany: Retreat to Victory* (Detroit: Wayne State Univ. Press, 1977), 161.

42. Tent, *Mission on the Rhine*, 39.

43. Ullrich Schneider, "The Reconstruction of the Universities in American Occupied Germany," in *Hochschuloffiziere und Wiederaufbau des Hochschulwesens in Westdeutschland, 1945–1952*, vol. 2: *Die US-Zone*, ed. Manfred Heinemann and Ullrich Schneider (Hannover: Veröffentlichung aus dem Forschungsschwerpunkt "Zeitgeschichte von Bildung und Wissenschaft" der Universität Hannover, 1990), 1–8. See also John Gimbel, "Science, Technology, and Reparations in Postwar Germany," in *American Policy and the Reconstruction of West Germany, 1945–1955*, ed. Jeffry M. Diefendorf, Axel Frohn, and Hermann-Josef Rupieper (Washington, DC: German Historical Institute, 1993), 177, 188.

44. Gimbel, "Science, Technology, and Reparations in Postwar Germany," 189.

45. Lansing, *From Nazism to Communism*, 147.

46. James F. Tent, "Denazification of Higher Education in U.S. Occupied Germany, 1945–1949," in *Hochschuloffiziere und Wiederaufbau des Hochschulwesens in Westdeutschland*, ed. Heinemann and Schneider, 2:12.

47. Remy, *Heidelberg Myth*, 189–90.

48. Ibid., 157.

49. John Gimbel, *The American Occupation of Germany: Politics and Military, 1945–1949* (Stanford, CA: Stanford Univ. Press, 1968), 240.

50. Christoph Führ, *The German Education System since 1945: Outlines and Problems* (Bonn: Inter Nationes, 1997), 13.

51. *Special Report of the Military Governor (Education & Cultural Relations), September 1948* (N.p.: Office of Military Government for Germany, 1948), 1.

52. Ibid.

53. Müller, *Schulpolitik in Bayern*, 255.

54. Gustav Kreuzer and Eduard Müller-Temme, *Geographische Weltkunde Lehr- und Arbeitsbuch für deutsche Schulen: Deutschland in Europa* (Baden: Badenia, 1958), 169.

55. The attempt to keep the Western Allies' zones of occupation cartographically distinguished from the Soviet zone reflected larger policy decisions and the desire (particularly by the Americans and the British) to divide Germany into two states. For more on that issue, see Carolyn Eisenberg, *Drawing the Line: The American Decision to Divide Germany, 1944–1949* (New York: Cambridge Univ. Press, 1996).

56. Hellmut Becker, "Retrospective View from the German Side," in *The British in Germany*, ed. Hearnden, 269.

57. Arthur Hearnden, "Education in the British Zone," in *The British in Germany*, ed. Hearnden, 11. Also see Kurt Jürgensen, "The Concept and Practice of 'Re-education' in Germany, 1945–50," in *Political Re-education of Germany*, ed. Pronay and Wilson, 86, 90.

58. Robert Fox, *Teubners Erdkundliches Unterrichtswerk für höhere Lehranstalten*, vol. 2: *Europa* (Leipzig: Teubner, 1931).

59. Quoted in Davis, "The Problem of Textbooks," 117.

60. Edith Davies, "British Policy and the Schools," in *The British in Germany*, ed. Hearnden, 102.

61. Davis, "The Problem of Textbooks," 109.

62. Geoffrey Bird, "The Universities," in *The British in Germany*, ed. Hearnden, 152. Also see Jürgensen, "Concept and Practice of 'Re-education,'" 90.

63. Tent, *Mission on the Rhine*, 314.

64. Frank G. Banta, "A Role in the Education Branch of the Office of the Military Government for Germany (US), 1945–1949," in *Hochschuloffiziere und Wiederaufbau des Hochschulwesens in Westdeutschland*, ed. Heinemann and Schneider, 2:39.

65. Peterson, *American Occupation of Germany*, 161.

66. Ibid.

67. Helen Liddell, "Education in Occupied Germany: A Field Study," in *L'education de l'Allemagne occupée*, ed. Helen Liddell (Paris: Librairie Marcel Riviére et Cie, 1949),

120–21. This use of specialists, of course, finally increased the number of officers per university to the one-to-one ratio the British had achieved years earlier.

68. D. G. Williamson, *Germany from Defeat to Partition, 1945–1963* (New York: Pearson, 2001), 14–15.

69. John Gimbel, *A German Community under American Occupation: Marburg, 1945–1952* (Stanford, CA: Stanford Univ. Press, 1961), 212.

70. Arthur Hearnden, "The Education Branch of the Military Government of Germany and the Schools," in *Political Re-education of Germany & Her Allies*, ed. Pronay and Wilson, 105.

71. Gimbel, *American Occupation of Germany*, 241.

72. Hearnden, "Education Branch of the Military Government," 105.

73. Müller, *Schulpolitik in Bayern*, 252, 255. In fact, in the American zone no history textbooks were used in classrooms prior to 1948 (Liddell, "Education in Occupied Germany," 120–21).

74. Josef Dietz, *Teure Heimat, sei gegrüsst* (1948), cited in Davis, "The Problem of Textbooks," 125.

75. Alonzo G. Grace, *Basic Elements of Educational Reconstruction in Germany* (Washington, DC: American Council on Education, 1949), 8–9.

76. Führ, *German Education System*, 13.

77. Schelhaas and Hönsch, "History of German Geography," 25. Also see Meynen, "Interrogation of January 30, 1947."

78. "Bericht über die Verhältnisse innerhalb der geographischen Wissenschaft in den letzten Jahren vor und nach dem Kriege (Geogr. Gesellschaft Magdeburg)," memo, May 9, 1948, Doc. 334-5, LIfL.

79. *Newsletter*, Nov. 8, 1947, Doc. 783-3/174, LIfL.

80. *Newsletter*, Apr. 2, 1948, Doc. 783-3/156, LIfL.

81. "Lectures and Seminars in Geography at German Universities," 1947, Doc. 805-3/98, LIfL.

82. "*Newsletter*, December '47–January '48," Feb. 1, 1948, Doc. 783-3/161, LIfL.

83. *Rundbrief* 4 (Aug. 14, 1948), Doc. 773-13/719, LIfL.

84. Wardenga et al., *Der Verband deutscher Berufsgeographen*, 30–31.

85. Brogiato et al., "'Ich kann sie nicht mehr gebrauchen, die Geographen, wie sie heute sind,'" 75.

86. Sandner, "Die unmittelbare Nachkriegszeit," 143.

87. Tucker, *War of Nerves*, 86.

88. "Top Secret Report: Conclusions," 8, Geoffrey Martin, personal archive, New Haven, CT.

89. "TOP SECRET: Professor Emil Meynen and Forschungsstaffel," Aug. 17, 1946, UK Foreign Office (FO) 1031/113, 2, National Archives of the United Kingdom, London.

90. Ibid., 4.

91. "Top Secret Report: Conclusions," 8.

92. Mechtild Rössler, "Secret Nazi Plans for Eastern Europe: Geography and Spatial Planning in the Third Reich," *Treballs de la Societat Catalana de Geografia* 35 (July 1993): 209.

93. "Interrogation of January 10, 1947: Personal Remarks Relating to the Subjects of the Interrogation," Jan. 11, 1947, Doc. 781-6/483, LIfL.

94. Untitled report on Emil Meynen, Doc. 818-3/155, LIfL. Also see A. F. Hennings (captain, Office of the Deputy Director of Intelligence) to "Whom It May Concern," May 9, 1947, Doc. 818-3/142, LIfL.

95. "Interrogation of Dec. 10, 1946 with Major Tilley and Mr. Bailey; Members of the 'Abteilung für Landeskunde' Being Also Members of the 'Forschungsstaffel zbV,'" Dec. 17, 1946, Doc. 781-7/559, LIfL.

96. "Notification of Information Concerning a Research Establishment," Apr. 1, 1947, Doc. 781-6/432, LIfL.

97. "Interrogation of Dec. 10, 1946 with Major Tilley and Mr. Bailey; Summary of the Homework of Dec. 10, 1946—Geographical and Cartographical Institutions and Organizations, Status 1944," Dec. 17, 1946, Doc. 781-7/562, LIfL.

98. Ibid.

99. For a great example of this approach, see Richard Hartshorne, "The Geopolitical Position of the United States and the Soviet Union," Oct. 1946, Manuscript Collection 28, Box 2, Folder 20, AGSL.

100. "Interrogation of Dec. 10, 1946 with Major Tilley and Mr. Bailey; Summary of the Homework of Dec. 10, 1946," Dec. 17, 1946.

101. "Interrogation of December 10, 1946 with Major Tilley and Mr. Bailey; List of Hiding Places as Far as Known to Members of the Abteilung für Landeskunde," Dec. 17, 1946, Doc. 781-7/518, LIfL.

102. "Interrogation of Dec. 27, 1946 with Lt. Hovsepian and Mr. Bailey; Supplement to the Report of Dec. 17, 1946. List of Hiding Places as Far as Known to Members of the Abteilung für Landeskunde," Dec. 28, 1946, Doc. 781-7/511, LIfL.

103. "Interrogation of January 10, 1947: Personal Remarks Relating to the Subjects of the Interrogation," Jan. 11, 1947.

104. Ibid.

105. Dr. Richard Shryock to Editha Meynen, May 29, 1947, Doc. 762-5/494, LIfL. Also see Emil Meynen to Dr. Richard Shryock, June 25, 1947, Doc. 762-5/489, LIfL.

106. "Homework—Die 'Forschungsgemeinschaften,'" Dec. 10, 1946, Doc. 781-7/623, LIfL. Also see "Interrogation of January 17, 1947: Second Accession List," Jan. 25, 1947, Doc. 781-6/453, LIfL.

107. "Interrogation of January 30, 1947: Calling of Mrs. Schulz-Kampfhenkel at Scheinfeld Early in 1946," Jan. 31, 1947, Doc. 781-6/447, LIfL.

108. Meynen, "Interrogation of January 30, 1947," Jan. 31, 1947.

109. Hennings to "Whom It May Concern," May 9, 1947.

110. Emil Meynen to Capt. Lloyd Black, June 25, 1947, Doc. 761-5/403, LIfL.

111. Emil Meynen to Prof. Rheinfelder (Bavarian State Ministry for Education and Culture), July 10, 1947, Doc. 761-5/386, LIfL.

112. R. A. Degraff to "Whom It May Concern," July 14, 1947, Doc. 780-1/113, LIfL.

113. Emil Meynen to Jan O. M. Broek, Dec. 30, 1947, Doc. 761-5/460, LIfL.

114. "Aktenvermerk," Mar. 5, 1947, Doc. 783-1/30, LIfL.

115. Untitled report, Aug. 23, 1947, Doc. 781-6/412, LIfL.

116. Emil Meynen to Dr. Fr. Hackmann, Dec. 29, 1947, Doc. 761-7/602, LIfL.

117. Emil Meynen, "Amt für Landeskunde / Office of Regional Geography," Oct. 8, 1947, Doc. 781-6/427, LIfL.

118. Erich Otremba to Dr. Glum (Bavarian State Chancellery), Apr. 4, 1947, Doc. 779-9/377, LIfL.

119. John P. Bradford (Chief, Governmental Structures Branch, Office of Military Government for Bavaria) to "Whom It May Concern," Apr. 2, 1947, Doc. 779-7/581, LIfL.

120. "Some Proposals Concerning the Abteilung für Landeskunde, Scheinfeld, in Her Collaboration with the State Department, Map Intelligence and Cartography," Dec. 7, 1946, Doc. 781-7/680, LIfL.

121. Untitled report, Aug. 23, 1947.

122. Ibid.

123. *Rundschreiben* 1 (Feb. 25, 1946), Doc. 334-4, LIfL.

124. *Rundschreiben* 2 (Mar. 10, 1946), Doc. 334-4, LIfL.

125. Untitled report, Aug. 23, 1947. Early versions of the *Berichte* were even published in English; see, for example, *News letter* [sic], Nov. 8, 1947, Doc. 783-3/174, LIfL, and *Newsletter*, Dec. 10, 1947, Doc. 783-3/178, LIfL.

126. Untitled report, Aug. 23, 1947.

127. Ibid.

128. "Annual Report Covering the Period 1 July 1948 to 30 June 1949," July 21, 1949, Doc. 781-4/244, LIfL.

129. *Berichte zur Deutschen Landeskunde* 36 (1966), Doc. 816-3/49, LIfL.

130. "Annual Report," July 1, 1947–June 30, 1948, Doc. 781-5/329, LIfL. Also see Emil Meynen, "Report," Oct. 22, 1951, Doc. 778-7/249, LIfL.

131. Emil Meynen, "Report," Oct. 22, 1951.

132. "Annual Report," July 1, 1947–June 30, 1948; Emil Meynen to Richard H. Shryock, Jan. 5, 1948, and Feb. 22, 1948, Docs. 762-5/485 and 762-5/484, LIfL.

133. "Annual Report," July 1, 1947–June 30, 1948.

134. "Map Department—Annual Report—Year Ending December 31st, 1947," Map Department Records, Box 1, Folder 34, AGSL.

135. D. W. McKenzie to Emil Meynen, Nov. 1, 1947, Doc. 762-2/254, LIfL.

136. D. W. McKenzie to Emil Meynen, Oct. 29, 1948, Doc. 762-2/244, LIfL.

137. Nordis Felland to Gerhard Schott, Mar. 15, 1948, Library Records, Box 5, Folder 34, AGSL.

138. Among the Americans listed were Chauncey Harris and George Cressey.

139. *Sonder-Rundbrief*, May 25, 1949, Doc. 773-13/670, LIfL. Meynen's English-language journal *Rundbrief* was hugely popular among German geography faculty (see Doc. 773-13/752, LIfL).

140. Emil Meynen to Dickson Y. Hovsepian, Dec. 28, 1948, Doc. 761-7/686, LIfL.

141. Emil Meynen to Jan O. M. Broek, Jan. 6, 1949, Doc. 761-5/454, LIfL.

142. Meynen to Hovsepian, Dec. 28, 1948.

143. In 2016, the Association of American Geographers changed its name to the American Association of Geographers. Because this book focuses on the institution prior to 2016, I refer to it by its original name—that is, the name used during the particular time period at issue.

144. See Emil Meynen to Capt. Lloyd Black, Apr. 1949, Doc. 761-5/398, LIfL; Emil Meynen to Dr. Gottfried Pfeiffer, Aug. 31, 1948, Doc. 762-6/394, LIfL; and Emil Meynen to Lloyd D. Black, Apr. 13, 1949, Doc. 761-5/401, LIfL.

145. Gimbel, *American Occupation of Germany*, 114.

146. "Reply of the Ministers-President to the Proposals Made by the Military Governors Following the London Decisions, 26 July 1948," in *Documents on the Creation of the German Federal Constitution*, comp. Office of Military Government for Germany, Civil Administration Division (Berlin: Office of Military Government for Germany [US], Sept. 1, 1949), 46–47. Also see "List of Resolutions Prepared by the Conference of Ministers President at Königstein and Submitted to the Military Governors for Consideration," Mar. 24, 1949, and "Washington Three-Power Meeting: Agreed Minute on Württemberg-Baden Plebiscite," Apr. 8, 1949, in *Documents on Germany under Occupation*, ed. von Oppen, 380.

4. The End of Occupation?

1. Wright, "Highlights in American Cartography," 299.

2. *Rundbrief* 10 (May 15, 1949), Doc. 773-13/675, LIfL.

3. Eckart Ehlers, "German Geography 1945–1992: Organizational and Institutional Aspects," in *40 Years After: German Geography: Development, Trends, and Prospects, 1952–1992*, ed. Eckart Ehlers (Bonn: Deutsche Forschungsgemeinschaft, 1992), 30.

4. Wilhelm von Nathusius to the Ministry for the Marshall Plan, Aug. 30, 1951, Doc. 778-7/264, LIfL.

5. George H. T. Kimble to Emil Meynen, Sept. 28, 1950, Doc. 783-4/190, LIfL.

6. *Rundbrief* 28 (Nov. 15, 1950), Doc. 773-12/561, LIfL.

7. List of delegations, in *Proceedings: Eighth General Assembly and Seventeenth International Congress, Washington, DC, Aug. 8–15, 1952* (Washington, DC: National

Academy of Sciences, 1952), 55. It should be noted, however, that the American report on German activity did make a clear distinction between East and West Germany. See Mildred A. Moorman, ed., "The Status of Geography in Countries Adhering to the International Geographical Union," Aug. 8–15, 1952, Box 83, Folder 4, AAG.

8. Edwin Fels, "Gesellschaft für Erdkunde (1828)," in *Proceedings: Eighth General Assembly*, 28.

9. Dr. Herbert Schlenger, "Die Ostforschung in den USA (Bericht über eine Reise durch die USA vom 24.7.–27.9.1952)," Doc. 802-2/88, LIfL. These libraries included the Library of Congress, the Public Library of Chicago, the Public Library of Buffalo, the Widener Library of Harvard University, the Public Library of New York, the Library of the American Geographical Society (New York City), and the Library of the National Geographical Society (Washington, DC). The research centers visited were the Russian Research Center at Harvard University, the Russian Institute at Columbia University, the Research Program on the USSR in New York City, the Mid-European Studies Center in New York City, the Institute of East European Studies at Indiana University, and the Russian Center for Languages at Syracuse University, among others.

10. "Memorandum: Problems Arising in Berlin in Connection with Immigration to USA under the Truman Directive," June 29, 1946, RG 84, Stack 350 58/11/05, Box 2, NARA.

11. "Questions Relating to Germany Territorial Reorganization: Statement by the Head of the U.S. Delegation," RG 84, Stack 350 57/30/05–07, Box 3, NARA, in *The Council of Foreign Ministers: Documents on Germany, Sessions I–VI, 1945–1949* (Washington, DC: Division of Historical Policy Research, US Department of State, Mar. 1950).

12. "Memorandum No. 55," Mar. 8, 1946, RG 84, Stack 350 58/11/05, Box 2, NARA.

13. George Haering to John F. Stone, June 15, 1946, RG 84, Stack 350 58/11/05, Box 2, NARA.

14. George Haering to Travers, Apr. 8, 1946, and Maurice Altaffer to George Haering, Apr. 10, 1946, RG 84, Stack 350 58/11/05, Box 2, NARA.

15. "Questions Relating to Germany: Statement by U.S. Delegation, Polish–German Frontier," Apr. 9, 1947, RG 84, Stack 350 57/30/05–07, Box 3, NARA, in *Council of Foreign Ministers*, 360.

16. "Territorial Reorganization," Apr. 2, 1947, RG 84, Stack 350 57/30/05–07, Box 3, NARA, in *Council of Foreign Ministers*, 299.

17. "Questions Relating to Germany: Territorial Reorganization of Germany, Statement by the Soviet Delegation," Mar. 15, 1947, RG 84, Stack 350 57/30/05–07, Box 3, NARA, in *Council of Foreign Ministers*, 106.

18. "Questions Relating to Germany: Form and Scope of the Provisional Political Organization of Germany, Statement by the Head of the French Delegation," Mar. 22, 1947, RG 84, Stack 350 57/30/05–07, Box 3, NARA, in *Council of Foreign Ministers*, 205.

19. Ibid.

20. "Questions Relating to Germany: Statement by the U.S. Delegation, Polish–German Frontier," Apr. 9, 1947, RG 84, Stack 350 57/30/05–07, Box 3, NARA, in *Council of Foreign Ministers*, 359.

21. Ibid., 359–62.

22. "Questions Relating to Germany: Memorandum by the French Delegation, Regime for the Saar," Apr. 10, 1947, RG 84, Stack 350 57/30/05–07, Box 3, NARA, in *Council of Foreign Ministers*, 365.

23. "Questions Relating to Germany: Future Frontiers of Germany, Statement by the Head of the French Delegation," Apr. 9, 1947, RG 84, Stack 350 57/30/05–07, Box 3, NARA, in *Council of Foreign Ministers*, 364.

24. Ibid., 362–65.

25. "Questions Relating to Germany: Statement by the Head of the French Delegation in Regard to Frontier Rectifications Claimed by Several Allied Countries," Apr. 11, 1947, RG 84, Stack 350 57/30/05–07, Box 3, NARA, in *Council of Foreign Ministers*, 413–15.

26. "Weekly Foreign Information Policy Guidance, No. 101," Mar. 12, 1952, 2, RG 335, Stack 631 46/43/05, Box 1, NARA.

27. "Council of Foreign Ministers (Questions Relating to Germany): Frontiers of Germany, Proposal of the U.K. Delegation," Nov. 28, 1947, RG 84, Stack 350 57/30/05–07, Box 3, NARA, in *Council of Foreign Ministers*, 516. Also see "Council of Foreign Ministers: Questions Relating to Germany: Preparation of the German Peace Treaty Frontiers, Statement Made by M. Georges Bidault, Chief of the French Delegation," Nov. 27, 1947, in RG 84, Stack 350 57/30/05–07, Box 3, NARA, *Council of Foreign Ministers*, 511–15.

28. For more on this period and the development of the permanent division, see Eisenberg, *Drawing the Line*.

29. Basic Law for the Federal Republic of Germany, in *Documents on the Creation of the German Federal Constitution*, comp. Office of Military Government for Germany, Civil Administration Division, 9.

30. Ibid., 11.

31. Ibid., 65.

32. Ibid., 11.

33. For more on the creation of Baden-Württemberg, see Karl Römer, "Die Geburtsstunde Baden-Württembergs: Die Gesetzgebung zur Bildung des Südweststaates," *Zeitschrift für Württembergische Landesgeschichte* 66 (2007): 475–96.

34. "Weekly Foreign Information Policy Guidance, No. 66," July 5, 1951, 3, RG 335, Stack 631 46/43/05, Box 1, NARA. Also see "National Affairs: War's End," *Time*, July 16, 1951.

35. "Weekly Foreign Information Policy Guidance, No. 74," Aug. 28, 1951, 2, RG 335, Stack 631 46/43/05, Box 1, NARA.

36. "Military Government—Germany, United States Area of Control, Law No. 23, Control of Scientific Research," effective Sept. 12, 1949, Doc. 782-4/163, LIfL.

37. Hearnden, *Education in the Two Germanies*, 67–68.

38. Jürgensen, "Concept and Practice of 'Re-education,'" 92.

39. Bird, "The Universities," 156.

40. Martin, *All Possible Worlds*, 184–85. The growth in geography's popularity after the Second World War is one quantifiable "success" James Tent overlooks in *Mission on the Rhine*, where he laments the absence of such evidence while arguing that—no matter—the Allied "influence was real" (312).

41. *Rundschreiben* 32 (Jan. 13, 1951), Doc. 761-7/652, LIfL.

42. *Berichte zur Deutschen Landeskunde* 36 (1966), Doc. 816-3/49, LIfL.

43. *Jahresbericht des Amtes für Landeskunde*, June 22, 1951, Doc. 781-3/181, LIfL.

44. Emil Meynen to Thomas R. Smith, Jan. 30, 1950, Doc. 762-5/504, LIfL.

45. Excerpt of the *Geographical Review* sent from Lloyd D. Black to the AfL, Oct. 10, 1949, Doc. 780-6/465, LIfL. For the full article, see Black, "Further Notes on German Geography."

46. Walter Ristow to George Kish, Oct. 13, 1950, Box 91, Folder 3, AAG.

47. Shannon McCune to Emil Meynen, May 21, 1950, Box 91, Folder 3, AAG.

48. Evelyn L. Petschek to George Kish, Dec. 30, 1950, Box 91, Folder 3, AAG.

49. Rebecca Boehling, "The Role of Culture in American Relations with Europe: The Case of the United States' Occupation of Germany," *Diplomatic History* 23, no. 1 (1999): 66.

50. Ibid.

51. Petschek to Kish, Dec. 30, 1950.

52. Robert E. Dickinson to Emil Meynen, Sept. 29, 1949, Doc. 781-8/763, LIfL. Also see John K. Wright to Emil Meynen, Oct. 3, 1949, Doc. 781-8/762, LIfL, and Thomas R. Smith to Emil Meynen, May 19, 1952, Doc. 762-5/502, LIfL.

53. Emil Meynen to Dr. Kessler, Feb. 17, 1950, Doc. 778-7/343, LIfL.

54. "Excerpt from Vol. XL, No. 3 (1950) of *The Geographical Review*," 1950 (specific date unavailable), Doc. 783-4/207, LIfL.

55. *Rundbrief* 23 (June 15, 1950), Doc. 773-12/590, LIfL.

56. Wardenga et al., *Der Verband deutscher Berufsgeographen*, 31. Also see Brogiato et al., "'Ich kann sie nicht mehr gebrachen, die Geographen, wie sie heute sind,'" 76.

57. Meynen to Kessler, Feb. 17, 1950.

58. Emil Meynen to Dr. Kessler, June 6, 1951, Doc. 778-7/298, LIfL.

59. Emil Meynen, "Die Situation der deutschen Landeskunde," *Tagungsberich und wissenschaftliche Abhandlungen, Deutscher Geographentag Frankfurt, 1951* (1951), Doc. 816-4/68, LIfL.

60. "Bericht über die Arbeitstagung der Landwirtschaftsgeographischen Arbeitsgemeinschaft am 25. und 26. April 1952 in Remagen," Doc. 804-7/332, LIfL.

61. "Niederschrift über die sechsts Mitgliederversammlung des Johann Gottfried Herder-Forschungsrates in Marburg/Lahn," May 2–3, 1952, Doc. 802-2/147, LIfL.

62. Larry Wolff, *Inventing Eastern Europe: The Map of Civilization on the Mind of the Enlightenment* (Stanford, CA: Stanford Univ. Press, 1994), 1.

63. Lutz Holzner, "The Role of History and Tradition in the Urban Geography of West Germany," *Annals of the Association of American Geographers* 60, no. 2 (1970): 322.

64. Berdahl, *Where the World Ended*, 144.

65. Ibid., 144–45.

66. For more on these arbitrarily drawn districts, see Karl-Heinz Hajna, "Zur Bildung der *Bezirke* in der DDR ab Mitte 1952," *Zeitschrift für Geschichtswissenschaft* 37, no. 4 (1989): 291–303.

67. Berdahl, *Where the World Ended*, 144–45.

5. Mapping and Selling the Two-State Solution

1. Eisenberg, *Drawing the Line*, 7.

2. Ibid., 9.

3. Ibid., 485.

4. Quoted in Richard Hartshorne, "U.W. Geography Professor Explains Why the Russians Pin Warmonger Label on Him," *Milwaukee Journal*, Sept. 10, 1950, Manuscript Collection 28, Box 8, Folder 12, AGSL.

5. Quoted in ibid.

6. Quoted in "UW Geographer Branded Top Foe by Russ. Magazine," *Milwaukee Sentinel*, July 30, 1950, Manuscript Collection 28, Box 8, Folder 12, AGSL.

7. The US Postal Service also withheld geographic material from George B. Cressey, who is quoted at the beginning of chapter 4. See Alan Reitman to George B. Cressey, Apr. 27, 1955, and Burton W. Adkinson to Theodore Herman, May 13, 1955, Box 83, Folder 1, AAG. Also see Burton W. Adkinson to George B. Cressey, Sept. 4, 1956, Box 69, Folder 4, AAG.

8. "'Europe Should Be Defended before Asia,' Says Geographer," *Columbia Missourian*, Apr. 17, 1951, Manuscript Collection 28, Box 8, Folder 12, AGSL.

9. Richard Hartshorne, "Analysis of the Heartland Theory," 1955, Manuscript Collection 28, Box 2, Folder 7, AGSL. One of the biggest problems with the Heartland Theory (Hartshorne admitted as much) was its underestimation of technological change, in particular the introduction of air power into geopolitical conflict.

10. Martin, *American Geography and Geographers*, 858.

11. J. Wreford Watson, "North America in the Changing World," *Journal of Geography* 57 (1958): 385, Manuscript Collection 28, Box 2, Folder 7, AGSL.

12. Emil Meynen to Richard H. Shryock, Jan. 5, 1948, Doc. 762-5/485, LIfL.

13. Emil Meynen, "Interrogation of January 30, 1947: My Personal Thoughts and Aspirations in Doing My Task since April 1945," Jan. 31, 1947, Doc. 781-6/448, LIfL.

14. Jakob Kaiser, "Address by Federal Minister for All-German Affairs Jakob Kaiser on the Need to Rehabilitate Zonal Border Areas Injured by Continuing Division (1 December 1952)," in *Documents on German Unity*, vol. 3 (Washington, DC: US Government Printing Office, 1953), 35.

15. For a great historical overview of the International Map of the World project, see Alastair Pearson, D. R. Fraser Taylor, Karen D. Kline, and Michael Heffernan, "Cartographical Ideals and Geopolitical Realities: International Maps of the World from the 1890s to the Present," *Canadian Geographer* 50, no. 2 (2006): 146–76.

16. See *Geographical and Cartographical Exhibition (International Section): Catalogue* (Rio de Janeiro: International Geographical Union, Brazilian National Committee, 1956).

17. See ibid. The Soviet Union also began sending delegates to the IGU Congress in 1956 (see V. V. Annenkov, "International Geographic Congresses," in *The Great Soviet Encyclopedia* [New York: Macmillan, 1973–83], 715–16).

18. Dr. Horst to Dr. J. Büdel, May 10, 1958, Doc. 812-4/58, LIfL.

19. "Report of the ad Hoc Statute Committee," May 1958, Doc. 812-4/47, LIfL.

20. Schelhaas, *Institutionelle Geographie*, 138.

21. Wilma B. Fairchild, "The Nineteenth International Geographical Congress, Stockholm, 1960," *Geographical Review* 51, no. 1 (1961): 110.

22. Erich Otremba to Herrn Bundesminister des Auswärtigen, "Stellung der Bundesrepublik Deutschland und der Sowjetischen Besatzungszone in der internationalen Geographen-Organisation," Aug. 9, 1960, Doc. 812-4/4, LIfL.

23. Emil Meynen to Bundesminister des Innern, Dec. 4, 1952, Doc. 778-7/181, LIfL. Meynen was often charged with making important changes to mappings of these corridors. In this particular example, he was instructed to make some alterations concerning the Hamburg–Berlin, Bückeburg–Berlin, and Frankfurt/Main–Berlin flight paths.

24. "Aerial Photography: Statement Made by the German Delegate at the Meeting of the Steering Committee on 3 December 1955," Dec. 3, 1955, RG 84, Stack 350 57/30/05–07, Box 7, NARA.

25. "Classification of Aerial Photographs," Nov. 30, 1955, RG 84, Stack 350 57/30/05–07, Box 1, NARA.

26. "German Forces Arrangements—Surveys," Nov. 12, 1955, RG 84, Stack 350 57/30/05–07, Box 14, NARA.

27. "Aerial Photography: Summary of the British Delegate's Statement at the Meeting of the Steering Committee on 5 December 1955," Dec. 14, 1955, RG 84, Stack 350 57/30/05–07, Box 1, NARA.

28. "Status Report on the New Forces Arrangements," Dec. 31, 1955, RG 84, Stack 350 57/30/05–07, Box 1, NARA.

29. "German Forces Arrangements—Surveys," Apr. 18, 1956, RG 84, Stack 350 57/30/05–07, Box 14, NARA.

30. John Hay to SeoState Washington, telegram, Feb. 6, 1959, RG 84, Stack 350 57/30/05–07, Box 1, NARA.

31. "Draft US–German Bilateral Administrative Agreement on Aerial Photography," July 1957, RG 84, Stack 350 57/30/05–07, Box 1, NARA.

32. Ray L. Thurston to David K. Bruce, Mar. 12, 1958, RG 84, Stack 350 56/35/04, Box 1, NARA.

33. Chauncy D. Harris, "Statement on the Sale and Exchange of the *Annals*," Mar. 26, 1959, Box 223, Folder 11, AAG.

34. Marie C. Goodman to Arch C. Gerlach, Aug. 11, 1958, Box 69, Folder 5, AAG.

35. *Rundbrief*, Feb.–Mar. 1953, Doc. 773-11/533, LIfL. Carl Troll was apparently very effective at convincing the Americans how important his work was while simultaneously making clear German dependence on American academic exchanges.

36. John A. Hostetler to Emil Meynen, Nov. 4, 1953, Doc. 761-7/679, LIfL.

37. Mildred B. Allport (US embassy, Office of Public Affairs) to the Association of American Geographers, Sept. 12, 1955, Box 69, Folder 2, AAG.

38. Even after the AAG exchanges were reevaluated and reapproved, material would still sometimes be lost owing to clerical error. An error could often mix up an exchange for years, as was the case with *Die Erde*, a publication maintained by the Berlin Geographical Society, a mix-up that was finally fixed after eight years in which *Die Erde* was sent to the AGS without reciprocation (Nordis Felland to Committee on Exchange of Publications, Association of American Geographers, Mar. 23, 1959, Box 69, Folder 5, AAG). The various name changes that the AfL went through, too, were problematic. After the name change from the Bundesanstalt für Landeskunde to the Institut für Landeskunde in 1959, the AAG publications stopped arriving until Meynen complained about the error and, of course, asked for back copies in 1960 (see Yetta G. Sternfeld to Emil Meynen, June 16, 1960, and Emil Meynen to Yetta G. Sternfeld, Sept. 26, 1960, Box 69, Folder 6, AAG).

39. Nordis Felland to Marie Goodman, Nov. 7, 1955, Box 69, Folder 2, AAG.

40. Marie C. Goodman, "The AAG Exchange Program—History," Box 69, Folder 2, AAG.

41. Felland to Goodman, Nov. 7, 1955.

42. Emil Meynen, "Institut für Landeskunde: Das erste Vierteljahrhundert seiner Tätigkeit, 1941–1966," *Berichte zur Deutschen Landeskunde* 36 (1966), Doc. 816-3/49, LIfL.

43. Dr. von Göler to Dr. F. Metz, July 31, 1952, Doc. 778-7/204, LIfL, and Dr. Dittrich to Dr. Schlösser, Nov. 13, 1952, Doc. 778-7/183, LIfL.

44. "Bundesanstalt für Landeskunde, Zentralarchiv für deutsche Landeskunde," June 9, 1953, Doc. 783-7/407, LIfL.

45. *Veröffentlichungen und Neuerscheinungen der Bundesanstalt für Landeskunde*, 1953, Doc. 786-3/153, LIfL.

46. Emil Meynen to Minister of Interior, "Militär-geographische Erhebungen der US-Armee," Feb. 24, 1954, Doc. 783-9/739, LIfL.

47. Emil Meynen, report, 1957–58, Doc. 786-6/424, LIfL.

48. "Geographische Landesaufnahme: Wirtschaftsräumliche Gliederung," June 1, 1956, Doc. 817-5/20, LIfL.

49. "ENTWURF: Wirtschaftsräumliche Gliederung," 1959, Doc. 785-1/1, LIfL.

50. It should be noted that the BfL considered the economic zones of Westfalen and Nordrhein to be two separate parts of one larger zone, but each of which deserved the same amount of study as the other zones listed here.

51. "ENTWURF für G.T.: Institut für Landeskunde," June 16, 1961, Doc. 786-5/334, LIfL.

52. Emil Meynen to D. W. McKenzie, Nov. 18, 1966, Doc. 762-9/22, LIfL.

53. Krygier and Wood, "Ce n'est pas le monde," 198–99.

54. For example, see Stephen P. Hanna and Vincent J. Del Casino Jr., "Introduction: Tourism Spaces, Mapped Representations, and the Practices of Identity," in *Mapping Tourism*, ed. Stephen P. Hanna and Vincent J. Del Casino Jr. (Minneapolis: Univ. of Minnesota Press, 2003), ix–xxvii, and Jonathan Culler, "The Semiotics of Tourism," in *Framing the Sign: Criticism and Its Institutions* (Norman: Univ. of Oklahoma Press, 1988), 153–67.

55. Edward Bernays, *Propaganda* (1928; reprint, New York: Ig, 2004), 44–45.

56. Edward Bernays, *Speak Up for Democracy! What You Can Do—a Practical Plan of Action for Every American Citizen* (New York: Viking Press, 1940), 20. It should be noted that Bernays was "no democrat" and "expressed little respect for the average person's ability to think out, understand, or act upon the world in which he or she lives" (Stuart Ewen, *PR! A Social History of Spin* [New York: Basic Books, 1996], 10).

57. Bernays, *Speak Up for Democracy!* 80.

58. Edward Bernays, *Public Relations* (Norman: Univ. of Oklahoma Press, 1952), 217.

59. Ibid., 293.

60. Brian C. Etheridge, "The Anti-German Wave, Public Diplomacy, and Intercultural Relations in Cold War America," in *Decentering America*, ed. Jessica C. E. Gienow-Hecht (Providence, RI: Berghahn Books, 2008), 79.

61. Ibid.

62. Scott M. Cutlip, *The Unseen Power: Public Relations. A History* (Hillsdale, NJ: Lawrence Erlbaum Associates, 1994), 73–74.

63. International Map Company, Inc., to W. L. Rehm, Aug. 25, 1942, RG 226, Stack 190 5/30/7, Box 229, NARA.

64. Rand McNally & Co. to Mr. William M. Drummond, Apr. 12, 1943, RG 226, Stack 190 5/30/7, Box 229, NARA.

65. D. W. G. to Mr. Charles V. Crittenden, Dec. 14, 1943, RG 226, Stack 190 5/30/7, Box 229, NARA.

66. "Public Relations Organization," Apr. 30, 1941, and "Memorandum for Colonel Hardin: Press Relations," Nov. 21, 1941, RG 77, Stack 390 1/07/02–03, Box 1, NARA.

67. "Memorandum: Reorganization of Public Relations Agencies," Sept. 21, 1942, RG 77, Stack 390 1/07/02–03, Box 1, NARA.

68. "Work Order No. DGN-3801: Demonstration of Equipment for Members of the Press," Aug. 17, 1944, RG 77, Stack 390 1/07/02–03, Box 2, NARA.

69. "Outgoing Classified Message No. WAR 84979," June 30, 1948, RG 335, Stack 490 8/35/03–07, Box 1, NARA.

70. Quoted in Rainer Epbinder, "The Role of Inter Nationes in Propagating an Image of Germany Abroad," in *Images of Germany: Perceptions and Conceptions*, ed. Peter M. Daly, Hans Walter Frischkopf, Trudis E. Goldsmith-Reber, and Horst Richter (New York: Peter Lang, 2000), 11, emphasis in original.

71. "Memorandum Concerning a Plan of Public Relations for Advancing the Interests of WEST GERMANY," Feb. 25, 1953, appendix A, p. 5, B145/777, Band (Bd.) I, Bundesarchiv (BArch), Koblenz, Germany.

72. Cutlip, *Unseen Power*, 83.

73. "Memorandum on: Editorial Publicity in the United States for the Federal Republic of Germany," Dec. 19, 1952, 2–3, B145/777, Bd. I, BArch.

74. Stephen Goerl to Willi Ritter, Chief of Press Department—Federal Republic of Germany, Sept. 10, 1952, 1–2, B145/777, Bd. I, BArch.

75. "Beglaubigte Abschrift: Contract between the Federal Republic of Germany and the Roy Bernard Co., Inc.," Jan. 8, 1952, 3, B145/3226, Bd. I, BArch.

76. Ibid., emphasis added.

77. Ibid., 3.

78. Bernard Gittelson to Baron Axel von dem Bussche, FRG embassy Press and Information Office, July 18, 1955, 1, B145/1277, Bd. I, BArch.

79. Herb, *Under the Map*, 184–85. Only in the 1980s would such maps again become regularly published in the FRG.

80. "Amerika wird das geteilte Deutschland gezeigt," unknown periodical, June 9, 1956, B145/1277, Bd. I, BArch.

81. Gittelson to Baron von dem Bussche, July 18, 1955.

82. FRG embassy Press and Information Office, "New Map of Germany," 1956, call no. 640 B-[1956]a, AGSL.

83. Mr. Charles E. Campbell to Mr. Georg von Lilienfeld, Aug. 20, 1952, 1–3, B145/775, Bd. I, BArch.

84. Ibid., 3.

85. "The United States Quartered / Democracy in Peril," 6, B145 1277, Bd. I, BArch.

86. Charles E. Campbell to Dr. Richard Mönnig, Sept. 16, 1952, B145 1277, Bd. I, BArch.

87. "The Foreign Legion of U.S. Public Relations," 17, B145 9764, Bd. III, BArch.

88. For more on the term *imagined communities*, see Anderson, *Imagined Communities*.

89. Etheridge, "Anti-German Wave," 81, 85.

90. Douglas Cater and Walter Pincus, "The Foreign Legion of U.S. Public Relations," *The Reporter*, Dec. 22, 1960, B145/9764, Bd. III, BArch. These concerns did not end with the *The Reporter*'s exposé. The use of PR in influencing foreign governments and American foreign policy remained a "hot topic" throughout the 1960s. One of the more interesting and least investigated incidents was the "Julius Klein Affair" of 1963, when the US Senate Committee on Foreign Affairs grilled Julius Klein, a prominent lobbyist for the organization Jewish War Veterans and a PR executive, over his relationship with the West German government and Konrad Adenauer. Many of Klein's papers can be found in the Wisconsin State Historical Archive, Madison.

91. Guntram Henrik Herb, "Double Vision: Territorial Strategies in the Construction of National Identities in Germany, 1949–1979," *Annals of the Association of American Geographers* 94, no. 1 (2004): 149–50.

92. Ibid., 158.

93. The man, Rudolf Urban, died one month later from complications caused by the injury from this jump.

94. Pertti Ahonen, *Death at the Berlin Wall* (New York: Oxford Univ. Press, 2011), 29–31, 38.

95. Pertti Ahonen, "The Curious Case of Werner Weinhold: Escape, Death, and Contested Legitimacy at the German–German Border," *Central European History* 45, no. 1 (2012): 80.

96. According to a poll of West Germans taken in 1952, 51 percent of the population claimed to value "security from the Russians" over "the unity of Germany." Each subsequent year the poll was taken, an increasing number of Germans prioritized their security over reunification. For more on political polling and German reunification, see Anja Kruke, "Western Integration vs. Reunification? Analysing the Polls of the 1950s," *German Politics and Society* 25, no. 2 (2007): 43–67.

6. Conclusion

1. Wolff, *Inventing Eastern Europe*, 3.

2. Mechtild Rössler, "Berlin or Bonn? National Identity and the Question of the German Capital," in *Geography and National Identity*, ed. David Hooson (Cambridge, MA: Blackwell, 1994), 94.

3. Ibid., 99. The vote count was 338 to 320 in favor of Berlin.

4. Carsten Volkery, "The Iron Lady's Views on German Reunification: 'The Germans Are Back!'" *Der Spiegel Online*, Sept. 11, 2009, at http://www.spiegel.de/international/europe/the-iron-lady-s-views-on-german-reunification-the-germans-are-back-a-648364.html.

5. Quoted in Klaus Wiegrefe, "Germany's Unlikely Diplomatic Triumph: An Inside Look at the Reunification Negotiations," *Der Spiegel Online*, Sept. 29, 2010, at http://www.spiegel.de/international/germany/germany-s-unlikely-diplomatic-triumph-an-inside-look-at-the-reunification-negotiations-a-719848-druck.html.

6. This type of rhetoric, however, has been employed throughout the early 2000s (especially in Great Britain). In 2006, for example, British newspapers claimed that a European Union initiative to encourage transnational tourism and environmentalism was a "German-led 'conspiracy of cartographers' [designed] to give Brussels the power to change national boundaries" (quoted in Mark Monmonier, *No Dig, No Fly, No Go: How Maps Restrict and Control* [Chicago: Univ. of Chicago Press, 2010], 31).

7. A. Dirk Moses, *German Intellectuals and the Nazi Past* (New York: Cambridge Univ. Press, 2007), 281–82. For an excellent analysis of how Germany's "multicultural" World Cup team influenced and was influenced by German identity, see Maria Stehle and Beverly M. Weber, "German Soccer, the 2010 World Cup, and Multicultural Belonging," *German Studies Review* 36, no. 1 (2013): 103–24.

8. Joshua Hagen, "Redrawing the Imagined Map of Europe: The Rise and Fall of the 'Center,'" *Political Geography* 22 (2003): 508.

9. D. J. Ziegler, "Post-Communist Eastern Europe and the Cartography of Independence," *Political Geography* 21 (2002): 677, 679–80.

10. Martin, *All Possible Worlds*, 437.

11. See Matthew D. Mingus, "Disseminating the Maps of a Postwar World: A Case Study of the University of Florida's Participation in Government Depository Programs," *Journal of Map and Geography Libraries* 8, no. 1 (2012): 5–20.

12. George L. Mosse, *Nationalism and Sexuality: Respectability and Abnormal Sexuality in Modern Europe* (New York: Fertig, 1985), 181.

13. Mark Mazower, *Dark Continent: Europe's Twentieth Century* (New York: Knopf, 1998), 401.

14. Eric Hobsbawm has also made this point in *Nations and Nationalism since 1780: Programme, Myth, Reality* (New York: Cambridge Univ. Press, 1992), although not specifically regarding mapmaking. For Hobsbawm, late-twentieth-century nationalism became a means to further developments and was no longer an end to itself. The postwar period was the clear turning point for this shift.

Bibliography

Archives

American Association of Geographers, Univ. of Wisconsin, Milwaukee.
American Geographical Society Library, Univ. of Wisconsin, Milwaukee.
Bundesarchiv, Koblenz, Germany.
Leibniz-Institut für Länderkunde, Archiv für Geographie, Leipzig, Germany.
Martin, Geoffrey. Personal archive, New Haven, CT.
National Archives and Records Administration, Washington, DC.
National Archives of the United Kingdom, London.
University of Florida Library and Archive, Gainesville.
University of Nebraska Library and Archive, Lincoln.

Published Sources

Ahonen, Pertti. "The Curious Case of Wener Weinhold: Escape, Death, and Contested Legitimacy at the German–German Border." *Central European History* 45, no. 1 (2012): 79–101.
———. *Death at the Berlin Wall.* New York: Oxford Univ. Press, 2011.
Anderson, Benedict. *Imagined Communities: Reflections on the Origin and Spread of Nationalism.* 1983. Rev. ed. New York: Verso, 2006.
Annenkov, V. V. "International Geographic Congresses." In *The Great Soviet Encyclopedia*, 715–16. New York: Macmillan, 1973–83.
Bachmann, Veit. "From Jackboots to Birkenstocks: The Civilianisation of German Geopolitics in the Twentieth Century." *Tijdschrift voor Economische en Sociale Geografie* 101, no. 3 (2009): 320–32.
Banta, Frank G. "A Role in the Education Branch of the Office of the Military Government for Germany (US), 1945–1949." In *Hochschuloffiziere und Wiederaufbau des Hochschulwesens in Westdeutschland, 1945–1952*, vol.

2: *Die US-Zone*, edited by Manfred Heinemann and Ullrich Schneider, 35–42. Hannover: Veröffentlichung aus dem Forschungsschwerpunkt "Zeitgeschichte von Bildung und Wissenschaft" der Universität Hannover, 1990.

Barnes, Trevor J. "Geographical Intelligence: American Geographers and Research and Analysis in the Office of Strategic Services, 1941–1945." *Journal of Historical Geography* 32, no. 1 (2006): 149–68.

Barten, Heinrich, ed. *Länder und Völker Erdkundliches Unterrichtswerk*. Vol. 5: *Deutschland, die Mitte Europas*. Stuttgart: Ernst Klett, 1951.

———, ed. *Länder und Völker Erdkundliches Unterrichtswerk*. Vol. 5: *Deutschland, die Mitte Europas*. Stuttgart: Ernst Klett, 1954.

———, ed. *Länder und Völker Erdkundliches Unterrichtswerk*. Vol. 5: *Deutschland, die Mitte Europas*. Stuttgart: Ernst Klett, 1956.

Becker, Hellmut. "Retrospective View from the German Side." In *The British in Germany: Education Reconstruction after 1945*, edited by Arthur Hearnden, 268–82. London: Hamish Hamilton, 1978.

Benjamin, Walter. *The Arcades Project*. Translated by Howard Eiland and Kevin McLaughlin. Cambridge, MA: Belknap Press of Harvard Univ. Press, 1999.

Berdahl, Daphne. *Where the World Ended: Re-unification and Identity in the German Borderland*. Berkeley: Univ. of California Press, 1999.

Bernays, Edward. *Propaganda*. 1928. Reprint. New York: Ig, 2004.

———. *Public Relations*. Norman: Univ. of Oklahoma Press, 1952.

———. *Speak Up for Democracy! What You Can Do—a Practical Plan of Action for Every American Citizen*. New York: Viking Press, 1940.

Bird, Geoffrey. "The Universities." In *The British in Germany: Educational Reconstruction after 1945*, edited by Arthur Hearnden, 146–57. London: Hamish Hamilton, 1978.

Black, Lloyd D. "Further Notes on German Geography." *Geographical Review* 37, no. 1 (1947): 147–48.

Blackbourn, David. *History of Germany, 1780–1918: The Long Nineteenth Century*. 2nd ed. Malden, MA: Blackwell, 2003.

Blackbourn, David, and Geoff Eley. *The Peculiarities of German History: Bourgeois Society and Politics in Nineteenth-Century Germany*. New York: Oxford Univ. Press, 1984.

Boehling, Rebecca. "The Role of Culture in American Relations with Europe: The Case of the United States' Occupation of Germany." *Diplomatic History* 23, no. 1 (1999): 57–69.

Braunreuther, Kurt. "Über die Bedeutung der Physiokratischen Bewegung in Deutschland in der Zweiten Hälfte des 18. Jahrhunderts." *Wissenschaftliche Zeitschrift der Humboldt-Universität zu Berlin* 5, no. 1 (1955): 15–65.

Breuilly, John. "The German National Question and 1848." *History Today* 48, no. 5 (1998): 13–20.

Brogiato, Heinz Peter, Dirk Hänsgen, Norman Henniges, Bruno Schelhaas, and Ute Wardenga. "'Ich kann sie nicht mehr gebrauchen, die Geographen, wie sie heute sind': Zur Gründungsgeschichte des DVAG." *Standort* 34 (2010): 74–79.

Brubaker, Rogers. *Citizenship and Nationhood in France and Germany.* Cambridge, MA: Harvard Univ. Press, 1998.

Buisseret, David. "Monarchs, Ministers, and Maps in France before the Accession of Louis XIV." In *Monarchs, Ministers, and Maps: The Emergence of Cartography as a Tool of Government in Early Modern Europe,* edited by David Buisseret, 99–123. Chicago: Univ. of Chicago Press, 1992.

Butzer, Karl W. "Practicing Geography in a Totalitarian State: (Re)Casting Carl Troll as a Nazi Collaborator?" *Erde* 135, no. 2 (2004): 223–31.

The Council of Foreign Ministers: Documents on Germany, Sessions I–VI, 1945–1949. Washington, DC: Division of Historical Policy Research, US Department of State, Mar. 1950.

Culler, Jonathan. *Framing the Sign: Criticism and Its Institutions.* Norman: Univ. of Oklahoma Press, 1988.

Cutlip, Scott M. *The Unseen Power: Public Relations. A History.* Hillsdale, NJ: Lawrence Erlbaum Associates, 1994.

Davies, Edith. "British Policy and the Schools." In *The British in Germany: Educational Reconstruction after 1945,* edited by Arthur Hearnden, 95–107. London: Hamish Hamilton, 1978.

Davis, Kathleen Southwell. "The Problem of Textbooks." In *The British in Germany: Educational Reconstruction after 1945,* edited by Arthur Hearnden, 108–30. London: Hamish Hamilton, 1978.

Deleuze, Gilles, and Félix Guattari. *On the Line.* Translated by John Johnston. New York: Semiotext(e), 1983.

Documents on German Unity. Vol. 3. Washington, DC: US Government Printing Office, 1953.

Dorpalen, Andreas. *The World of General Haushofer: Geopolitics in Action.* New York: Farrar and Rinehart, 1942.

Ehlers, Eckart. "German Geography 1945–1992: Organization and Institutional Aspects." In *40 Years After: German Geography: Development, Trends, and Prospects, 1952–1992*, edited by Eckart Ehlers, 11–32. Bonn: Deutsche Forschungsgemeinschaft, 1992.

Eisenberg, Carolyn. *Drawing the Line: The American Decision to Divide Germany, 1944–1949*. New York: Cambridge Univ. Press, 1996.

Eisfeld, Rainer. "Mitteleuropa in Historical and Contemporary Perspective." *German Politics and Society* 28 (Spring 1993): 39–52.

Eley, Geoffrey. *From Nazism to Unification*. Boston: Allen and Unwin, 1985.

Epbinder, Rainer. "The Role of Inter Nationes in Propagating an Image of Germany Abroad." In *Images of Germany: Perceptions and Conceptions*, edited by Peter M. Daly, Hans Walter Frischkopf, Trudie E. Goldsmith-Reber, and Horst Richter, 11–17. New York: Peter Lang, 2000.

Etheridge, Brian C. "The Anti-German Wave, Public Diplomacy, and Intercultural Relations in Cold War America." In *Decentering America*, edited by Jessica C. E. Gienow-Hecht, 73–106. Providence, RI: Berghahn Books, 2008.

Evans, Richard J. "The New Nationalism and the Old History: Perspectives on the West German *Historikerstreit*." *Journal of Modern History* 59, no. 4 (1987): 761–97.

Ewen, Stuart. *PR! A Social History of Spin*. New York: Basic Books, 1996.

Fahlbusch, Michael. "Emil Meynen." In *Handbuch der völkischen Wissenschaften: Personen-Institutionen-Forschungsprogramme-Stiftungen*, 422–28. Munich: Saur, 2008.

Fairchild, Wilma B. "The Nineteenth International Geographical Congress, Stockholm, 1960." *Geographical Review* 51, no. 1 (1961): 109–13.

Fox, Robert. *Teubners Erdkundliches Unterrichtswerk für höhere Lehranstalten*. Vol. 2: *Europa*. Leipzig: Teubner, 1931.

Franklin, William M. "Zonal Boundaries and Access to Berlin." *World Politics* 16, no. 1 (1963): 1–31.

Führ, Christoph. *The German Education System since 1945: Outlines and Problems*. Bonn: Inter Nationes, 1997.

Gay, Peter. *Weimar Culture: The Outsider and Insider*. Westport, CT: Greenwood Press, 1981.

Gellner, Ernest. *Nations and Nationalism*. 1983. 2nd ed. Malden, MA: Blackwell, 2006.

Geographical and Cartographical Exhibition (International Section): Catalogue. Rio de Janeiro: International Geographical Union, Brazilian National Committee, 1956.

"A Geography Lesson for Young Germany." *New York Times*, Mar. 17, 1935.

"Geography-Teaching in Germany." *Science* 7, no. 161 (1886): 209–10.

Giles, Geoffrey. *Students and National Socialism in Germany*. Princeton, NJ: Princeton Univ. Press, 1985.

Gimbel, John. *The American Occupation of Germany: Politics and Military, 1945–1949*. Stanford, CA: Stanford Univ. Press, 1968.

———. *A German Community under American Occupation: Marburg, 1945–1952*. Stanford, CA: Stanford Univ. Press, 1961.

———. *Science, Technology, and Reparations: Exploitation and Plunder in Postwar Germany*. Stanford, CA: Stanford Univ. Press, 1990.

———. "Science, Technology, and Reparations in Postwar Germany." In *American Policy and the Reconstruction of West Germany, 1945–1955*, edited by Jeffry M. Diefendorf, Axel Frohn, and Hermann-Josef Rupieper, 175–96. Washington, DC: German Historical Institute, 1993.

Grace, Alonzo G. *Basic Elements of Educational Reconstruction in Germany.* Washington, DC: American Council on Education, 1949.

Hackmann, Jörg. "German East or Polish West? Historiographical Discourse on the German–Polish Overlap between Confrontation and Reconciliation, 1772–2000." In *Disputed Territories and Shared Pasts: Overlapping National Histories in Modern Europe*, edited by Tibor Frank and Frank Hadler, 92–124. New York: Palgrave Macmillan, 2011.

Hagen, Joshua. "Redrawing the Imagined Map of Europe: The Rise and Fall of the 'Center.'" *Political Geography* 22 (2003): 489–517.

Hajna, Karl-Heinz. "Zur Bildung der *Bezirke* in der DDR ab Mitte 1952." *Zeitschrift für Geschichtswissenschaft* 37, no. 4 (1989): 291–303.

Hamerow, Theodore S. *Restoration, Revolution, Reaction: Economics and Politics in Germany, 1815–1871*. Princeton, NJ: Princeton Univ. Press, 1958.

Handbuch der völkischen Wissenschaften: Personen-Institutionen-Forschungsprogramme-Stiftungen. Munich: Saur, 2008.

Hanna, Stephen P., and Vincent J. Del Casino Jr. "Introduction: Tourism Spaces, Mapped Representations, and the Practices of Identity." In *Mapping Tourism*, edited by Stephen P. Hanna and Vincent J. Del Casino Jr., ix–xxvii. Minneapolis: Univ. of Minnesota Press, 2003.

Hearnden, Arthur, ed. *The British in Germany: Educational Reconstruction after 1945*. London: Hamish Hamilton, 1978.

———. "Education in the British Zone." In *The British in Germany: Education Reconstruction after 1945*, edited by Arthur Hearnden, 11–45. London: Hamish Hamilton, 1978.

———. *Education in the Two Germanies*. Boulder, CO: Westview Press, 1974.

Heinemann, Manfred, and Ullrich Schneider, eds. *Hochschuloffiziere und Wiederaufbau des Hochschulwesens in Westdeutschland, 1945–1952*. Vol. 2: *Die US-Zone*. Hannover: Veröffentlichung aus dem Forschungsschwerpunkt "Zeitgeschichte von Bildung und Wissenschaft" der Universität Hannover, 1990.

Herb, Guntram Henrik. "Double Vision: Territorial Strategies in the Construction of National Identities in Germany, 1949–1979." *Annals of the Association of American Geographers* 94, no. 1 (2004): 140–64.

———. *Under the Map of Germany: Nationalism and Propaganda, 1918–1945*. New York: Routledge, 1997.

Hesse, Carla. *The Other Enlightenment: How French Women Became Modern*. Princeton, NJ: Princeton Univ. Press, 2001.

Hobsbawm, Eric. *Nations and Nationalism since 1780: Programme, Myth, Reality*. New York: Cambridge Univ. Press, 1992.

Holzner, Lutz. "The Role of History and Tradition in the Urban Geography of West Germany." *Annals of the Association of American Geographers* 60, no. 2 (1970): 315–39.

Howard, Michael Eliot. *The Franco-Prussian War: The German Invasion of France, 1870–1871*. New York: Macmillan, 1961.

Hudson, Alice. "The New York Public Library's Map Division Goes to War, 1941–1945." *Bulletin: Special Library Association, Geography and Map Division* 182 (Spring 1996): 2–25.

Judson, Pieter M. *Guardians of the Nation: Activists on the Language Frontiers of Imperial Austria*. Cambridge, MA: Harvard Univ. Press, 2006.

Judt, Tony. *Postwar: A History of Europe since 1945*. New York: Penguin, 2005.

Jürgensen, Kurt. "The Concept and Practice of 'Re-education' in Germany, 1945–50." In *The Political Re-education of Germany & Her Allies after World War II*, edited by Nicholas Pronay and Keith Wilson, 83–96. Totowa, NJ: Barnes & Noble Books, 1985.

Kaiser, Jakob. "Address by Federal Minister for All-German Affairs Jakob Kaiser on the Need to Rehabilitate Zonal Border Areas Injured by Continuing

Division (1 December 1952)." In *Documents on German Unity*, vol. 3, 35. Washington, DC: US Government Printing Office, 1953.

Karl, Ernst, and Franz Schneider. *Geographie Welkunde Lehr- und Arbeitsbuch für deutsche Schulen: Deutschland, eine geographische Zusammenschau.* Baden: Badenia, 1953.

Kettenacker, Lothar. *Germany since 1945.* New York: Oxford Univ. Press, 1997.

———. "The Planning of 'Re-education' during the Second World War." In *The Political Re-education of Germany & Her Allies after World War II*, edited by Nicholas Pronay and Keith Wilson, 59–81. Totowa, NJ: Barnes & Noble Books, 1985.

Kiss, George. "Political Geography into Geopolitics: Recent Trends in Germany." *Geographical Review* 32, no. 4 (Oct. 1942): 632–45.

Kjellén, Rudolf. *Der Staat als Lebensform.* Leipzig: Hirzel, 1917.

Knowles, Anne Kelly. *Placing History: How Maps, Spatial Data, and GIS Are Changing Historical Scholarship.* Redlands, CA: ESRI Press, 2008.

Kocka, Jürgen. "German History before Hitler: The Debate about the German *Sonderweg*." *Journal of Contemporary History* 23, no. 1 (1988): 3–16.

Kollen, Christine, Wangyal Shawa, and Mary Larsgaard. *Cartographic Citations: A Style Guide.* 2nd ed. Chicago: American Library Association, 2010.

Kreuzer, Gustav, and Eduard Müller-Temme. *Geographische Weltkunde Lehr- und Arbeitsbuch für deutsche Schulen: Deutschland in Europa.* Baden: Badenia, 1958.

Kruke, Anja. "Western Integration vs. Reunification? Analysing the Polls of the 1950s." *German Politics and Society* 25, no. 2 (2007): 43–67.

Krygier, John, and Denis Wood. "Ce n'est pas le monde (This Is Not the World)." In *Rethinking Maps*, edited by Martin Dodge, Rob Kitchin, and Chris Perkins, 189–219. New York: Routledge, 2009.

Lang, Herbert. *Deutschlands Vermessungs- und Kartenwesen Aspekte seiner Entwicklung seit Reichsgründung 1871.* Dresden: Schütze, Engler, Weber, 2008.

Lansing, Charles B. *From Nazism to Communism: German Schoolteachers under Two Dictatorships.* Cambridge, MA: Harvard Univ. Press, 2010.

Lefebvre, Henri. *The Production of Space.* Translated by Donald Nicholson-Smith. Malden, MA: Blackwell, 1991.

Liddell, Helen. "Education in Occupied Germany: A Field Study." In *L'education de l'Allemagne occupée*, edited by Helen Liddell, 95–148. Paris: Librairie Marcel Riviére et Cie, 1949.

Madajczyk, Piotr. "Generalplan Ost." In *Handbuch der völkischen Wissen-schaften: Personen-Institutionen-Forschungsprogramme-Stiftungen*, 187–93. Munich: Saur, 2008.

Martin, Geoffrey. *All Possible Worlds: A History of Geographical Ideas*. New York: Oxford Univ. Press, 2005.

———. *American Geography and Geographers: Toward Geographical Science*. New York: Oxford Univ. Press, 2015.

———. *The Life and Thought of Isaiah Bowman*. Hamden, CT: Archon Books, 1980.

———. *Mark Jefferson, Geographer*. Ypsilanti: Eastern Michigan Univ. Press, 1968.

Matloff, Maurice. *Strategic Planning for Coalition Warfare, 1943–1944*. Washington, DC: Office of the Chief of Military History, US Department of the Army, 1959.

Mazower, Mark. *Dark Continent: Europe's Twentieth Century*. New York: Knopf, 1998.

Meyer, Henry Cord. *Mitteleuropa in German Thought and Action, 1815–1945*. The Hague: Martinus Nijhoff, 1955.

Meynen, Emil. *Amtliche und private Ortsnamenverzeichnisse des Großdeutschen Reiches und der mittel- und osteuropäischen Nachbargebiete, 1910–1941*. Leipzig: Hirzel, 1942.

Mingus, Matthew D. "Disseminating the Maps of a Postwar World: A Case Study of the University of Florida's Participation in Government Depository Programs." *Journal of Map and Geography Libraries* 8, no. 1 (2012): 5–20.

Monmonier, Mark. *How to Lie with Maps*. 2nd ed. Chicago: Univ. of Chicago Press, 1996.

———. "Mapping under the Third Reich: Nazi Restrictions on Map Content and Distribution." *Coordinates*, Series B, no. 2 (Jan. 2005): 1–4.

———. *No Dig, No Fly, No Go: How Maps Restrict and Control*. Chicago: Univ. of Chicago Press, 2010.

Moses, A. Dirk. *German Intellectuals and the Nazi Past*. New York: Cambridge Univ. Press, 2007.

Mosley, Philip E. "The Occupation of Germany: New Light on How the Zones Were Drawn." *Foreign Affairs* 28, no. 4 (1950): 580–604.

Mosse, George L. *Nationalism and Sexuality: Respectability and Abnormal Sexuality in Modern Europe*. New York: Fertig, 1985.

Müller, Winfried. *Schulpolitik in Bayern im Spannungsfeld von Kulturbürokratie und Besatzungsmacht, 1945–1949*. Munich: Oldenbourg, 1995.

Murdock, Caitlin. *Changing Places: Society, Culture, and Territory in the Saxon-Bohemian Borderlands, 1870–1946*. Ann Arbor: Univ. of Michigan Press, 2010.

Murphy, David Thomas. *The Heroic Earth: Geopolitical Thought in Weimar Germany, 1918–1933*. Kent, OH: Kent State Univ. Press, 1997.

———. "Hitler's Geostrategist? The Myth of Karl Haushofer and the 'Institut für Geopolitik.'" *The Historian* 76, no. 1 (2014): 1–25.

———. "A Sum of the Most Wonderful Things: 'Raum,' Geopolitics, and the German Tradition of Environmental Determinism, 1900–1933." *History of European Ideas* 25, no. 5 (1999): 121–33.

Murphy, Mary. "History of the Army Map Service Map Collection." In *Federal Government Map Collecting: A Brief History*, edited by Richard W. Stephenson, 1–6. Washington, DC: Special Libraries Association, 1969.

Murray, George. "The Training of Teachers." In *The British in Germany: Educational Reconstruction after 1945*, edited by Arthur Hearnden, 131–45. London: Hamish Hamilton, 1978.

Naimark, Norman M. *Fires of Hatred: Ethnic Cleansing in Twentieth-Century Europe*. Cambridge, MA: Harvard Univ. Press, 2001.

Natter, Wolfgang. "Geopolitics in Germany, 1919–1945: Karl Haushofer and the *Zeitschrift für Geopolitik*." In *A Companion to Political Geography*, edited by John Agnew, Katharyne Mitchell, and Gerard Toal, 187–202. Malden, MA: Blackwell, 2003.

Nicoletti, Frank T. "U.S. Army Topographic Command College Depository Program." *Bulletin: Special Library Association, Geography and Map Division* 86 (Dec. 1971): 2–8.

Nipperdey, Thomas. *Germany from Napoleon to Bismarck*. Translated by Daniel Nolan. Princeton, NJ: Princeton Univ. Press, 1996.

Office of Military Government for Germany, Civil Administration Division, comp. *Documents on the Creation of the German Federal Constitution*. Berlin: Office of Military Government for Germany (US), Sept. 1, 1949.

Office of Strategic Services, Division of Map Intelligence and Cartography. *April 7, 1947 Report: Allan Evans (Director, Office of Intelligence Research) to Mr. C. Hitchcock (American Geographical Society): "German Cartographic and Map Collecting Agencies: Controlling Laws and Regulatory Statutes."* Washington, DC: Office of Strategic Services, Feb. 5, 1947.

Olson, Everett C., and Agnes Whitmarsh. *Foreign Maps*. New York: Harper and Brothers, 1944.

Otte, Max. A *Rising Middle Power? German Foreign Polity in Transformation, 1989–1999*. New York: St. Martin's Press, 2000.

Pearson, Alastair, D. R. Fraser Taylor, Karen D. Kline, and Michael Heffernan. "Cartographical Ideals and Geopolitical Realities: International Maps of the World from the 1890s to the Present." *Canadian Geographer* 50, no. 2 (2006): 146–76.

Peterson, Edward N. *The American Occupation of Germany: Retreat to Victory*. Detroit: Wayne State Univ. Press, 1977.

Pickles, John. A *History of Spaces: Cartographic Reason, Mapping, and the Geocoded World*. New York: Routledge, 2004.

Plewe, Ernst. "Heinrich Schmitthenner, 3.5.1887–18.2.1957." *Mitteilungen Universitätsbund Marburg* 2–3 (1957): 3–19.

Presner, Todd. "Remapping German-Jewish Studies: Benjamin, Cartography, Modernity." *German Quarterly* 82, no. 3 (2009): 293–315.

Proceedings: Eighth General Assembly and Seventeenth International Congress, Washington, DC, Aug. 8–15, 1952. Washington, DC: National Academy of Sciences, 1952.

Pronay, Nicholas, and Keith Wilson, eds. *The Political Re-education of Germany & Her Allies after World War II*. Totowa, NJ: Barnes & Noble Books, 1985.

Puhle, Hans-Jürgen. "Die neue Ruhelosigkeit: Michael Stürmers nationalpolitischer Revisionismus." *Geschichte und Gesellschaft* 13, no. 3 (1987): 382–99.

"Ratzel's 'Political Geography.'" *Geographical Journal* 13, no. 2 (1899): 171–73.

Reisser, Wesley. *The* Black Book: *Woodrow Wilson's Secret Plan for Peace*. New York: Lexington Books, 2012.

Remy, Steven P. *The Heidelberg Myth: The Nazification and Denazification of a German University*. Cambridge, MA: Harvard Univ. Press, 2002.

Römer, Karl. "Die Geburtsstunde Baden-Württembergs: Die Gesetzgebung zur Bildung des Südweststaates." *Zeitschrift für Württembergische Landesgeschichte* 66 (2007): 475–96.

Rössler, Mechtild. "'Area Research' and 'Spatial Planning' from the Weimar Republic to the German Federal Republic: Creating a Society with a Spatial Order under National Socialism." In *Science, Technology, and National Socialism*, edited by Monika Renneberg and Mark Walker, 126–38. New York: Cambridge Univ. Press, 1994.

———. "Berlin or Bonn? National Identity and the Question of the German Capital." In *Geography and National Identity*, edited by David Hooson, 92–103. Cambridge, MA: Blackwell, 1994.

———. "Geography and Area Planning under National Socialism." In *Science in the Third Reich*, edited by Margit Szöllösi-Janze, 59–78. New York: Berg, 2001.

———. "Secret Nazi Plans for Eastern Europe: Geography and Spatial Planning in the Third Reich." *Treballs de la Societat Catalana de Geografia* 35 (July 1993): 203–10.

Sammartino, Annemarie H. *The Impossible Border: Germany and the East, 1914–1922.* Ithaca, NY: Cornell Univ. Press, 2010.

Sandner, Gerhard. "Die unmittelbare Nachkriegszeit: Personelle, institutionelle und fachlichinhaltliche Aspekte 1945–1950." In *Kontinuität und Diskontinuität der deutschen Geographie in Umbruchphasen: Studien zur Geschichte der Geographie*, edited by Ute Wardenga and Ingrid Hönsch, 141–50. Munster: Institut für Geographie der Westfalischen Wilhelm-Universität, 1995.

Schelhaas, Bruno. *Institutionelle Geographie auf dem Weg in die wissenschaftspolitische Systempaltung: Die Geographische Gesellschaft der DDR bis zur III. Hochschul- und Akademie-reform, 1968/69.* Leipzig: Leibniz-Institut für Länderkunde, 2004.

Schelhaas, Bruno, and Ingrid Hönsch. "History of German Geography: Worldwide Reputation and Strategies of Nationalisation and Institutionalisation." In *Geography: Discipline, Profession, and Subject since 1870*, edited by Gary Dunbar, 9–44. Norwell, MA: Kluwer Academic, 2001.

Schissler, Hanna, and Yasemin Nuhoglu Soysal, eds. *The Nation, Europe, and the World: Textbooks and Curricula in Transition.* New York: Berghahn Books, 2005.

Schivelbusch, Wolfgang. *The Railway Journey: The Industrialization of Time and Space in the 19th Century.* Berkeley: Univ. of California Press, 1986.

Schneider, Ullrich. "The Reconstruction of the Universities in American Occupied Germany." In *Hochschuloffiziere und Wiederaufbau des Hochschulwesens in Westdeutschland, 1945–1952*, vol. 2: *Die US-Zone*, edited by Manfred Heinemann and Ullrich Schneider, 1–8. Hannover: Veröffentlichung aus dem Forschungsschwerpunkt "Zeitgeschichte von Bildung und Wissenschaft" der Universität Hannover, 1990.

Schulz, Hans-Dietrich. "Fantasies of *Mitte*: *Mittellage* and *Mitteleuropa* in German Geographical Discussion in the 19th and 20th Centuries." *Political Geography Quarterly* 8, no. 4 (1989): 315–39.

Smith, Helmut Walser. *The Continuities of German History: Nation, Religion, and Race across the Long Nineteenth Century.* New York: Cambridge Univ. Press, 2008.

Smith, John. *The Generall Historie of Virginia, New-England, and the Summer Isles* (1624). In *The Complete Works of Captain John Smith (1580–1631) in Three Volumes*, edited by Philip L. Barbour, 2:27–487. Chapel Hill: Univ. of North Carolina Press, 1986.

Smith, Neil. *American Empire: Roosevelt's Geography and the Prelude to Globalization*. Berkeley: Univ. of California Press, 2004.

Special Report of the Military Governor (Education & Cultural Relations), September 1948. N.p.: Office of Military Government for Germany, 1948.

Stehle, Maria, and Beverly M. Weber. "German Soccer, the 2010 World Cup, and Multicultural Belonging." *German Studies Review* 36, no. 1 (2013): 103–24.

Stone, Dan. *Histories of the Holocaust*. New York: Oxford Univ. Press, 2010.

Stürmer, Michael. *Das ruhelose Reich: Deutschland, 1866–1918*. Berlin: Severin und Siedler, 1983.

Szaz, Zoltan Michael. *Germany's Eastern Frontier: The Problem of the Oder-Neisse Line*. Chicago: Regnery, 1960.

Tang, Chenxi. *The Geographic Imagination of Modernity: Geography, Literature, and Philosophy in German Romanticism*. Stanford, CA: Stanford Univ. Press, 2008.

Tent, James F. "Denazification of Higher Education in U.S. Occupied Germany, 1945–1949." In *Hochschuloffiziere und Wiederaufbau des Hochschulwesens in Westdeutschland, 1945–1952*, vol. 2: *Die US-Zone*, edited by Manfred Heinemann and Ullrich Schneider, 9–15. Hannover: Veröffentlichung aus dem Forschungsschwerpunkt "Zeitgeschichte von Bildung und Wissenschaft" der Universität Hannover, 1990.

———. *Mission on the Rhine: Reeducation and Denazification in American-Occupied Germany*. Chicago: Univ. of Chicago Press, 1982.

Tichy, Franz. "Leben und Werk Heinrich Schmitthenners." In *Heinrich Schmitthenner Gedächtnisschrift*, edited by Helmut Blume and Herbert Wilhelmy, 9–21. Stuttgart: Steiner, 1987.

Tietze, Wolf. "A Politically Distorted Self-Portrait of German Geography." *GeoJournal* 57 (2002): 313–15.

Tucker, Jonathan. *War of Nerves: Chemical Warfare from World War I to al-Qaeda*. New York: Pantheon Books, 2006.

Volkery, Carsten. "The Iron Lady's Views on German Reunification: 'The Germans Are Back!'" *Der Spiegel Online*, Sept. 11, 2009. At http://www.spiegel.de/international/europe/the-iron-lady-s-views-on-german-reunification-the-germans-are-back-a-648364.html.

Von Oppen, Beate Ruhm, ed. *Documents on Germany under Occupation, 1945–1954.* New York: Oxford Univ. Press, 1955.

Wardenga, Ute. "Emil Meynen—Annäherung an ein Leben." *Geographisches Taschenbuch* 23 (1995–96): 18–41.

Wardenga, Ute, Norman Henniges, Heinz Peter Brogiato, and Bruno Schelhaas. *Der Verband deutscher Berufsgeographen, 1950–1979: Eine sozialgeschichtliche Studie zur Frühphase des DVAG.* Leipzig: Leibniz-Institut für Länderkunde, 2011.

Watson, J. Wreford. "North America in the Changing World." *Journal of Geography* 57 (1958): 381–89.

Wawro, Geoffrey. *The Franco-Prussian War: The German Conquest of France in 1870–1871.* New York: Cambridge Univ. Press, 2003.

Wegner, Gregory Paul. *Anti-Semitism and Schooling under the Third Reich.* New York: RoutledgeFalmer, 2002.

Wiegrefe, Klaus. "Germany's Unlikely Diplomatic Triumph: An Inside Look at the Reunification Negotiations." *Der Spiegel Online,* Sept. 29, 2010. At http://www.spiegel.de/international/germany/germany-s-unlikely-diplomatic-triumph-an-inside-look-at-the-reunification-negotiations-a-719848-druck.html.

Wildt, Michael. *An Uncompromising Generation: The Nazi Leadership of the Reich Security Main Office.* Translated by Tom Pampert. Madison: Univ. of Wisconsin Press, 2009.

Williamson, D. G. *Germany from Defeat to Partition, 1945–1963.* New York: Pearson, 2001.

Wilson, Leonard S. "Lessons from the Experience of the Map Information Section, OSS." *Geographical Review* 39, no. 2 (1949): 298–310.

Wingfield, Nancy M. *Flag Wars and Stone Saints: How the Bohemian Lands Became Czech.* Cambridge, MA: Harvard Univ. Press, 2007.

Wolff, Larry. *Inventing Eastern Europe: The Map of Civilization on the Mind of the Enlightenment.* Stanford, CA: Stanford Univ. Press, 1994.

Wood, Denis. *The Power of Maps.* New York: Guilford Press, 1992.

———. *Rethinking the Power of Maps.* New York: Guilford Press, 2010.

Wright, John K. "Highlights in American Cartography, 1939–1949." In *Comptes rendus du Congés International de Géographie: Lisbon 1949,* vol. 1, 298–314. Lisbon: Centro Tip. Colonial, 1950.

———. "The Sixteenth International Geographical Congress: Lisbon, 1949." *IGU Newsletter: Bulletin of the International Geographical Union* 1, no. 1 (1950): 5–7.

Wyman, Mark. *DP: Europe's Displaced Persons, 1945–1951.* Philadelphia: Balch Institute Press, 1989.

Zahra, Tara. *Kidnapped Souls: National Indifference and the Battle for Children in the Bohemian Lands, 1900–1948.* Ithaca, NY: Cornell Univ. Press, 2011.

Ziegler, D. J. "Post-Communist Eastern Europe and the Cartography of Independence." *Political Geography* 21 (2002): 671–86.

Index

Matthew D. Mingus is assistant professor of history at the University of New Mexico at Gallup. He loves living in New Mexico and spending time with his wife, Lindsey, their son, Isaac, and their dogs, Dixie and Oakley. When Professor Mingus is not busy teaching, he brews beer, plays board games, and hikes.